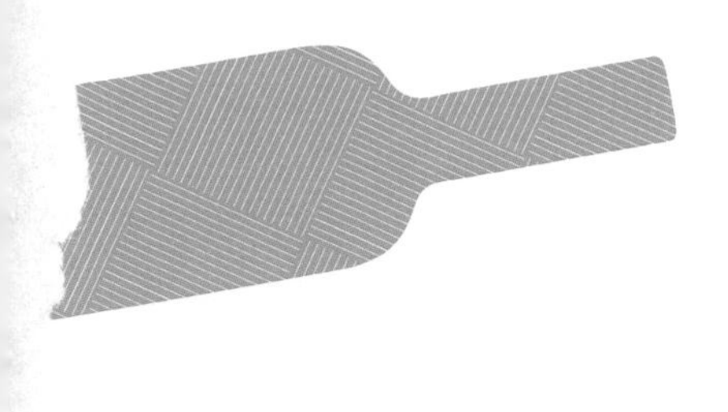

WINE TRAILS
AUSTRALIA & NEW ZEALAND

PLAN 40 PERFECT WEEKENDS IN WINE COUNTRY

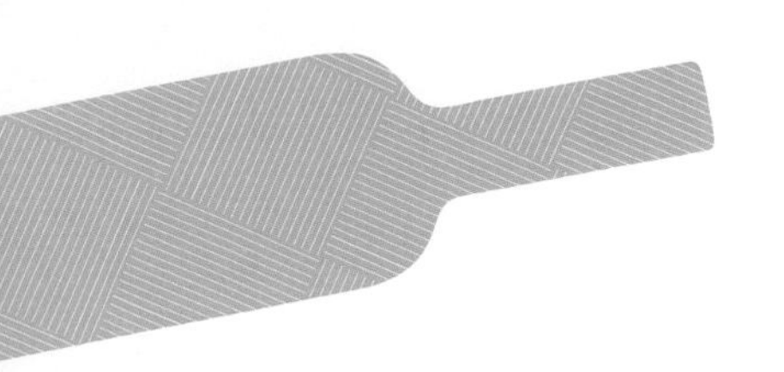

INTRODUCTION

We've all experienced it on our travels - whether watching a sunset in Margaret River with a glass of chilled Chardonnay or at a barbeque in Barossa Valley with a beefy Shiraz - when a local wine could not be more perfectly suited to the moment.

Tasting wine in the place it was made can be a revelation. This book plots a course through 40 of Australia and New Zealand's greatest wine regions, with weekend-long itineraries in each. We encounter Tasmania's terrific Pinot Noirs, rivalled by the wondrous wines coming out of New Zealand. We venture into historic, world-famous wineries and cutting-edge cellar doors, and in Victoria's Pyrenees and South Australia's Clare Valley we discover some unsung heroes. In each region, our expert writers - including the critics and columnists Huon Hooke and Bob Campbell, and wine buyer Michael Ellis - review the most rewarding wineries to visit and the most memorable wines to taste.

This is a book for casual quaffers; there's no impenetrable language about malolactic fermentation or scoring systems. Instead, we meet some of the world's most enthusiastic and knowledgeable winemakers and learn about each region's wines in their own words. It is this personal introduction to wine, in its home, that is at the heart of wine-touring's appeal.

CONTENTS

AUSTRALIA

ACT

NEW SOUTH WALES

QUEENSLAND

SOUTH AUSTRALIA

TASMANIA

VICTORIA

WESTERN AUSTRALIA

NEW ZEALAND

AUSTRALIA & NEW ZEALAND

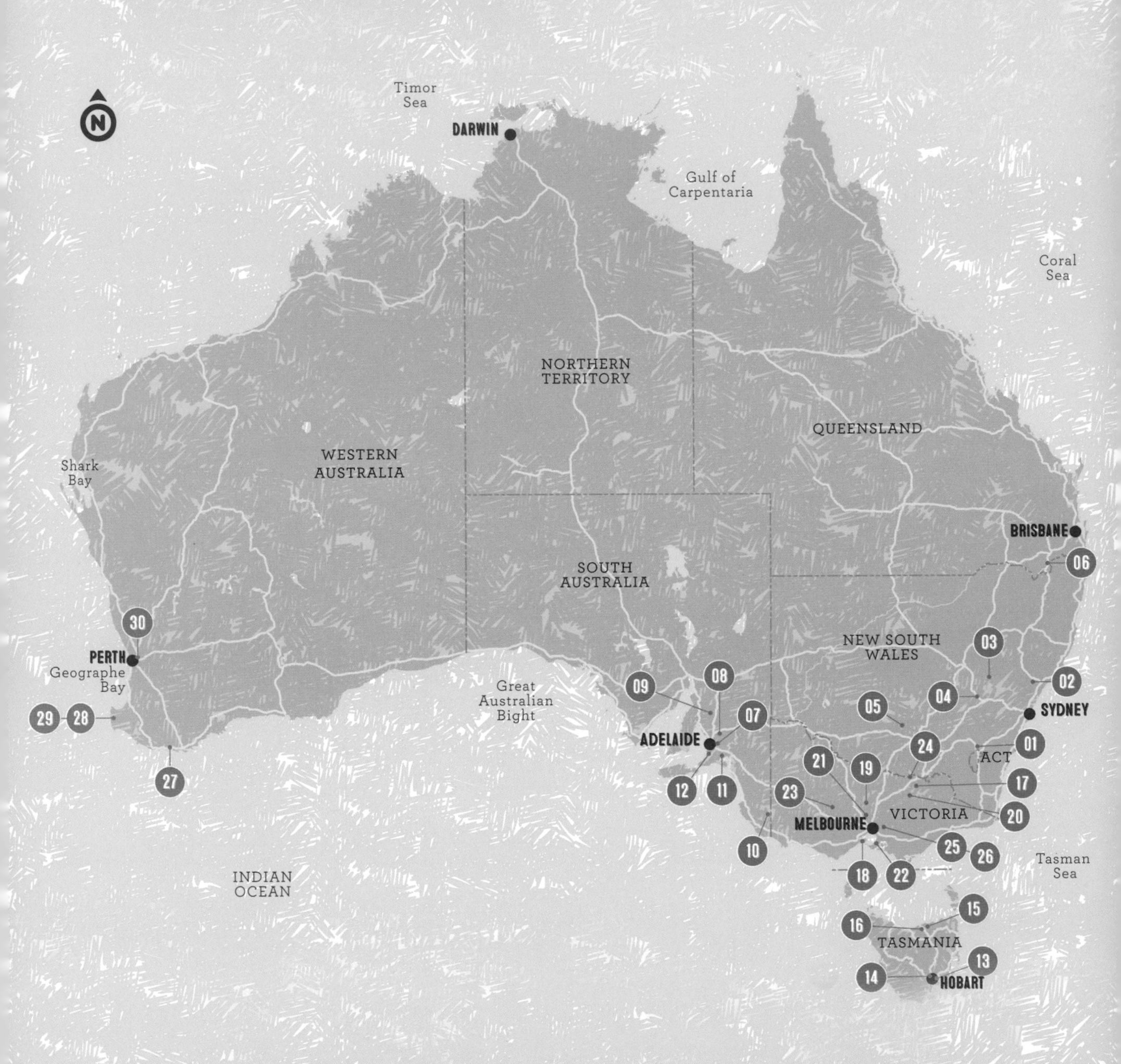

NORTHLAND
38
WHANGAREI
36
AUCKLAND
AUCKLAND
31
HAMILTON
TAURANGA
BAY OF PLENTY
NORTH ISLAND
WAIKATO
GISBORNE
GISBORNE
NEW PLYMOUTH
HAWKE'S BAY
33
Tasman Sea
TARANAKI
HASTINGS
WANGANUI
MANAWATU-WANGANUI
34
TASMAN
37
NELSON
35
40
WELLINGTON
MARLBOROUGH
GREYMOUTH
39
WEST COAST
SOUTH ISLAND
CANTERBURY
CHRISTCHURCH
SOUTH PACIFIC OCEAN
OTAGO
32
SOUTHLAND
DUNEDIN
INVERCARGILL

Courtesy of Terindah Estate

AUSTRALIA

01

Courtesy of Mount Majura / Simon Hughes

[ACT/NSW]

CANBERRA

Wines from up-and-coming Canberra are making a splash locally and globally – even if most of the wineries are actually in New South Wales.

Canberra's cool-climate wine region is one of the nation's youngest, but what it lacks in maturity, or geographical cohesion, it makes up for in exuberance and a willingness to experiment. You'll find some of Australia's most authentic cellar door experiences here, where owners and winemakers loiter eagerly behind counters, excited to offer the incoming punter a sample of their labour.

The Canberra District's first vines were planted in 1971 at the region's showcase winery, Clonakilla, in Murrumbateman. John Kirk, Clonakilla's founder, was among a small group of individuals pivotal to the careful planning and development of the region. They noted that the continental climate, with warm summers accompanied by cool nights and plummeting winter temperatures, provided the perfect conditions for killer Shiraz and crisp, floral Riesling. And from this, another Australian wine region was born.

GET THERE
Canberra airport has plenty of car rental options. Murrumbateman is a 30min drive away.

Despite the Canberra District moniker, there's only a sprinkling of wineries inside the Australian Capital Territory border. Most of the cellar door action takes place in Murrumbateman, New South Wales, a half hour's drive from Canberra on the road to Yass. There's a second cluster of wineries around the almost waterless yet very green Lake George, northeast of Canberra – the fluctuating water levels of this million-year-old lake have given rise to all sorts of tall tales, from lurking beasts to alien visits, and when near-dry it does make for an eerie sight.

Canberra itself, Australia's manufactured capital, is a city on the up. Much maligned in the past, it's in the midst of a massive transformation, with new boutique hotels opening and plenty of fine-dining possibilities. Home to an enormous cache of Australia's national treasures, the 'berra provides a great base to explore one of Australia's cheekiest new wine regions.

01 Mount Majura vineyards

02 Putting up netting at Clonakilla

03 Kangaroos at Mount Majura

04 Mount Majura reds

05 Ken Helm, owner of Helm Wines

01 FOUR WINDS VINEYARD

There's quite a buzz around this boutique family-oriented vineyard, underlined by owner Sarah Collingwood being crowned owner/operator of the year at the 2017 Australian Women in Wine Awards. And it's easy to see why this laid-back operation secured her such an accolade. Four Winds Vineyard is an intergenerational business where Sarah's father slaves away to create the perfect wood-fired pizzas to accompany his daughter's delicious liquid offerings. 'What better way to spend a weekend than drinking beautiful wine, eating amazing wood-fired pizzas and looking over the picturesque Riesling vines,' wonders Sarah. The selection of six tastings at the stylish cellar door includes regional specialities Riesling and Shiraz but also extends to varietals such as a Sangiovese and a much-anticipated, soon-to-be-added sparkling Riesling. A sense of warmth and community permeates the whole of Four Winds, where the winemaker and her family are as much a part of the joyful experience as the wines and food.

www.fourwindsvineyard.com.au; tel 02-6227 0189; 9 Patemans Ln, Murrumbateman; 10am–4pm Thu–Mon, pizzas weekends noon–3pm

02 CLONAKILLA

Kangaroos cluster in the paddocks surrounding the lane that leads to Clonakilla's cellar door. The pioneer of this relatively young wine region, Clonakilla is much admired for having produced some of Australia's best and most groundbreaking Shiraz. Being the first vineyard in the Canberra cool-climate wine region, with its original vines laid in 1971, the success of these celebrated drops, according to winemaker Tim Kirk, is derived specifically from the land beneath and around the vineyard. Kirk explains that harnessing the unique features of the setting, where there's an abundance of granitic soil, is the core component of his winemaking mission.

Although the region is known for its Riesling, Clonakilla's elegant Viognier, bursting with pear, apricot and ginger notes, has national

The changing water levels of the million-year-old lake have given rise to all sorts of tall tales, and when near-dry it's an eerie sight

critics singing its praises as the best of its varietal in Australia. It's no coincidence that you'll find Clonakilla's wines on the first-class passenger menus on the likes of Emirates and Singapore Airlines. *www.clonakilla.com.au; tel 02-6227 5877; 3 Crisps Ln, Murrumbateman; 11am–4pm Mon–Fri, 10am–5pm Sat–Sun*

03 LERIDA ESTATE

Blue wren dance around the courtyard, hopping among the potted herbs and olive trees, and panoramic views sweep around the expanse of Lake George – yes, Lerida Estate provides the perfect excuse to break up your road trip along the Federal Highway.

Taking its name from that first given to the region, Lerida established itself in the late '90s as a small-batch boutique operator focused on delivering world-class Pinot Noir. Find out more on one of the two types of vineyard tours on offer. The hour-long tour (AU$12.50 per person) includes a 20min stroll through the vineyard, winery and barrel room topped off with a tasting of six wines selected specifically from their Super Premium and Proprietor's Selection range. Alternatively sit back and enjoy one of Australia's best sparkling brut rosés and dig in to Café Lerida's seasonal, something-for-everyone menu. *www.leridaestate.com.au; tel 02-6295 6640; Federal Hwy, Lake George; 10am–5pm daily*

From top left: courtesy of Clonakilla / David Reist; Mount Majura / Beth Jennings (2); Helm Wines / Irene Dowdy

06 Ken and family at Helm

07 An aerial view of capital city Canberra

04 MOUNT MAJURA VINEYARD

Gumboot tour, anyone? One of the few wineries of the Canberra cool-climate wine region actually located within the borders of the tiny Australian Capital Territory, Mount Majura is another pioneering establishment and offers a brilliant, free, self-guided trail through the single-site vineyard. In fact, this place prides itself on visitors being able to see everything right from the cellar door, including, if you time it right, all the feverish handpicking and hand-pruning.

Mount Majura is all about the Tempranillo where the elegant finish of the Rock Block Tempranillo has to be compared to the dense and brooding notes of the Little Dam Tempranillo, demonstrating the team's passion for producing a brilliant selection from this Spanish varietal. The seated tasting of 15 (yes, that's 15) wines occurs over a relaxed half hour and is best accompanied by a tasting plate piled with local delicacies, such as beef and kangaroo prosciutto. *www.mountmajura.com.au; tel 02-6262 3070; 88 Lime Kiln Rd, Majura; 10am–5pm daily*

05 HELM WINES

Divert off the main road on the outskirts of Murrumbateman, snake down a dirt track and seek out local winemaking royalty, in the form of Ken Helm. After prising open the creaking door of the reclaimed 1888 Toual Public School House, which acts as Helm Wines' tasting room, you'll likely find Ken settled behind the counter where he's eager to show off his gorgeous wines and regale you with stories of his winery and the bush surrounds. His delicate and floral Rieslings are the best this boutique region has to offer. Given Ken's ancestral connection to Germany's Rhineland, this really should come as no surprise. *www.helmwines.com.au; tel 02-6227 5953; 19 Butts Rd, Murrumbateman; 10am–5pm Thurs–Mon*

06 POACHERS PANTRY & WILY TROUT VINEYARD

From its humble beginnings as a smokehouse, the Poachers Pantry has flourished over the past two decades and now comprises the Wily Trout vineyard and cellar door, a farm shop and one of the region's favourite weekend restaurants. This all-bases-covered set-up allows for pairings that carnivores will savour, such as a peppery Wily Trout Shiraz with the pantry's artisanal smoked meats.

If you're that way inclined, there's no better way to impress your significant other than with the romantic 'Picnic Package': after a meander through the vineyard on a personalised tour you'll be treated to a comprehensive tasting, including the sparkling Pinot Chardonnay, followed by the ultimate gourmet picnic among the pretty vines. *www.poacherspantry.com.au; tel 02-6230 2487; 431 Nanima Rd, Springrange; cellar door 9.30am–5pm daily; restaurant 12pm–3pm Fri–Sun, brunch 9.30am–11.30am Sat–Sun*

ESSENTIAL INFORMATION

WHERE TO STAY

HOTEL HOTEL
Boutique Canberra at its best, where individually styled rooms blend a Scandi aesthetic with elements of the Australian bush. There's a gallery and library to browse, plus apartments and split-level lofts if you fancy more privacy. *www.hotel-hotel.com.au; tel 02-6287 6287; 25 Edinburgh Ave, Canberra*

LITTLE NATIONAL HOTEL
Boutique Canberra at its smallest. With a nod to compact Japanese hotels, the tiny rooms at the Little National are brilliant for a solo traveller, and have plenty of enticing freebies. *www.littlenationalhotel.com.au; tel 02-6188 3200; 21 National Circuit, Barton*

WHERE TO EAT

EIGHTYSIX
Well-established eightysix boasts a stellar menu consisting of consistently high-quality meals, delivering modern Australian dining with a punch.

07

www.eightysix.com.au; tel 02-6161 8686; Cnr Elouera & Lonsdale Sts, Braddon; dinner 6pm–late daily

AKIBA
Whether you're craving dim sum or a dip into the vast sake selection, this Canberra institution offers pan-Asian perfection and works particularly well for larger groups. *www.akiba.com.au; tel 02-6162 0602; 40 Bunda St, Canberra; 11.30am–3pm, 5.30pm–midnight Mon–Wed, till 2am Thu–Sat*

THE CUPPING ROOM
A breakfast and brunch favourite for Canberrans. Devised by the people behind speciality roasters, ONA Coffee, this is the place to get your morning coffee buzz and brekkie bowl. *www.thecuppingroom.com.au; 1/1–13 University Ave, Canberra; 7am–4pm Mon–Fri, 8am–3pm Sat, Sun and hols*

WHAT TO DO

THE TRUFFLE FARM
Time for a treasure hunt, of sorts. Team up with Australia's best truffle dog team on the ultimate truffle hunt through dense oak and hazelnut forest, followed by a tasting (if you've been successful). If you're feeling flush, opt for the AU$138 truffle hunt and brunch which includes chef Damian Brabender preparing your meal, while answering all your truffle-infused questions. *www.thetrufflefarm.com.au; tel 02-400 483 082; Mount Majura Rd, Canberra*

TIDBINBILLA NATURE RESERVE
Abutting the Namadgi National Park, 40km southwest of Canberra, this reserve is rich in Australian wildlife including kangaroos and emus, and platypuses and lyrebirds at dusk. Check online for ranger-guided activities. *www.tidbinbilla.ac.gov.au; tel 02-6205 1233; Tidbinbilla Reserve Rd; 7.30am–6pm Apr–Nov, to 8pm Oct–Mar, visitor centre 9am–5pm*

CELEBRATIONS

CANBERRA DISTRICT WINE WEEK
The 'week' stretches for 10 days during this April harvest festival that features wine tastings, food and tours. *www.canberrawines.com.au*

01

Courtesy of Tyrell's Wines

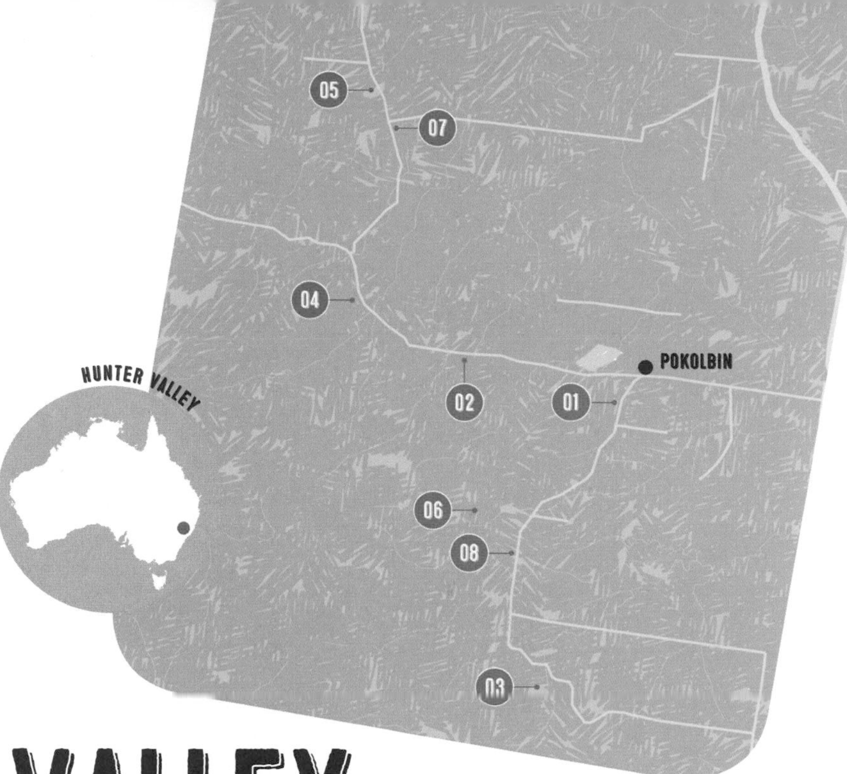

[New South Wales]

HUNTER VALLEY

Expect a warm welcome in the Hunter Valley, home to some of Australia's oldest vines and sublime wineries, large and small.

With age, comes experience. The first vines were planted in the Hunter Valley in the 1860s and today the region is superbly set up for wine tourism, its 110 cellar doors accompanied by excellent restaurants and places to stay, and everything from hot-air-balloon rides to horse-drawn carriage tours. The landscape of lush vineyards framed by the Brokenback Range is picturesque, but it's the wine – plus the cheese, beer, olives and chocolate – that visitors come to feast on.

Each of the Valley's seven sub-regions has its own character but most cellar doors are in the central Pokolbin/Rothbury and Lovedale areas. The wineries are a blend of old family estates, such as Tyrrell's and Mount Pleasant, and modernists including Usher Tinkler and De Iuliis. Some places, such as Bimbadgen and Tempus Two, host regular concerts in the vineyards, and vintage time (Feb–Mar) features all sorts of winery events to celebrate the harvest.

The Hunter has two distinct soil types: the red loams of volcanic origin found mainly on the lower slopes of the Brokenback Range are prized for red grapes, especially Shiraz, while the low-lying white, sandy soils found alongside creeks and in ancient river-beds are well suited to white varieties, especially Semillon. Nipping at the heels of the valley's mainstays, dry Semillon and medium- to full-bodied Shiraz, are increasingly refined, subtly oaked Chardonnay and Verdelho, as well as relative novices including Pinot Gris/Grigio, Sangiovese and Tempranillo. Merlot, Cabernet Sauvignon and sparkling wines are also widely found.

Come in the cooler months to avoid the crowds and the summer heat. The Hunter is pretty in winter and thanks to its even year-round rainfall distribution, it's often no wetter then than in other seasons.

GET THERE
The Hunter Valley is only two hours' drive north from Sydney.

01 BROKENWOOD

Established in 1970, Brokenwood has risen to be one of the Hunter's most respected wineries, largely thanks to the drive and talent of long-serving chief winemaker and CEO Iain Leslie Riggs. The winery's bestselling Semillon, ILR, is named after him, and is simply one of the Hunter's best. Issued at five to six years' age, it's an intense, toasty, lemony marvel that matures to twenty years and beyond.

A full range of wines are made, including several from Beechworth, McLaren Vale and Orange, but Shiraz and Semillon are the staples. The top Shiraz is Graveyard, from a patch beside the winery which was once designated for a parish cemetery.

Brokenwood recently started work on a new cellar door, which will only add to the winery's massive appeal and extensive wine club membership.

www.brokenwood.com.au; tel 02-4998 7559; 401-427 McDonalds Rd, Pokolbin; 9.30am-5pm Mon-Sat, 10am-5pm Sun $

02 TYRELL'S WINES

The Tyrrells are one of the oldest and most distinguished wine families in the region, established in 1858, now with the fifth generation at work. Founder Edward Tyrrell's one-roomed ironbark slab hut still stands on the property, and his influence runs deep. 'Behind everything we do is a complete commitment to quality at the very top end,' says patriarch Bruce Tyrrell. 'We will only take grapes from the best vineyards we can find, and we will only bottle a wine if we believe it's good enough.'

You can hear all about the history of the site and the family's winemaking experience by joining one of the daily winery tours, and round off your visit with a sip or two of their iconic Semillons, which consistently reel in awards.

www.tyrells.com.au; tel 02-4993 7028; 1838 Broke Rd, Pokolbin; 9am-5pm Mon-Sat, 10am-4pm Sun $

03 MOUNT PLEASANT

Few Hunter vineyards are as picturesque as Mount Pleasant, tucked immediately beneath the

01 Bruce Tyrell, family head of Tyrell's Wines

02 The hilltop Audrey Wilkinson winery

03 A tasting platter at Audrey Wilkinson

04 Grapes at Tyrell's

05 Harvesting at Tyrell's Wines

06 Balloons above Hunter Valley

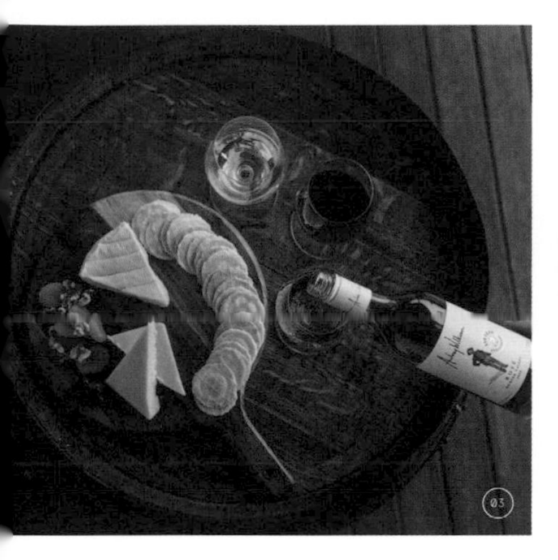

Brokenback Range, on slopes of red volcanic soil ideal for Shiraz. The awe-inspiring mountain provides an unforgettable setting for the cellar door.

Another Hunter Valley institution, these vineyards were first planted in the 1880s, and later made famous by legendary winemaker Maurice O'Shea. O'Shea established the Lovedale and Rose Hill vineyards, the first famous as the source of the classic Mount Pleasant Semillon, the second a single-estate Shiraz to stand beside the Old Paddock and Old Hill Shirazes grown on the original property.

Looking beyond these celebrated Shiraz and Semillon vintages, the younger members of chief winemaker Jim Chatto's team have experimented with a limited range called B-Side, which includes a light red blended from Montils and Shiraz, revisiting a style from a bygone era. *mountpleasantwines.com.au; tel 02-4998 7505; 401 Marrowbone Rd, Pokolbin; 10am–4pm daily*

04 DE LULIIS

The De Iuliis family embraced the new millennium with a striking new winery and light-filled cellar door. A past winner of the Hunter's Cellar Door of the Year award, you're guaranteed a warm welcome here as you sip a selection of wines and nibble local cheeses. There are also awesome views to soak up from the observation tower.

Rich, chocolatey Shiraz and floral Semillon are top of the list, but Mike De Iuliis also makes an elegant Chardonnay and in recent years has been turning heads (and winning trophies) with an innovative Shiraz Touriga blend, made in a soft, medium-bodied style which drinks well young. *www.dewine.com.au; tel 02-4993 8000; 1616 Broke Rd, Pokolbin; 10am–5pm daily*

05 THOMAS WINES

Andrew Thomas made the move from McLaren Vale in South Australia to the Hunter Valley, determined to focus on the region's two signature grapes, Semillon and Shiraz. Having cut his teeth at Tyrrell's, he struck out on his own in 1997, renting space in another winery until 2016 when he built a new winery and cellar door in the Tuscany Estate complex.

Thomas has been a spearhead for the new, modern style of Hunter Semillon: a delicate wine that ages well yet is beautifully drinkable, soft and fruity upon release just a few months after the harvest. That accessibility is deceptive – Thomas is a details guy and a perfectionist. About

From top left: courtesy of Audrey Wilkinson / Josh Hill (2); Tyrell's Wines

Courtesy of Tyrell's Wines

Hunter Semillon, he explains, 'The vineyard is paramount: you can't make a silk purse out of a sow's ear. It's about preserving the potential quality from vine to bottle. That's the task.'

As with may wineries today, Thomas Wines charges a fee for group tastings and for sampling the premium flight of single-vineyard wines (the $10 fee for this is redeemable against any purchases). With the calibre and professionalism of the staff, you won't be complaining.
www.thomaswines.com.au; tel 02-4998 1734; In Estate Tuscany, Corner Hermitage Rd & Mistletoe Lane, Pokolbin; 10am–5pm daily

06 AUDREY WILKINSON

A pioneer Hunter winemaker, from the late 19th to the mid-20th century, Audrey Wilkinson's legacy is a cellar door with a stunning hilltop outlook, one side overlooking the vast, contour-planted estate vineyards. The ruins of the original winery serve as a base for today's impressive building, which houses a museum where the old tanks and foundations are on display.

Current winemakers Jeff Byrne and Xanthe Hatcher create such gems as the Winemaker's Selection Semillon and earthy, regional Shiraz, as well as others at the associated winery Poole's Rock, downhill on De Beyers Road. The two properties and the brands were acquired by the Agnew family in 2004.
www.audreywilkinson.com.au; tel 02-4998 1866; 750 De Beyers Rd, Pokolbin; 10am–5pm daily

07 KEITH TULLOCH WINE

Keith Tulloch is a fourth-generation winemaker bringing experience gleaned in the Rhone Valley and Sonoma to bear on a blossoming estate. The extensive complex on Hermitage Road includes a two-storey cellar door – visitors are treated to an in-depth 'educational but fun' experience, not to mention fantastic views across the vineyard. A stone's throw away is an excellent lunch spot, Muse Kitchen, operated by the same team as the Hunter's award-winning restaurant, Muse at Hungerford Hill.

Keith owns vines on the sandy creek-bed soil near the winery, which he calls the Hunter's 'grand cru' strip. It's where many of the greatest Semillon wines are grown – including his own Field Of Mars. 'White sand gives low vigour. The vines are in balance and they give wines of great purity,' Tulloch says. He has planted Chardonnay there expecting it to be similarly stellar.
www.keithtullochwines.com.au; tel 02-4998 7500; Corner Hermitage & Deasys Rd, Pokolbin; 10am–5pm daily

08 USHER TINKLER

Another winemaker with strong family roots in the Hunter Valley, Usher Tinkler likes to do things a bit differently – be it by converting a former church into a welcoming cellar door, or in his innovative take on Hunter favourites. Choose from an excellent reserve Chardonnay, a statuesque reserve Shiraz, or an eye-catchingly packaged sweet fortified Verdelho, Mr T's Very Rare 20 Year Old. Bold label design is a strong point, and extends to the secondary range, Nose To Tail. With an eye on prevailing trends, they also produce a La Volpe Prosecco.

The platter of hams on offer alongside the wines hail from Jamon Iberico, Parma, Bayonne – unmistakably the good stuff, to savour as you sink back into the plush leather sofas, glass in hand.

Usher also makes the wine for his family's Tinkler Wines, established in 1946, on Pokolbin Mountains Road. They have their own cellar door, open daily 10am–5pm.
www.ushertinklerwines.com; tel 02-4998 7069; 97 McDonalds Rd, Pokolbin; 10am–5pm daily, salumi & cheese 10am–3pm

ESSENTIAL INFORMATION

WHERE TO STAY

TONIC

The polished-concrete floors and urban minimalist style of this handsome hotel work a treat in the vivid Hunter light. There's a lovely outlook over a dam into the sunset from the rooms and the two-bedroom apartment. *www.tonichotel.com.au; tel 02-4930 9999; 251 Talga Rd, Lovedale*

SPLINTERS GUEST HOUSE

These comfy cottages are some of the Hunter's best, with beautiful decor and smart furniture. The owners provide a generous breakfast in the fridge plus wine and cheese, a dessert wine and other details. Three B&B rooms and one self-catering cottage, sleeping up to six, are available. *www.splinters.com.au; tel +64 02 6574 7118; 617 Hermitage Rd, Pokolbin*

WHERE TO EAT

MUSE RESTAURANT

Inside the Hungerford Hill winery is the area's highest-rated restaurant, offering sensational contemporary fare and top-notch service in an attractive modern space. Presentation is exquisite, especially for dishes on the degustation menu, which is compulsory on Saturday ($125, with wine $185). There's a separate vegetarian menu (two/three courses $60/$80). *www.musedining.com.au; tel 02-4998 6777; 1 Broke Rd, Pokolbin; lunch 12pm–3pm Sat & Sun; dinner 6.30pm–10pm Wed–Sun*

06

BISTRO MOLINES

Set in the Tallavera Grove winery, this French restaurant run by Robert Molines, the Hunter Valley's most storied chef, has a seasonally driven menu that is nearly as impressive as the vineyard views. Daily specials supplement the main menu. *www.bistromolines.com.au; tel 02-4990 9553; Tallavera Grove, 749 Mt View Rd, Mt View; lunch 12pm–3pm Thu–Mon; dinner 7pm–9pm Fri–Sat*

WHAT TO DO

Big international names (think Springsteen, Stones) regularly drop by for weekend concerts at the larger vineyards. If there's something special on, accommodation books up well in advance. *Check for info at www.winecountry.com.au*

BALLOON ALOFT

Take to the skies for a sunrise hour-long hot-air-balloon ride over the vineyards. The jaunt is followed up with bubbles and breakfast at Petersen House Winery. *www.balloonaloft.com; tel 02-4990 9242*

TWO FAT BLOKES

These immersive gourmet experiences are a great way to discover the region. Upbeat guided tours take you to some excellent vineyards, but there's plenty more besides the wine, with cheese, beer, lunch and plenty of entertaining background information. *www.twofatblokes.com.au; tel 02-4998 6699; 1616 Broke Rd, Pokolbin*

CELEBRATIONS

HUNTER VALLEY WINE FESTIVAL

An annual event bringing together the region's best wineries, along with beer and cider tastings and the finest local food, plus plenty of family-friendly entertainment. *www.huntervalleywinefestival.com*

01

Courtesy of Gilbert Family Wines

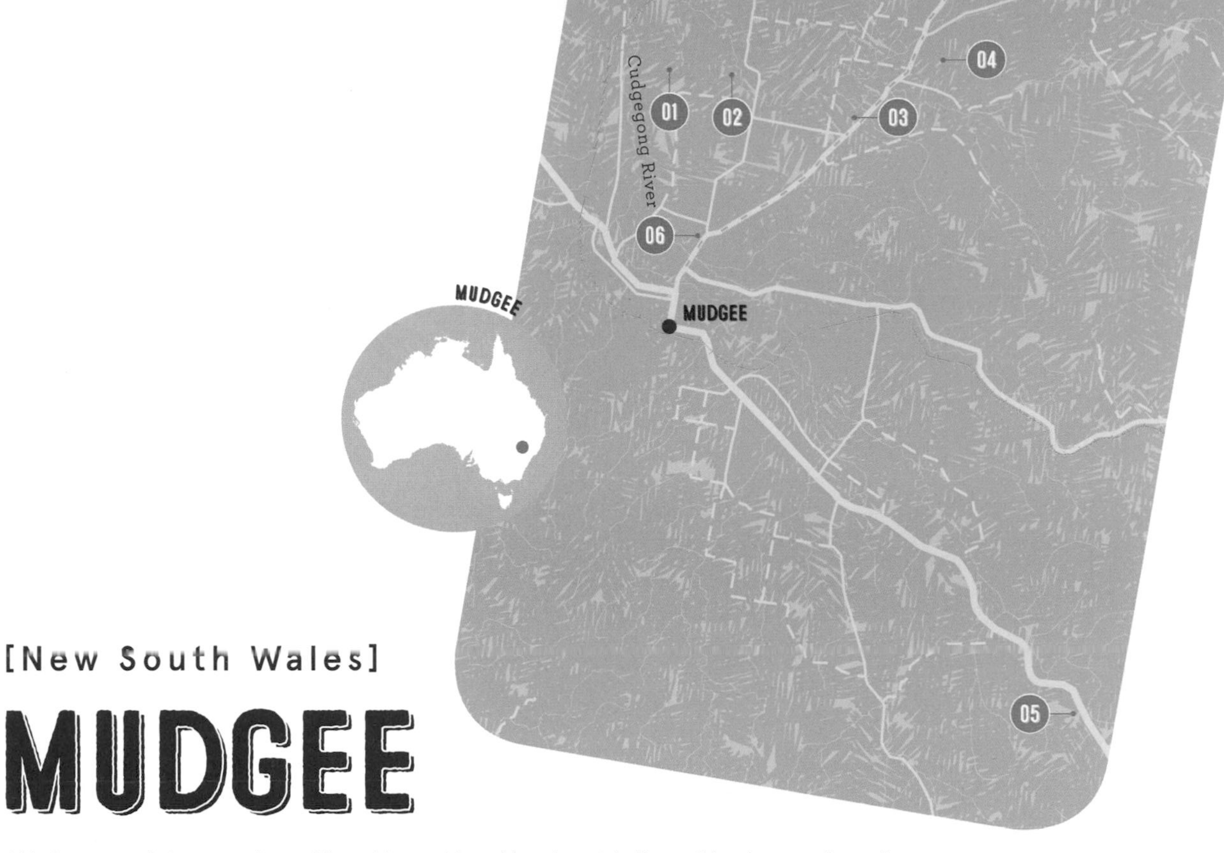

[New South Wales]

MUDGEE

Higher, colder and wetter than the Hunter Valley, Mudgee stands distinct from its well-established neighbour, and it's a region on the rise.

Is there a more quintessentially Australian country town than Mudgee? It takes its name from the Indigenous Wiradjuri word '*moothi*' meaning 'nest in the hills' and you can see why. With its historic early stone buildings, Cudgegong River, big eucalypts, undulating pasture, vineyard country and forested surrounds, Mudgee is pretty indeed.

The Hunter Valley was Mudgee's closest wine region for most of its history, but the two could not be more different. While the Hunter's weather is influenced by the Pacific Ocean, Mudgee is on the western slopes of the Great Dividing Range and its weather more westerly influenced: hotter summers, colder winters, less rain in the growing season and less humidity. It's also higher altitude at 400m to 500m, with vines as high as 1100m in the Rylstone area, at Nullo Mountain. This combination of continental climate and well-drained sandy loam or slightly acidic soils, over clay, is suited to robust red wines – deep crimson Cabernet Sauvignons lead the way.

Mudgee has a rich past and was a notable gold-mining area. Poet Henry Lawson is one of its favourite sons. The local wine industry recently went through a period of radical restructuring during which a third of its vines were uprooted; what remains should be the cream of the crop. Certainly, the wine quality, winery tourism and optimism of the vignerons are all on a high, with confident investment in cellar doors and some fine restaurants opening.

Mudgee is the first Australian wine region to be known for organic wine, due to pioneer Botobolar – claiming to be Australia's oldest organic vineyard, established in 1971 – and later subscribers Lowe, Thistle Hill and Broombee. At under four hours' drive from Sydney and with some 35 cellar doors, it's a great winery-hopping weekend destination.

GET THERE

Mudgee is 128km north of Lithgow. From Sydney, it offers a drive through the Blue Mountains and Great Dividing Range.

01 LOWE WINES

The Lowe family property Tinja has been in the family for five generations but David Lowe was the first to plant vines here. A charismatic 'flying winemaker' (someone who has gained and shared expertise across continents), he wears his reputation lightly, encouraging clear, jargon-free appreciation of the splendid wines at Lowe's award-winning cellar door.

The vineyards are in two discrete locations: at the winery on Tinja Lane where Shiraz and Zinfandel are grown, and secondly in a recently acquired vineyard at Nullo Mountain, near Rylstone. This 1100m high-altitude vineyard excels with Riesling, Chardonnay and Pinot Gris. Lowe also produces wine from grapes grown at Orange. All the vineyards are certified organic and Lowe also makes some no-preservative-added wines.

Renowned chef Kim Currie runs an outstanding restaurant, The Zin House, in the former Lowe family homestead, overlooking the Zinfandel vineyard. You can also follow a walking and cycling trail through the orchards and vines, past donkeys and chickens to wooded picnic grounds.

www.lowewine.com.au; tel 02-6372 0800; Tinja Lane, Mudgee; 10am–4.30pm daily

02 ROBERT OATLEY VINEYARDS

The Oatley family, founders of the well-established Rosemount Estate, still have two wineries in Mudgee: Montrose and Craigmoor. The latter is Mudgee's oldest winery and vineyard, established in 1858, and now hosts the cellar door, a large and noisy family restaurant and wine museum, in what was once the underground barrel cellar.

The full selection of Robert Oatley wines, from Mudgee to as far afield as Western Australia's Margaret River, is available to taste. This includes the Wild Oats range, named after founder Bob Oatley's fleet of racing yachts, winners of several Sydney to Hobart races.

www.robertoatley.com.au; tel 02-6372 2208; Craigmoor Rd, Mudgee; 10am–4pm daily

01 Evening session at Gilbert Family Wines

02 Gathering in the Gilbert gardens

03 Gilbert Family fare

04 Three generations of Steins at the eponymous winery

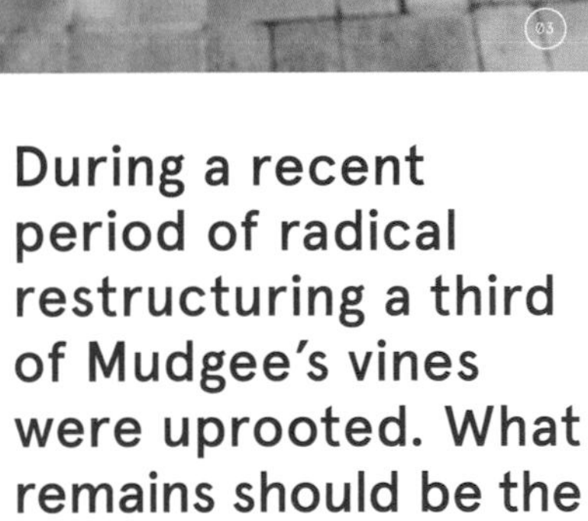

During a recent period of radical restructuring a third of Mudgee's vines were uprooted. What remains should be the cream of the crop

03 HUNTINGTON ESTATE

One of Mudgee's most famous wineries, Huntington Estate changed hands in 2005, when Bob Roberts retired and passed the reins to his neighbours, Tim and Nicky Stevens. The estate's renowned full-bodied, long-aging reds, made from Cabernet Sauvignon and Shiraz, are still here but the focus has shifted a little, with Tim adding some lighter-bodied reds to the portfolio – such as a juicy, succulent little Grenache. Older vintages are available at the cellar door and the Stevens are still dedicated to bottles that stand the test of time. Mudgee's firm tannins are a pet project: while respecting what the region naturally produces, Tim experiments with fermenting whole bunches and whole berries, as well as making an Amarone-style red from partially sun-dried grapes.

The annual week-long Huntington Music Festival, initiated by the music-loving Roberts family, attracts some of the best chamber musicians in the world. In partnership with Musica Viva, it is more popular than ever.

huntingtonestate.com.au; tel 02-6373 3825; 641 Ulan Rd, Buckaroo; 10am–4pm Mon–Fri & Sun, 10am–5pm Sat

04 ROBERT STEIN

Winegrowing in Mudgee was established by a German viticulturist named Roth, brought to Australia in the 1830s to work for one of the industry founders,

From top left: courtesy of Gilbert Family Wines (2); Robert Stein / Amanda Davenport / Str udge Publishing

05 Working the vineyard at Logan Wines

06 Grape gathering at Robert Stein

John Macarthur. Another of those German 'vine-dressers' was an ancestor of Robert Stein, but it wasn't until 1976 that Stein moved from Sydney to Mudgee to return to the family's roots. He planted the vines that his grandson Jacob Stein manages today, producing a flagship, award-winning Riesling range and full-blooded reds from Shiraz and Cabernet Sauvignon.

Robert Stein had another passion beside wine – motorcycles – and you can check out his vintage collection at the free on-site museum. Also in the grounds, the Pipeclay Pumphouse restaurant has high standards to match the wines. Much of the produce is grown on the farm, including pork from Jacob's own pigs. *robertstein.com.au; tel 02-6373 3991; Pipeclay Lane, Mudgee; 10am–4.30pm daily*

05 LOGAN WINES

The modern, stylishly designed Logan cellar door puts paid to any notions of Mudgee as a staid old wine region. Winemaker and owner Peter Logan holds court in this sunny space with its panoramic view over the Cudgegong Valley. He swapped pharmaceuticals for the wine industry, setting up Logan in 1997 to specialise in wines made from Mudgee and Orange grapes.

Logan's schtick is all about wines that accompany food, wines that people enjoy drinking, as opposed to wines that win medals. To that end he's added a skin-fermented Pinot Gris: an amber-coloured wine with tannin, texture and the backbone to partner stronger food flavours better than most white wines. The quirky range Weemala, named after the Logan vineyard in Mudgee, includes Shiraz Viognier and Tempranillo. Of special interest is a pair of super-premium Shirazes named Ridge Of Tears, one each from Mudgee and Orange, a fascinating taste comparison. *loganwines.com.au; tel 02-6373 1333; 1320 Castlereagh Hwy, Apple Tree Flat, Mudgee; 10am–5pm daily*

06 GILBERT FAMILY WINES

A descendant of Joseph Gilbert, who first planted Pewsey Vale in South Australia's Eden Valley in 1842, Simon Gilbert is almost wine royalty. He has made wine in Mudgee most of his life, and with his son, sixth-generation winemaker Will, on board, has opened a smart new cellar door in prime position out of Mudgee town on the Ulan Road.

Will Gilbert worked several vintages in Canada's Okanagan and Niagara regions before returning to the family business in 2016. Acknowledging recent trends, he's broadened the range to include a sparkling Riesling pét-nat (*pétillant naturel*), a skin-contact rosé and skin-fermented white wines. These are well-made drops that will appeal to followers of the natural wine movement. An alternative draw might be the Goose apple cider, also available at the cellar door. *www.gilbertfamilywines.com.au; tel 02-6372 1325; 137 Ulan Rd, Mudgee; 10am–6pm Sun–Thurs, 10am–10pm Fri–Sat*

Courtesy of Logan Wines

ESSENTIAL INFORMATION

WHERE TO STAY

PERRY STREET HOTEL

Stunning apartment suites make a sophisticated choice in town. The attention to detail is outstanding, right down to the kimono bathrobes, Nespresso machine and free gourmet snacks. *www.perrystreethotel.com.au; tel 02-6372 7650; Corner Perry & Gladstone Sts, Mudgee*

WILDWOOD GUESTHOUSE

This rustic homestead has four comfortable bedrooms individually styled with big downy beds, fine linens and an eclectic mix of antiques. Each opens out onto the wraparound verandah overlooking the tranquil countryside. *www.wildwoodmudgee.com.au; tel 02-6373 3701; Henry Lawson Dr, Mudgee*

WHERE TO EAT

ZIN HOUSE

A highlight of vineyard dining: long, leisurely six-course lunches of simply prepared local

produce (either home-grown, from honey and eggs to figs, quinces and persimmons, or impeccably sourced). Diners share farmhouse tables in a beautifully designed home. *zinhouse.com.au; tel 02-6372 1660; 329 Tinja Ln, Mudgee; noon–3pm & 5pm–10pm Fri–Sat, noon–3pm Mon*

PIPECLAY PUMPHOUSE

On the grounds of the Robert Stein Winery, this farm-to-table stunner is the talk of Mudgee, serving to-die-for weekend breakfasts featuring the likes of bacon and egg gnocchi with truffles, light lunches made using a wealth of local produce, and two-to-three course and degustation dinners, paired of course with Robert Stein wines. *www.pipeclaypumphouse.com.au; tel 02-6373 3998; 1 Pipeclay Ln, Mudgee; noon–3pm & 6pm–9pm Thu–Fri, 8.30am–3pm & 6pm–9pm Sat–Sun*

ALBY & ESTHERS

Down an alleyway is this supremely pretty courtyard café, serving up fine local fare and good coffee. It morphs into a wine bar on Friday and Saturday nights. *www.albyandesthers.com.au; tel 02-6372 1555; 8am–5pm Mon–Thu, to late Fri & Sat*

WHAT TO DO

CYCLING

One of the best ways to explore the region is on two wheels – clear your head with a relaxed ride around town, or saddle up for the more challenging 25km Rocky Waterhole loop. *www.visitmudgeeregion.com.au/explore-absorb*

PUTTA BUCCA WETLANDS

Swap wine tasting for birdwatching at this wildlife park, just north of Mudgee, on the site of an old quarry.

CELEBRATIONS

MUDGEE WINE FESTIVAL

This popular festival celebrating the region's 35 wineries, local farms and paddock-to-plate restaurants runs through the month of September and features live music, cellar-door events, tastings and special lunches and dinners. Check the website for full details and book accommodation well in advance. *www.mudgeewine.com.au*

LONG
ANGULLONG

Courtesy of Angullong

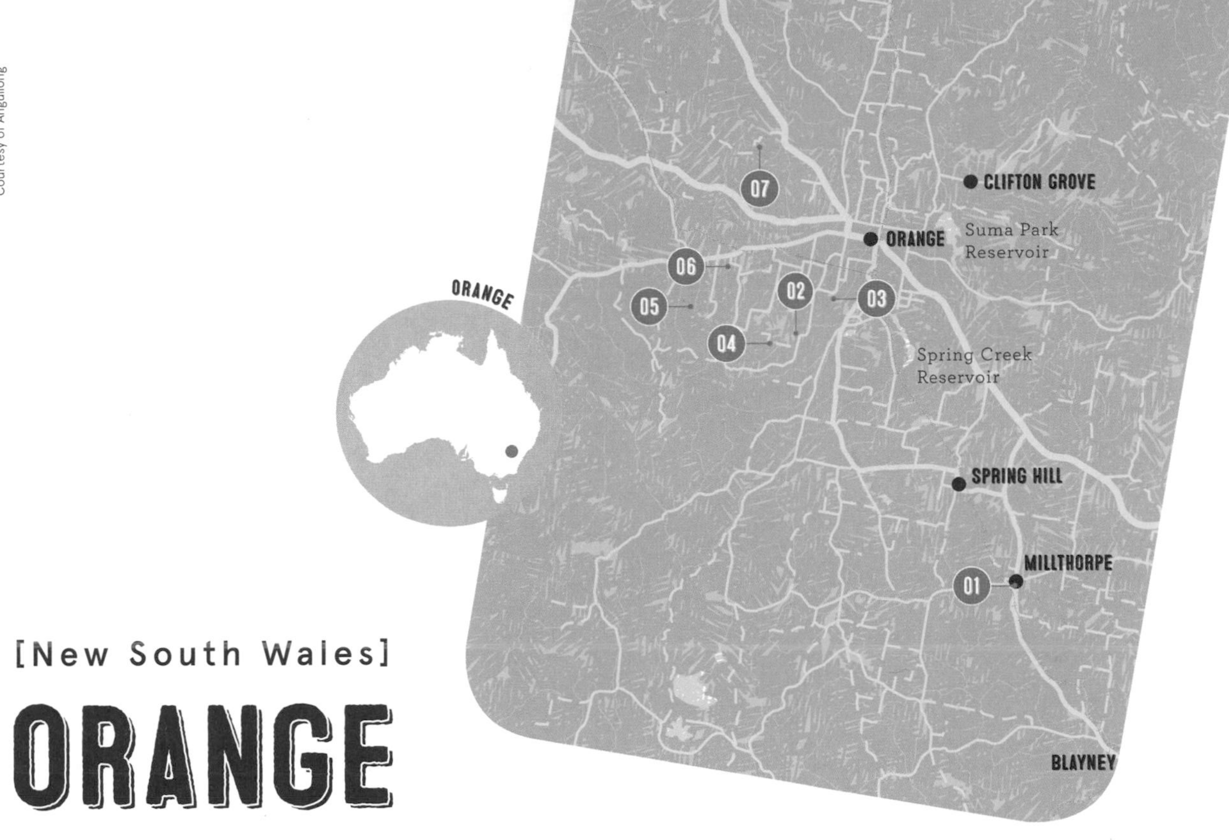

[New South Wales]

ORANGE

Cool-climate wine regions are rare in New South Wales, but due to its cold winters and sunny summers, Orange is one of the state's rising stars.

Orange might just be the prettiest regional centre in New South Wales. It has fine heritage architecture, a mild, high-elevation climate and enough going on to make it a great place to visit, or live – with its booming food-and-wine scene, the city of Orange is attracting well-heeled retirees and refugees from the Sydney rat race.

A thriving wine industry has blossomed where once there were only orchards and grazing lands. Fruits, berries and nuts are still grown here and many farms throw open their gates to visitors.

The first modern-day vineyards were planted in the late 1970s to early '80s by Sons & Brothers, Bloodwood, Cargo Road and Forest Edge; today there are more than 80 vineyards comprising over 15sq km of vines. What makes the difference here is altitude. Vineyards are all at least 600m above sea level and peak at 1100m, many right on the slopes of the extinct Mt Canobolas, the highest mountain in the region. The cool temperatures afford slow ripening and potential for fine table wines and delicate sparkling wines. The main grape varieties are the cool-climate specialists Chardonnay, Pinot Noir and Sauvignon Blanc, but Shiraz and Merlot deliver good results too. Exciting alternative varieties such as Barbera, Nebbiolo, Tempranillo, Zinfandel and even Sagrantino are gaining a strong foothold. Key Alsace white varieties also do well, with the emphasis on Pinot Gris, Riesling and Gewürztraminer.

Typically for a newer Australian region, the wineries tend to be widely dispersed, to the north, south, east and west of Orange, although there is a nucleus of excellent producers quite close to town. At just over three hours' drive from the big smoke, this all adds up to make Orange another prime long-weekend wine-tasting destination.

GET THERE
The drive from Sydney is about 3.5hrs. There are daily flights from Sydney, Melbourne and Brisbane.

01 ANGULLONG

Established by the Crossing family on its extensive cattle grazing and cropping property 50km from Orange in the Belubula Valley, this large (by Orange standards) 220-hectare vineyard is the source of some outstanding value-for-money wines. Its distance from town inspired the Crossings to set up their cellar door sales in Millthorpe, a historic village on the main Sydney–Orange road. The atmospheric venue is a 19th-century bluestone stables, which originally serviced the hotel next door.

The wines are made by contract winemakers, chiefly Liz Silkman at First Creek in the Hunter Valley, and the quality is as reliable as it is impeccable. Italian varieties are a speciality, notably Barbera, Sangiovese and Sagrantino, while the Chardonnay, Shiraz Viognier and Sauvignon Blanc are also notable. The main range of wines is branded Fossil Hill, a reminder that the region is rich in fish fossils. The Age of Fishes museum in nearby Canowindra is well worth a detour.
www.angullong.com.au; tel 02-6366 4300; The Old Bluestone Stables, Victoria St, Millthorpe; 11am–5pm daily

02 COLMAR ESTATE

Bill and Jane Shrapnel bought a six-hectare vineyard in 2013 and named it after an old town in Alsace, the region which inspired their passion for winemaking. They were wisely led by the land, and its 980m elevation, replacing ill-suited varieties (Cabernet Sauvignon, Shiraz and Merlot) with Chardonnay, Pinot Noir and Pinot Gris, among others,

Their wines have done well in competitions, for which the local contract winemakers Chris Derrez and Lucy Maddox must share some of the glory – ask to taste the lauded, effusively floral, green-citrus scented Block 6 Riesling from 2016. The Block 3 Pinot Noir from the same year was also superb: cherry- and charcuterie-perfumed and full of esay-drinking, medium-bodied charm.
www.colmarestate.com.au; tel 0419 977 270; ; 790 Pinnacle Rd, Orange; 10.30am–5pm weekends & public hols or by appt

01 Alfresco tastings at Angullong

02 Enjoying the Angullong varietals

03 Colmar Estate

04 Preparing to entertain at Angullong

03 PHILIP SHAW

Philip Shaw is one of Australia's most distinguished winemakers, having been chief winemaker for Rosemount Estate and then the Southcorp group in his previous lives. He began establishing vineyards at Orange in the late 1980s while still at Rosemount, and later made the move to devote himself full-time to the fledgling, hand-tended site.

The 47 hectares of vines in the Koomooloo vineyard peak at 900m. They provide two ranges of wines, the first numbered (the No 11 Chardonnay is outstanding), the second bearing nicknames which presumably reflect facets of the multitalented and somewhat idiosyncratic man himself. These include The Dreamer, The Wire Walker, The Architect, The Conductor and even The Idiot!

The winery grounds have recently been landscaped so that they resemble something between an ancient Roman ruin and a croquet lawn. Two rustic outbuildings have been transformed into a kitchen and a public eating area.
www.philipshaw.com.au; tel 02-6362 0710; 100 Shiralee Rd, Orange; 11am–5pm daily

04 ROSS HILL

The Robson family planted their first vines at their Griffin Road property in 1994, and have always taken great care to minimise the impact of their winemaking on the environment. These efforts continued at their next site at Wallace Lane, a previous apple and cherry orchard on rich, volcanic soil and positioned high up at 1020m above sea level. This cooler-climate vineyard specialises in Chardonnay, Pinot Noir and Pinot Gris.

The Ross Hill winery, housed inside a former apple-packing shed at Wallace Lane, recently achieved carbon neutral status, the first winery to do so in the whole country. Their top range is the Pinnacle Series, not to be confused with the Pinnacle Lane sub-region of Orange. The red wines are powerfully structured and often exhibit strong eucalyptus nuances. Pick of the bunch is The Griffin, a statuesque red blended from Cabernet Sauvignon, Merlot and

05 On guard at Rowlee

06 Angullong's cosy interior

Cabernet Franc.

The Robsons also keep busy growing olives and fresh cherries, producing extra virgin olive oil and running the Barrel & Larder School of Wine and Food.
www.rosshillwines.com.au; tel 02-6365 3223; 134 Wallace Ln, Orange; 10.30am–5pm daily

05 DE SALIS WINES

This is one of the highest altitude wineries and vineyards in the region, on the northern slope of Mt Canobolas. It's no accident that owners Charlie and Loretta Svenson specialise in generously matured, bottle-fermented sparkling wines, although table wines from Pinot Noir, Chardonnay and Sauvignon Blanc are also high on the agenda. The latter is made as a white Bordeaux style, barrel-fermented and exceedingly complex wine.

The vineyard, which sits at 1050m, is named Lofty, as is the top rung of wines. The dirt access road winds lazily up the hill, but the view from the tasting room and deck is definitely worth the trip.
www.desaliswines.com.au; tel 02-5310 6752; Lofty Vineyard, 125 Mt Lofty Rd, Nashdale; 11am–5pm daily

06 ROWLEE

Rowlee is one of Orange's newest wine names, the first vintage being 2013, although the grazing property on which it was established dates back to the 1850s. The vines grow in rich volcanic soil on the lower slope of the extinct Mt Canobolas at an altitude of 920m. The grapes are hand-harvested and all the wines produced from this single vineyard. Pinot Noir is an important varietal at Rowlee, as are Pinot Gris and Chardonnay. Less predictable perhaps is Nebbiolo, which prefers more heat, although it is starting to bed down here.

Continuing the Piedmontese theme, the white grape Arneis is also grown, and makes a very presentable dry white wine.
www.rowleewines.com.au; tel 02-6365 3047; 19 Lake Canobolas Rd, Orange; 11am–5pm daily

07 BLOODWOOD

Stephen and Rhonda Doyle are Orange region pioneers, having established Bloodwood in 1983. Despite not hosting a regular cellar door, they are renowned hosts and Stephen is well-known for his witty winery newsletter, the *Bloodwood Bible*.

When it comes to wine, they are deadly serious, though. All grapes are grown on the 8.4-hectare Bloodwood vineyard, which has an altitude varying from 810 to 860m above sea level. The soils here are not the volcanic basalt found closer to Mt Canobolas, but well-drained and gravelly. Riesling, Chardonnay, the Malbec rosé, Big Men In Tights, and sparkling Chirac are their most noted wines. The Chirac was named so that the nuclear testing at Mururoa Attol in the Pacific Ocean, authorised by the then French president, would not be forgotten.
www.bloodwood.biz; tel 02-6362 5631; 231 Griffin Rd, Orange; by appt only

ESSENTIAL INFORMATION

WHERE TO STAY

DE RUSSIE BOUTIQUE HOTEL

As good as anything in Sydney, this little slice of hotel heaven in Orange has boutique written all over it. It has luxe mod cons, including kitchenettes in every studio (a hamper of breakfast supplies is included). *www.derussiehotels.com.au; tel 02-6360 0973; 72 Hill St, Orange*

ARANCIA B&B

Set in rolling green hills, this Orange B&B has hotel-worthy facilities on a smaller scale; five spacious rooms with big beds, en suites and classy furnishings. Breakfasts here are renowned. It's adults only, with a two-night minimum on weekends. Packages are available. *www.arancia.com.au; tel 02-6365 3305; 69 Wrights Lane, Nashdale*

WHERE TO EAT

LOLLI REDNI

See Orange's finest produce wrapped in all its glory at this much-praised restaurant (bookings essential). The matching of food with wines is well thought-out, the setting and service are exemplary, and the kitchen creations (including many for vegetarians) sing with flavour. *www.lolliredini.com.au; tel 02-6361 7748; 48 Sale St, Orange; 6–9pm Tue–Sat & noon–2pm Sat*

06

AGRESTIC GROCER

'This is what happens when shopkeepers and farmers unite,' says the flyer. The results are pretty wonderful. This rustic cafe-grocer celebrates local produce a few kilometres north of town on the Mitchell Hwy (known as Molong Rd at this point). Breakfast on house-made crumpets, lunch on Italian panzanella salad or Korean barbecue burger. It's all delicious. *www.facebook.com/theagresticgrocer; tel 02-6360 4604; 426 Molong Rd; 8.30am–5.30pm Mon–Fri, to 4pm Sat & Sun*

WHAT TO DO

MT CANOBOLAS

Southwest of Orange, this conservation area encompasses waterfalls, views, walking trails and bike paths. Swimmer-friendly Lake Canobolas is a great place to start with plenty of picnic areas and a lakeside children's playground – the turn-off to the lake is on the extension of Coronation Rd, 8km west of town.

ORANGE REGIONAL MUSEUM

This fabulous free museum – in a brand new architecturally designed building with a sloping grass roof – is the city's cultural pride and joy, with permanent exhibits on local history, as well as visiting exhibitions.

CELEBRATIONS

ORANGE WINE FESTIVAL

This popular boozy festival celebrating the region's excellent vineyards through more than 80 events is held each October. *brandorange.com.au*

F.O.O.D WEEK

Book your accommodation in advance if you plan to visit for this foodie fest (running from late March to mid-April) highlighting local produce. *www.orangefoodweek.com.au*

01

Courtesy of De Bortoli / Guy Lavoipierre

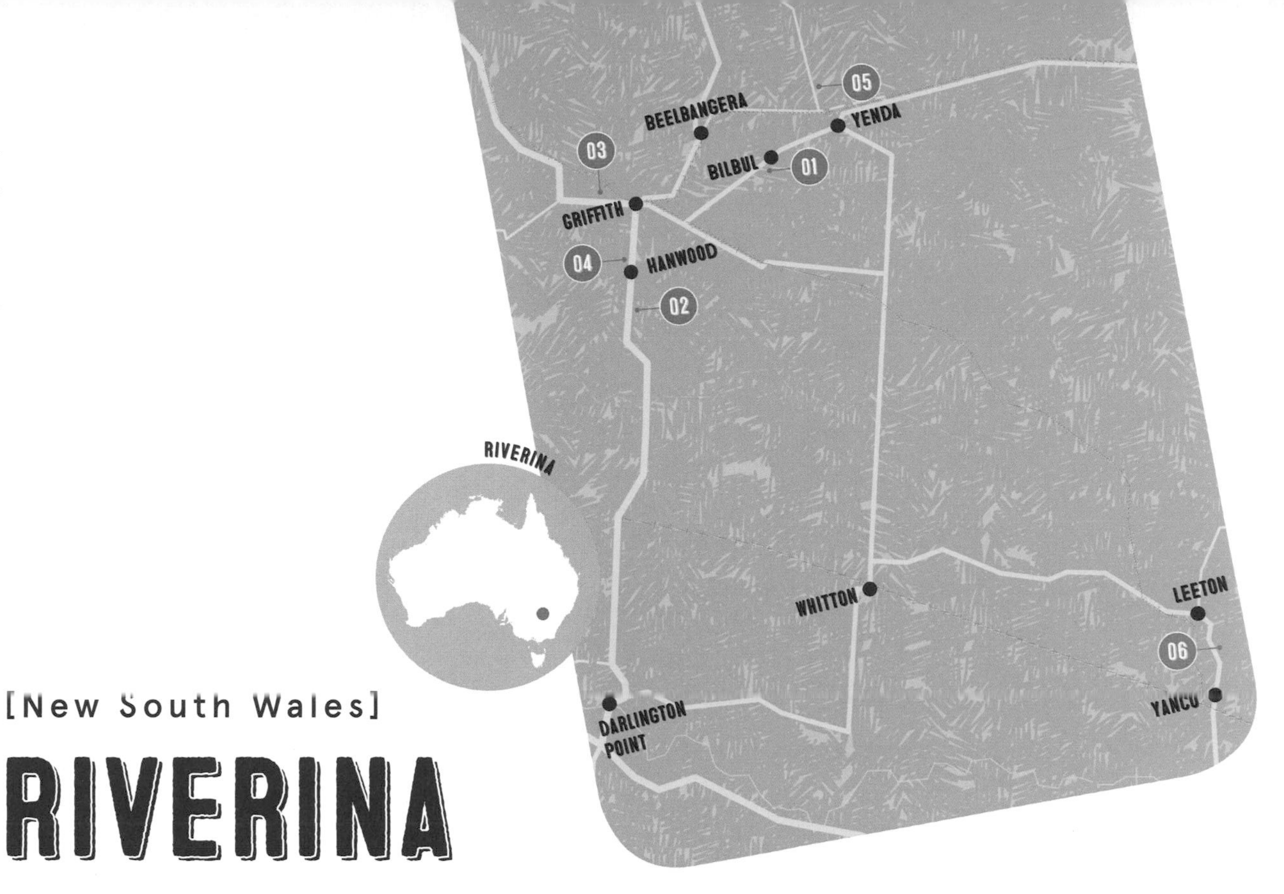

[New South Wales]

RIVERINA

Veer away from the middle of the wine road to track down Riverina's gems, stopping off for authentic Italian food en route.

Australia's second-longest river, the Murrumbidgee, meanders through the flat landscape of the Riverina in southwestern New South Wales, bordered by massive red gum trees. This is the region's lifeline, a vital resource harnessed by the creation of irrigation weirs, canals and a network of channels. These transformed what was once a semi-desert into arable land whose rich soils proved ideal for growing fruit trees, vegetable gardens, cereal crops including rice, and wine grapes.

A wave of Italian immigrants arriving after WWII immediately showed their enterprising spirit and drive, setting to work in developing vineyards and wineries, often alongside diverse horticultural and agricultural activities. Among those families were the De Bortolis, Casellas, Calabrias, Mirandas and Rossettos, names you'll soon spot on signs welcoming you to wineries across the region.

Summers here are hot and dry, but the plentiful water supplies forestall any concerns about drought, and in fact the high temperatures grant a disease-free growing season for the grapes. The upshot is that the Riverina produces 25% of all Australia's wine, the majority of it inexpensive, everyday stuff, with the occasional gem. Chief among the gems is the sweet wine made from botrytis-affected grapes – the fungus *botrytis cinerea* is ushered in with the humid autumn conditions, shrivelling the grapes and intensifying their sweetness. These outstanding, luscious wines, usually but not solely made from Semillon, can be world-beaters. Other frontrunners to sample include the first-rate Chardonnay and the Shiraz.

Most cellar doors across Riverina offer complimentary tastings and put the wine centre stage, although very few of them have restaurants.

GET THERE
Daily flights to Griffith from Sydney take just over an hour. Car hire is available.

01 DE BORTOLI

Simply put, De Bortoli is one of the most successful wine companies in Australia. Family-owned and run today by third-generation Darren De Bortoli, it began in the Riverina, later expanding to the Yarra Valley. The Riverina operation remains the foundation, a large concern producing inexpensive bottle and cask wines – sparkling, still and fortified, many of which deliver surprising quality for the prices.

De Bortoli's most famous product is Noble One Botrytis Semillon, a Sauternes-style barrel-fermented sweet wine which is one of the country's most successful show wines. The Deen De Bortoli Vat Series is often exceptional value, with full-bodied reds from Durif, Petit Verdot and Shiraz, dry white Verdelho and a botrytis Semillon which is a little brother to Noble One. The premium fortifieds, including dessert muscat and tawny, are outstanding. And on top of all that, it also produces a very smart beer: William's Pale Ale.

You're encouraged to bring along a picnic to the cellar door – a family-friendly set-up complete with a kids' playground.
www.debortoli.com.au; tel 02-6966 0111; De Bortoli Rd, Bilbul; 9am–5pm Mon–Sat, 9am–4pm Sun

02 MCWILLIAM'S

The McWilliam family has a history as distinguished as any New South Wales wine company, beginning in the late 19th century in Junee, southeast towards Canberra, before moving to Griffith in 1916. Today, it has winemaking interests in the Hunter Valley (Mount Pleasant), Hilltops (Barwang) and Margaret River (Evans & Tate) and takes grapes from other regions for its eclectic array of wines. The Riverina wines, however, provide the foundations, in particular the modestly priced Hanwood and Inheritance ranges which deliver great value for money. One example is Hanwood Durif, an inky, densely fruity red wine, sold young.

Visitors to the award-winning cellar door at Hanwood, Griffith, find themselves in a large barrel-shaped building with a striking painted-glass mural which depicts a vineyard scene. Constructed

01 Darren De Bortoli

02 De Bortoli vineyards

03 Jim Brayne and Jim Chatto of McWilliam's

04 A refill at De Bortoli's cellar door

A wave of Italian immigrants arriving after WWII showed their enterprising spirit and drive, setting to work in developing vineyards and wineries

to scale, the Hanwood Barrel has been serving customers since 1973. *mcwilliams.com.au; tel 02-6963 3400; Jack McWilliams Rd, Hanwood; 10am–4pm Wed–Sat*

03 CALABRIA FAMILY WINES

Formerly known as Westend Estate, Calabria has reverted to its original family name – a nod to its heritage and yet another example of Riverina's Italian-origin, historic wineries embracing both tradition and the dynamism of younger generations. The company was established in 1945 by Francesco and Elisabetta, whose son Bill heads things up today, and is a high-profile figure in the region.

Calabria sources grapes from various regions including the Barossa Valley (where it has a vineyard), while the core wines, mainly under the Three Bridges label, rely on varieties that flourish in the Riverina. These include Durif, Shiraz, Nero d'Avola, Aglianico and Saint Macaire, which was once grown in Bordeaux but has almost vanished: Calabria's two hectares constitute the biggest planting in the world.

www.calabriawines.com.au; tel 02-6969 0800; 1283 Brayne Rd, Griffith; 9am–5pm Mon–Fri, 10am–4pm Sat–Sun

04 NUGAN ESTATE

A Spanish immigrant, Alfredo Nugan arrived in Australia in 1940 and established a fruit and vegetable packing business in Griffith. This

From top left: courtesy of De Bortoli / Guy Lavoipierre; McWilliam's; De Bortoli / Guy Lavoipierre

05 Yarran Wines

06 The Murrumbidgee river and its trail

led to winemaking, on which in recent years the company has been increasingly focused, to the extent that it owns nearly 500 hectares of vineyards in the Riverina, King Valley and McLaren Vale.

Tastings take place in the estate's prized restaurant, Michelin, with the choice of tapas or a full meal alongside. The top wines to try are botrytis Semillon and full-bodied reds made from Durif and Shiraz. Their modestly priced Cookoothama range is especially good value for money.
www.nuganestate.com.au; tel 02-6964 9006; 72 Banna Ave, Griffith; 12pm–3pm Tues–Sun

05 YARRAN WINES

Yarran is a recent entrant into the Riverina winemaking scene, producing its first wine in 1998 and now offering varietals including Pinot Grigio, Petit Verdot, some fortified blends and the Riverina speciality, botrytis Semillon.

Winemaker Sam Brewer studied oenology and gained experience working for De Bortoli and Southcorp as well as overseas in China and California's Sonoma Valley, before returning to the family business in 2009. Gradually, more of the fruit from the family vineyards is being channelled into the wines. Sam's magic touch is clear in the Sauvignon Blanc which is aromatic and tropical-fruity. Like many other Riverina wineries, Yarran also sources some grapes from other regions such as Heathcote, and these appear under the Leopardwood label.

The modern but unobtrusive cellar door building sits picturesqely on the edge of the vineyard, amid the vines. Bring a picnic to enjoy on the veranda, while you soak up the views of Cocoparra National Park.
www.yarranwines.com.au; tel 02-6968 1125; 178 Myall Park Rd, Yenda; 10am–5pm Mon–Sat

06 LILLYPILLY ESTATE

In another tale of expansion and ambition, the Fiumara winery sprang out of the family's main business, the Golden Apple supermarket. From fruit and veg to growing vines, sixth son Robert Fiumara's passion for winemaking put Lillypilly on the map, and he's been in place as the winemaker since 1982.

There's a solid range of table wines, notably a Traminer-Semillon blend, trademarked as Tramillon, but best are the botrytis-affected sweet white wines. While most Riverina wineries offer one or two of these 'stickies', usually made from pure Semillon, Lillypilly makes several, employing a range of grapes. The mainstay is the Noble Blend, from Sauvignon Blanc and Semillon, but there's also Noble Harvest, fashioned from Sauvignon Blanc, Semillon and Gewürztraminer, and the refreshing Noble Muscat of Alexandria. The cellar door is attached to the supermarket, and sells a range of liquor besides the Lillypilly Estate wines.
www.lillypilly.com.au; tel 02-6953 4069; 47 Lillypilly Rd, Leeton; 10am–5.30pm Mon–Sat, Sun by appt

ESSENTIAL INFORMATION

WHERE TO STAY

YAMBIL INN

The owners of this little motel keep the place immaculate. Its 16 large, tidy, renovated rooms have all that you need for a good night's sleep, including air-conditioning and flat-screen TV, and a small salt-water pool is perfect for cooling off at the end of the day. There are BBQ facilities too. *www.yambilinn.com.au; tel 02-6964 1233; 155 Yambil St, Griffith*

WISTERIA COTTAGE, NARRANDERA

Not far from Lillypilly Estate in the town of Narrandera, this quaint and comfortable two-bedroomed B&B makes a good base for Riverina winery-hopping, with plenty of shopping and dining options on the doorstep. *tel 0418 441 142; 54 Whitton St, Narrandera*

WHERE TO EAT

BERTOLDO'S BAKERY

You will likely spot a theme in Griffith – the town's Italian-descended population have helped

06

to make it the food-and-wine capital of the Riverina. This Italian patisserie and *panetteria*, which have been firm favourites since the 1950s, are certain to have you drooling, whether it's over the cream-stuffed cannoli, savoury rolls or traditional pasta dishes. *www.bertoldos.com; 324 Banna Ave, Griffith; 8.30am–5pm daily*

ZECCA

Zecca serves up handmade pasta and Italian meals in the funky modern setting of a converted 1940s Rural Bank building. The kitchen uses local ingredients where possible, working with farmers to showcase the best regional produce. *www.zeccagriffith.com.au; tel 02-6964 4050; 239 Banna Ave, Griffith; 11am–4pm Tues–Wed, to 11pm Thu & Fri, 6pm–11pm Sat*

LA SCALA

Expect old-school family recipes, mural-covered walls and cheap house wine by the glass. Simple and brilliant. *tel 02-6962 4322; 455b Banna Ave, Griffith; 6pm–9.30pm Tue–Sat*

WHAT TO DO

COCOPARRA NATIONAL PARK

Stretch your legs along a walking trail and climb Mt Brodgen to admire views of the Murrumbidgee river, without which there would be no Riverina wine to be had. Less than half an hour's drive from Griffith, the park is a delight in springtime, when flowers temper the rugged landscape. *www.nationalparks.nsw.gov.au/visit-a-park/parks/cocoparra-national-park; tel 02-6966 8100; 200 Yambil St, Griffith*

HERMIT'S CAVE LOOKOUT

This panoramic lookout is located about the fascinating Hermit's Cave, which was inhabited for decades in the early 20th century by Italian-born Valerio Riccetti, a miner from Broken Hill; make sure you watch out for snakes.

CELEBRATIONS

UNWINED

An October festival of local wine and produce featuring wine tastings, lunches and live music. *www.unwined-riverina.com*

FERRIER
015 WILD YEAST
VIOGNIER
YEAST
1/3
18.2.15
01

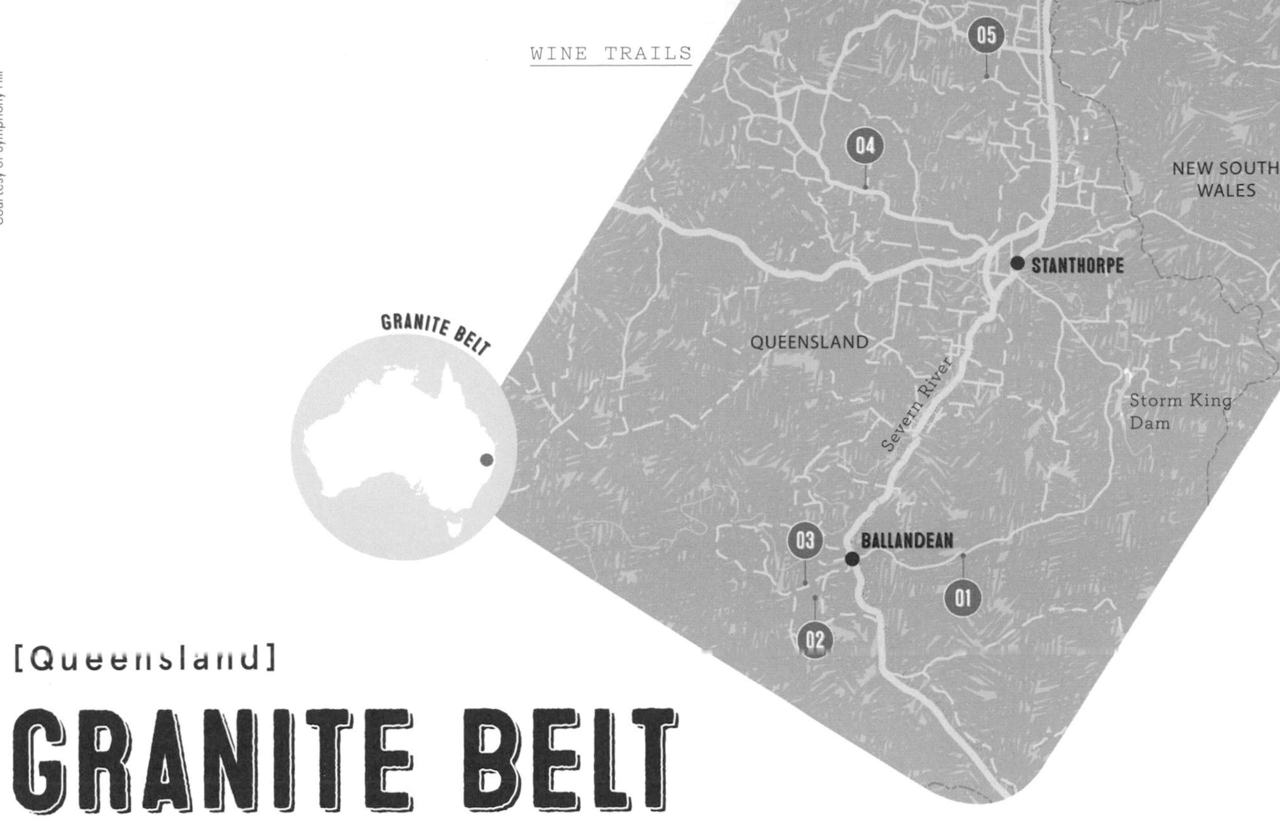

[Queensland]

GRANITE BELT

Spring flowers, autumn colours and even the chance of snow – the Granite Belt's distinct seasons are a tourist draw as well as a recipe for unique and unusual wines.

Dappling the western flanks of the Great Dividing Range about 210km southwest of Brisbane, the Granite Belt is Queensland's only real wine region, where hillsides are lined with vineyards, olive groves and orchards growing apples, pears, plums and peaches.

It's located just north of the New South Wales border in a mountainous area where the 1000m altitude affords Queensland's coolest grape-growing climate. In 1905 the state government decreed the Granite Belt Queensland's official health resort on account of its fresh, clean air. The mountainous terrain and high altitude are good news for the vines, too. The soils are predominantly decomposed granite, hence the region's name, and quite rocky, which favours high-quality wines, especially reds.

There are 25 wineries with cellar-door sales and the biggest nearby town, Stanthorpe, has some boutique accommodation and decent places to eat. Aside from the wineries' wares, craft beer and cider flow liberally. Stanthorpe is also the gateway to two scenic national parks, Sundown and Girraween, the latter featuring bulbous granite outcrops and, in spring, a blanketing of wild flowers.

Mainstream varieties such as Shiraz, Cabernet Sauvignon, Merlot, Chardonnay and Riesling are produced, and a recent new initiative, the StrangeBirds Wine Trail, champions lesser-known types. The trail leads you to wineries producing 'alternative' varieties, defined as representing no more than 1% of the total Australian grape harvest. In the Granite Belt these include Barbera, Sangiovese, Malbec, Tempranillo, Durif, Nero d'Avola, Nebbiolo and Mourvèdre in reds; in whites, Chenin Blanc, Fiano, Gewürztraminer, Savagnin, Vermentino, Verdelho, Viognier and Marsanne.

GET THERE
Queensland's Granite Belt is a 230km drive southwest of Brisbane, where car hire is available.

01 Winemaker Mike Hayes of Symphony Hill

02 Cabernet Merlot from Ballandean Estate

03 The cafe and lake at Robert Channon

04 Ballandean tastings Channon

01 SYMPHONY HILL

Back when they started out, Ewen and Elissa Macpherson planted over 40 less mainstream grape varieties in their research and development block. Thankfully their long-serving winemaker/viticulturist at Symphony Hill, Mike Hayes, likes to dabble with alternative varieties – his Gewürztraminers have done especially well, one of them nabbing the top gold medal at the Royal Melbourne Wine Awards, and Hayes himself was the surprise winner of the Australian Society for Viticulture and Oenology's 2017 winemaker of the year.

Other interesting varietals worth trying include Petit Manseng, Vermentino, Viognier, Verdelho, and in the red camp, Tempranillo, Nero d'Avola, Montepulciano, Saperavi, Lagrein, Tannat, Nebbiolo, Sangiovese and Petit Verdot.

Winery tours are part of the service, and the funky cellar door provides a bright contemporary setting in which to savour their remarkable wines; for large group tastings, the backdrop is the candlelit barrel room.

symphonyhill.com.au; tel 07-4684 1388; 2017 Eukey Rd, Ballandean; 10am–4pm daily

02 GOLDEN GROVE ESTATE

The Costanzos are one of the longest-standing wine families of the region. They first arrived in 1946 as fruit growers, planted grapevines in 1972 and, two generations of Charles Sturt University-trained family winemakers later, Golden Grove Estate is firmly on the map. Like others in the region, it is part of the StrangeBirds Wine Trail promoting less familiar varieties. The Vermentino is their star turn, a flinty, barrel-fermented style with crisp refreshing acidity. There's also a joven ('young') style Tempranillo, Malbec, Mourvèdre, Sangiovese and Nero d'Avola. The bold and brassy Malbec is especially good.

www.goldengroveestate.com.au; tel 07-4684 1291; 337 Sundown Rd, Ballandean; 9am–4pm daily, till 5pm Sat

03 BALLANDEAN ESTATE

Another well-established family-run concern, Ballandean's wines just keep getting better. The

Courtesy of Ballandean Estate; Robert Channon; Ballandean Estate

04

05 Angelo Puglisi, owner of Ballandean

06 Ewen MacPherson, Symphony Hill co-owner

Puglisi family's 2012 Malbec, under the Messing About label, was the champion wine at the 2014 New England Wine Show.

The modern winery is well-equipped but also embraces the past: in pride of place in the restaurant are the oldest working wine barrels in the state, 150-year-old vats holding maturing Muscat and port. Angelo and Mary are the friendly hosts, with Mary selling her own home-made products at the cellar door, alongside those of other local food artisans. The restaurant, The Barrelroom, serves modern Australian food with a low carbon footprint, and food, wine and music combine at annual charity event Opera in the Vineyard, held in conjunction with Queensland's state opera company. *www.ballandeanestate.com; tel 07-4684 1226; 354 Sundown Rd, Ballandean; 9am–5pm daily; restaurant open for lunch Thurs–Mon, dinner Thurs–Sun*

04 ROBERT CHANNON

Robert Channon is probably Queensland's most awarded winery, the Verdelho attracting special attention over the many years – the 2015 Verdelho bagged the trophy for best white wine at the 2015 Queensland Wine Awards. It could also be the only winery whose winemaker moonlights as a talented cook – Paola Cabezas does guest chef gigs in the winery's Singing Lake Cafe, which overlooks a serene expanse of water.

With a busy events calendar including concerts, stand-up comedy nights and themed dinners, there's almost always something besides wine tasting going on. The monthly concerts are staged in the appropriately named Swigmore Hall. *www.robertchannonwines.com; tel 07-4683 3260; 32 Bradley Ln, Stanthorpe; 11am–4pm Mon, Tues & Fri, 10am–5pm weekends; cafe open for lunch 11am Fri–Mon*

05 BOIREANN

'For Lovers of Red Wine' is the Boireann slogan, and when it comes to exceptional reds, Boireann is regarded by some experts as making the very best in the region.

The tiny 1.6-hectare vineyard is at 870m altitude at the northern end of the Granite Belt, a true micro-boutique. Set on a larger, 10-hectare property, dotted with the ubiquitous granite boulders, the vineyard has no fewer than 11 grape varieties planted, which means only small quantities of each wine are produced. The bottle label design is pared back and restrained, adorning the usual French varieties Shiraz, Merlot, Mourvèdre and Cabernet Sauvignon, but also the Italians Nebbiolo, Barbera and Sangiovese. Don't expect bells and whistles, this place is simply all about the wine. *www.boireannwinery.com.au; tel 07-4683 2194; 26 Donnellys Castle Rd, The Summit; 10am–4pm Fri–Mon*

ESSENTIAL INFORMATION

WHERE TO STAY

DIAMONDVALE B&B COTTAGES

In atmospheric bushland outside of Stanthorpe (expect to see kangaroos, koalas and echidnas), Diamondvale consists of four lovely private cottages and a four-bedroom lodge, each with old-fashioned details, a wood-burning fireplace, kitchen and verandah. The communal barbecue hut is a winner, as is the hospitality of owners Tony and Kerryn. Walk 2km along the creek into town or simply jump in for a swim. *www.diamondvale cottages.com.au; tel 07-4681 3367; 26 Diamondvale Rd, Stanthorpe*

WHERE TO EAT

BRASS MONKEY BREW HOUSE

Chef Gia Rokashvili and his team do incredible work here; with wine pairings in mind, they craft fresh, innovative dishes deeply informed by tradition and supplied by the local market. In summer, the large private outdoor patio, equally suited to intimate diners and large groups, provides spectacular views and, often, spontaneous and joyful live music. *www.brassmonkeybrew houseptyltd.com; tel 0488 967 401; 106 Donges Rd, Severnlea; 10am-6pm Thu-Mon*

06

Courtesy of Symphony Hill / Erik Williamson

AUSSIE BEEF STEAKHOUSE

A modest, family-friendly eatery serving impressive bits of beef (rib, rump, eye or porterhouse fillets), plus other meaty mains like beef-cheek and Shiraz pie or pork loin with a maple and paprika glaze. The steakhouse is tacked onto the side of a motel on the northern edge of town. *www.aussiebeefsteak house.com.au; tel 07-4681 1533; 1 High St, Stanthorpe; 6pm-7.30pm Tue-Thu, to 8pm Fri & Sat*

WHAT TO DO

STANTHORPE HERITAGE MUSEUM

This curio-crammed museum on Stanthorpe's northern outskirts gives a comprehensive insight into the town's tin-mining and grazing past. Well-preserved old buildings from the 1800s include a slab-timber jail, a shepherd's hut and a schoolhouse. There's a moving display on Stanthorpe's wartime losses, and an exhibit featuring ingenious homemade 'make-do' pieces, as well as others showcasing period fashions and the area's Italian heritage. *www.halenet.com.au/ ~jvbryant/museum.html; tel 07-4681 1711; 12 High St, Stanthorpe; 10am-4pm Wed-Fri, 1-4pm Sat, 9am-1pm Sun*

GIRRAWEEN NATIONAL PARK

A short drive east of Ballandean, Girraween National Park is home to some astonishing granite boulders, pristine forests and brilliant blooms of springtime wildflowers (Girraween means 'place of flowers'), all of which make a marvellous setting for a bushwalk.

Wildlife is abundant and there are 17km of trails to take you around and to the top of some of the surreal granite outcrops. Although winter nights can be cold here, it's hot work scaling the boulders, so make sure you bring plenty of water if you're hiking. *www.npsr.qld.gov.au/ parks/girraween*

HHW

Courtesy of Hahndorf Hill

[South Australia]

ADELAIDE HILLS

Discover a different side to Australia in this cool-climate region where jacaranda trees, fruit orchards and weekend cyclists offer a distinctly European vibe.

Think of all the tourist-board images of Australia: endless, red-rocked deserts, surfers on a cresting wave, perhaps a didgeridoo playing in the background. Now recalibrate – and welcome to a side of Australia that's not often presented to the rest of the world. From the jacaranda-lined streets of Adelaide's CBD, the M1 freeway climbs southeastward and the trees get thicker, the road quieter. You'll probably pass a few cyclists out for a spin, and apple or cherry orchards. Just half an hour later you'll be in the heart of the Adelaide Hills.

This part of South Australia was settled in the 19th century by Germans and Lutherans fleeing persecution and there's a certain European feel to the pretty winding roads that link twee towns like Hahndorf. These days it's a popular weekending destination for residents of the South Australian state capital, intent on trying and buying some up-and-coming wines from the Hills' small-scale producers. This is a true cool-climate region; as other grape-growing regions in Australia wonder about rising temperatures, the Adelaide Hills enjoys ideal growing conditions for Sauvignon Blanc and a fresher form of Shiraz. There's not much of a Germanic connection in the vineyards (Australia's best Riesling is still found in Clare Valley, see p51) but some have had success with Grüner Veltliner. The Hills is a young, compact wine region but it's growing up fast; only a few years ago, there were no signposts to the wineries on the roads – but that's changing.

Adelaide itself is a city for gourmands, with one of Australia's best food markets and a thriving farm-to-fork local produce scene. The only time the city gets busy is during the Adelaide Festival in March. The rest of the year, this sedate city makes a great base.

GET THERE
Adelaide has the closest airport with car rental and is about 40min from Hahndorf. Tours from the city are also available.

01 GOLDING WINES

Although Golding Wines' first vintage was in 2002, the winery has close connections to the fruit-growing heritage of the Adelaide Hills; Darren Golding's father was a local apple and pear merchant. Together they designed and built the cellar door with an Aussie aesthetic: a tin roof, bare wood, brick and stone.

They started with parcels of Pinot Noir and Sauvignon Blanc but quickly became more adventurous, including planting what they thought was Albariño. 'The plants were given to Australia by the Spanish government,' says Darren. 'It was only a few years later that we were alerted that the Albariño was in fact Savignan, a grape from the Jura in France, where it makes *vin jaune*. Michael Sykes, Golding's winemaker, uses it to make Lil' Late (Harvest), a sweet wine with tropical flavours.

But the staples of the winery are the Handcart Shiraz, which shows the fruity spicy side of Shiraz, and a Burgundy-style Pinot Noir. 'The cool nights in the Adelaide Hills preserve the acidity,' explains Darren, 'leading to vibrant, elegant wines, red or white.' The Hills, reckons Darren, have a huge future. So where else would he recommend in the region? 'Head up to Mt Lofty Ranges,' suggests Darren. 'The wines are good and if you go out the back you can look over Piccadilly Valley.'

www.goldingwines.com.au; tel 08-8389 5120; 52 Western Branch Rd, Lobethal; 11am-5pm daily

02 MT LOFTY RANGES

'All I want is to produce wines representative of this place,' says owner Garry Sweeney, whose wife, Sharon, decided on the location for Mt Lofty Ranges. She chose well because the cellar door's location is enviable, with views down into a small, verdant valley from its perch at 550m.

Growing grapes gives entry into a close-knit community. 'Everyone lends a hand,' he says. 'If your tractor breaks down, someone will come round. In my first year I didn't know how to prune and other winemakers came over to show me.' Their lessons were learned: Mt

01 Hahndorf Hill cellar door

02 Shaw + Smith

03 Darren Golding of Golding Wines

04 Bird In Hand

05 Tasting platter at Shaw + Smith

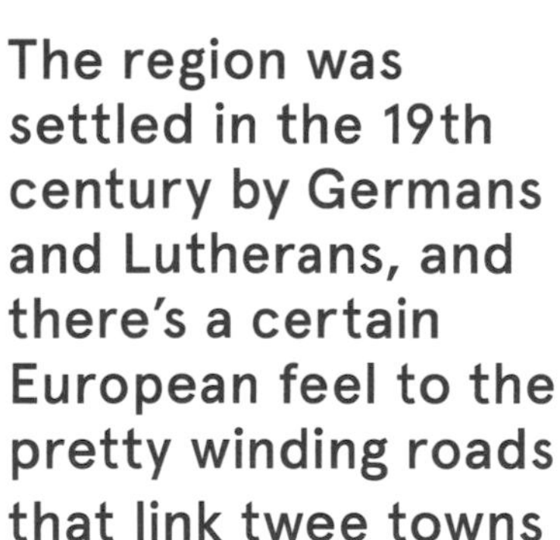

The region was settled in the 19th century by Germans and Lutherans, and there's a certain European feel to the pretty winding roads that link twee towns

Lofty Ranges' Pinot Noir, Riesling and Chardonnay are delicious.

The tasting room features reclaimed materials, an open fireplace and a terraced decking that leads down to the vines. If you arrive any time from mid-March to early April you may catch Garry and the team among the vines, hand-picking the year's harvest. *www.mtloftyrangesvineyard.com.au; tel 08-8389 8339; 166 Harris Road, Lenswood; 11am-6pm Fri-Sun, 11am-5pm Thu & Mon*

03 BIRD IN HAND

Set back from the road, the first impression of Bird in Hand winery is of the pair of ancient shutters that owner Andrew Nugent and his wife Susie brought back from France

and which now hang on the cellar door. The entire venue has a French feel, thanks to a shady terrace. In the vineyard the winery hosts live music occasionally.

There's plenty happening with the wine too, with three levels to taste: the Two in the Bush entry-level wines, the premium Bird in Hand range (which includes Shiraz, a Merlot Cabernet and a Montepulciano), and in certain years, the Nest Egg series for cellaring. The Shiraz, in particular, is an exemplary cool-climate red, fruity and spice without being overblown.
www.birdinhand.com.au; tel 08-8389 9488; Bird In Hand Rd & Pfeiffer Rd, Woodside; 10am-5pm Mon-Fri, 11am-5pm Sat & Sun

04 SHAW + SMITH

Shaw + Smith is one of the larger cellar doors in the Hills. The focus is on five wines: a Sauvignon Blanc, a Chardonnay, a Riesling, a Pinot Noir and a Shiraz. For $20 you can taste a flight of all five with a platter of local cheeses; the Sauvignon Blanc is perhaps the most successful, lying someway between a fruity Marlborough, New-Zealand style and a spartan Sancerre from France.
www.shawandsmith.com; tel 08-8398 0500; 136 Jones Road, Balhannah daily 11am-5pm

05 HAHNDORF HILL

At Hahndorf Hill, which is pioneering several Austrian grape varieties, you'll not only be testing your tastebuds with interesting wines but also some tongue-twisting names. The warm days and cool nights of the Hills suit Grüner Veltliner, which owners Larry Jacobs and Marc Dobson first planted in 2006; South Australia's first Grüner Veltliner vintage was released in 2010. Blaufrankisch, the red version of the grape, has been grown at Hahndorf for more than 20 years – both benefit from the high mineral content of the blue slate, quartz and ironstone soil. The pair also make a pear-scented Pinot Grigio, and a great cool-climate Shiraz to try while enjoying the views over the vines and gum trees.
www.hahndorfhillwinery.com.au; tel 08-8388 7512; 38 Pains Rd, Hahndorf; 11am-5pm daily

06 Wine flights with a view at Shaw + Smith

07 Spot wildlife on beautiful Kangaroo Island

ESSENTIAL INFORMATION

WHERE TO STAY

AMBLE AT HAHNDORF

At Amble's country-luxe base in Hahndorf there's the Fern studio, the Wren cottage and an apartment (Amble Over). Wren features a spa bathroom and private deck; Fern a private courtyard with a barbecue. *www.amble-at-hahndorf.com.au; tel 0408 105 610; 10 Hereford Avenue, Hahndorf*

FRANKLIN BOUTIQUE HOTEL

The Franklin is the hip, new option in Adelaide, a much-needed meeting of demand for twee-free accommodation. The basic ('deluxe') rooms are small but so stylish that you won't mind; pay more for bigger bathrooms and more inventive lighting in the premium and superior rooms. *www.thefranklinhotel.com.au; tel 08-8410 0036; 92 Franklin Street*

WHERE TO EAT

CHIANTI

With local growers as suppliers, the chefs at Chianti, Adelaide's long-standing and much-loved Italian restaurant, are spoiled for choice. And they could probably tell you where the crispy pig's ear in the *risoni con frattaglie* or the garfish fillets in the *pesce al cartoccio* came from. *www.chianti.net.au; tel 08-8232 7955; 160 Hutt Street, Adelaide*

WHAT TO DO

Kangaroo Island is a popular excursion from Adelaide. It's not only inhabited by kangaroos but lots of amazing marsupials, and, in the ocean, dolphins and seals. *www.tourkangaroo-island.com.au*

CELEBRATIONS

The Adelaide area has not one but two annual festivals. In the summer, the Crush festival takes over more than 30 wineries for three days in January. It's not just tastings; there's food, music and an Alice in Wonderland-themed ball to finish the weekend. In winter, July's Winter Reds Weekend has become a regular fixture, again with around 30 local wineries participating and plenty of log fires crackling. *www.crushfestival.com.au*

01

Courtesy of Rockford

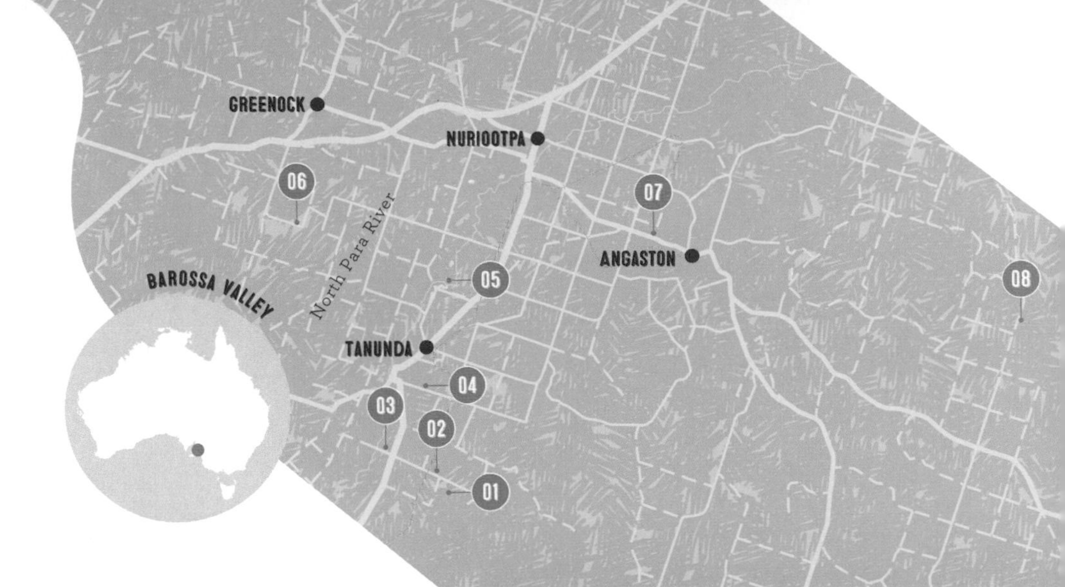

[South Australia]

BAROSSA VALLEY

More than just a wine region, the Barossa has a proud history, a rich culinary culture, and despite its small size manages to produce over one fifth of the country's wine.

One of the world's great wine regions, and Australia's best-known, the Barossa is just a 90min drive northeast of Adelaide. It's a compact valley, only 25km long, set in open, undulating pastureland with a backdrop provided by the Barossa Ranges, which skirt its eastern side. Nestled in the ranges is the Eden Valley, a separate region but one included in the Barossa zone – wines blended from Barossa Valley and Eden Valley grapes can still be labelled Barossa. The northern Barossa is more spread out than the south, a little warmer and a little drier, the source of heroic, full-bodied reds which sometimes qualify for the epithet of 'blockbuster'. The Eden Valley's vineyards, meanwhile, are more scattered and cover a smaller area; its altitude is higher and climate cooler, a combination which suits white wines and more medium-bodied, spicy reds.

The regional hub, leafy Tanunda, is arguably the most picturesque town in the Barossa, with bakeries, butchers and other shops that probably haven't changed much in a century. The local towns have a distinctly German heritage, dating back to 1842 when settlers fleeing religious persecution in Prussia and Silesia created a Lutheran heartland where German traditions endure today – gothic church steeples and stone cottages are everywhere. Cultural legacies of the early days include a dubious passion for oom-pah bands, and an appetite for wurst, pretzels and sauerkraut. Of course the settlers also brought their vine cuttings with them.

This trail focuses on the Tanunda area, including Bethany, south as far as Krondorf Road and east as far as Angaston, gateway to the Eden Valley. This is rich territory for the great, the venerable, the well-established and the famous. It's also the most historic part of the Barossa: the first European settlements were at Bethany, Langmeil, Hoffnungsthal and environs.

GET THERE
Adelaide, 65km southwest, has the closest airport with car hire. The route through the Adelaide Hills is super-scenic.

01 CHARLES MELTON

Charlie Melton's Nine Popes is the wine that kick-started the renaissance of interest in Rhône-style dry reds in the late 1980s – the Grenache-Shiraz-Mourvèdre blend remains a standard-bearer. In Melton's rustic, Krondorf Road cellar door you'll find a range of solid Barossa reds as well as one of its most famous pink wines (is it a rosé or a light red?), named Rose of Virginia after Charlie's wife, and a unique sweet white modelled on Tuscany's vin santo, made using air-dried grapes. At the cellar door you'll also find light meals, platters and tutored tastings.
www.charlesmeltonwines.com.au; tel 08-8563 3606; 194 Krondorf Rd, Krondorf; 11am–5pm daily

02 ROCKFORD

It's unlikely a more fascinating winery visit exists, especially if you're a nostalgia nut. At Rockford they make small-range wines using old, discarded machinery and equipment, and you can see it all in action during the vintage. The buildings were erected by founder Rob O'Callaghan and his mates from local stone. The wines are just as distinctive as the place: high quality but again, old-fashioned, which is no criticism. Sparkling, spicy Black Shiraz is a cult wine; Basket Press Shiraz the flagship red wine.

Stonewallers Club (Rockford's wine society) members queue for the regular in-house lunches concocted from ingredients grown in the organic garden. Heirloom tomatoes and other produce are often available to buy.
www.rockfordwines.com.au; tel 1800 088 818; 131 Krondorf Rd, Tanuda; 11am–5pm daily

03 ST HALLETT

This winery, established in 1944 and revived in the 1980s, is now part of the large Accolade group but run quite independently, with long-serving winemaker Toby Barlow in charge. No one has been a stauncher promoter of the Barossa than St Hallett: all its wines are 100% Barossa/Eden Valley, and sub-regional and single vineyard differences are explored by the winemakers under their diverse labels. While Grenache is making a determined comeback, Shiraz is

01 Rockford's local-stone-built home

02 Tending vines at Peter Lehmann

03 A fresh haul

04 Rockford's singular cellar door

the speciality, with the iconic Old Block at the top and descending through the single-vineyard wines to Blackwell and Faith and the very affordable Gamekeepers.
www.sthallett.com.au; tel 08-8563 7070; 100 St Hallett Rd, Tanuda; 10am–5pm daily

04 TURKEY FLAT

Timeless old stone buildings are everywhere in the Barossa, a reminder of its rustic, subsistence-farming past. The Schulz family first came here in 1870 as butchers, acquiring a vineyard originally planted in 1847, making it one of the valley's oldest. These vines have been augmented by other plantings and the range of wines incudes a very popular rosé and the flagship Turkey Flat Shiraz.

The old family butcher's shop has been repurposed as Turkey Flat's cellar door, with the original butcher's block still in situ. This also lends its name to an affordably priced range of wines, the red and white both excellent blends of Rhône varieties and representing fantastic value for money.
www.turkeyflat.com.au; tel 08-8563 2851; 67 Bethany Rd, Tanuda; 11am–5pm daily

05 PETER LEHMANN

Barossa doyen Peter Lehmann may no longer be with us but his winery and memory live on. Enter via a long, tree-lined driveway which crosses the Para River by an impossibly narrow bridge. The cellar door, its nucleus an 1880s stone building, doubles as a meditative art gallery, set among spacious green lawns and gardens where picnickers are welcome. Visit the stone weighbridge where Lehmann used to hold court, sharing a 'shluck and a schnitter' and many a laugh with his grape-growers as their trucks and trailers queued up to deliver fruit.

Rich Shirazes are the signature wines; together with the Rieslings vintages, these are probably the most consistent, affordable and widely distributed wines in the Barossa.
www.peterlehmannwines.com; tel 08-8565 9555; Para Rd, Tanuda; 9.30am–5pm Mon–Fri, 10.30am–4.30pm Sat–Sun

From top left: courtesy of Peter Lehmann / Jonathan van der Knaap (2); Rockford

05-06 Ledger and logo, Turkey Flat

07 Transporting grapes at Peter Lehmann

06 SEPPELTSFIELD

If there is one Barossa winery you have to visit, it is Seppeltsfield. Established in 1850 by the pioneering Seppelt family, it was a village in itself, with the employees and their families living on the property, and maintaining a butchery, bakery, distillery and much else alongside the winery. Current owner Warren Randall has recently undertaken a comprehensive revival of the estate, including the gardens and surrounds of the 100-hectare property. Heritage-listed buildings and mature trees stand side by side with newer developments.

Fortified wines are the longstanding speciality here, but a range of table wines is also produced in the recommissioned 1888 gravity-flow winery. The whole visitor experience is second to none, with a slick cellar door, the outstanding Fino restaurant, and lively Jam Factory contemporary art and design studios, gallery and shop.
www.seppeltsfield.com.au; tel 08-8568 6200; 730 Seppeltsfield Rd, Seppeltsfield; 10.30am–5pm daily

07 SALTRAM

One of the historic wineries of the Barossa, established by the Salter family in 1859, Saltram is the place that helped cultivate the legendary Peter Lehmann in the 1960s. Today it's part of Treasury Wine Estates and is riding high again after something of a lull period. Part of the winning formula was refocusing on traditional, high quality, exclusively Barossa wines.

Hearty Barossa Shirazes stand out: No 1 Shiraz is a deeply coloured wine of rich plum/chocolate fruit and soft tannins; The Journal Centenarian Shiraz is produced in the best vintage years, an exceptionally concentrated wine made from a single 100-year-old vineyard and released only after five years of maturation. Pepperjack, the base range of mid-priced reds, is widely distributed and good value for money.

The old stone barrel cellar was remodelled to house a top-notch restaurant, open daily for lunch. The cellar door is on a pretty section of the Nuriootpa-Angaston road, just as you drive into Angaston – a beautiful property, redolent with more than 150 years of winemaking history.
www.saltramwines.com.au; tel 08-8561 0200; Murray St, Angaston; 10am–5pm daily

08 HENSCHKE

Detour about 10km southeast of Angaston to the Eden Valley to reach old-school Henschke. The renowned Hill of Grace Shiraz produced here today level-pegs with Penfolds Grange as Australia's most iconic wine.

It's the sixth generation of the Henschke family who are now at work, and the stone cellars evoke a long and distinguished history. They're not resting on their laurels though, with the wine range continually growing and viticulturist Prue Henschke's commitment to biodynamic practices and sustainable agriculture reaping rewards.

While you're in the area, pay a visit the Hill of Grace vineyard and admire the beautiful stone Gnadenberg church – the name originates from a region in Silesia and translates as 'Hill of Grace'.
www.henschke.com.au; tel 08-8564 8223; 1428 Keyneton Rd, Keyneton; 9am–4.30pm Mon–Fri, 9am–noon Sat

Courtesy of Turkey Flat, Courtesy of Peter Lehmann

ESSENTIAL INFORMATION

WHERE TO STAY

THE KIRCHE @ CHARLES MELTON

Knocked together in 1964, this old stone Lutheran church – the Zum Kriplein Christi church, in fact – is now a fabulous boutique B&B. It's a few minutes' drive south of central Tanuda, on the same road as a string of good wineries. Inside you'll find black leather couches, a marble-tiled bathroom, two bedrooms and a cranking wood-heater. Two-night minimum. *meltons.com.au; tel 08-8563 3606; 192 Krondorf Rd, Tanuda*

MARBLE LODGE

A grandiose 1915 Federation-style villa on the (reasonably steep!) hill behind the town, built from local pink and white granite. Accommodation is in two plush suites behind the house (high-colonial or high-kitsch, depending on your world view). Breakfast is served in the main house – a candlelit, buffet-style experience. *www.marblelodge.com.au; tel 08-8564 2478; 21 Dean St, Angaston*

WHERE TO EAT

FINO SEPPELTSFIELD

From a humble start in a little stone cottage on the Fleurieu Peninsula, Fino has evolved into one of Australia's best restaurants, now ensconced in the gorgeous 1851 Seppeltsfield estate west of Tanuda. Food from the understated, deceptively simple menu highlights local ingredients, and is designed to be shared. *www.fino.net.au; tel 08-8562 8528; 730 Seppeltsfield Rd, Seppeltsfield; noon–3pm daily, 6pm–8.30pm Fri–Sat*

VINTNERS BAR & GRILL

One of the Barossa's landmark restaurants, Vintners stresses simple elegance in both food and atmosphere. The dining room has an open fire, vineyard views and bolts of crisp white linen; menus concentrate on local produce and conjure up sensational dishes. *www.vintners.com.au; tel 08-8564 2488; cnr Stockwell and Nuriootpa Rds, Angaston; noon–2.30pm daily, 6.30pm–9pm Mon–Sat*

WHAT TO DO

BAROSSA FARMERS MARKET

Occupying a big farm shed behind Vintners Bar & Grill, head to this weekly market for hearty Germanic offerings, coffee, flowers and lots of local produce. The Facebook page is updated weekly on Thursdays with a list of each week's stallholders. *www.barossafarmersmarket.com; cnr Stockwell and Nuriootpa Rds, Angaston; 7.30am–11.30am Sat*

MENGLER'S HILL LOOKOUT

From Tanuda, take the scenic route to Angaston via Bethany for hazy valley views (just bypass the naff sculptures). Menglers Hill Rd tracks through beautiful rural country, studded with huge eucalyptus.

CELEBRATIONS

BAROSSA GOURMET WEEKEND

Fab food matched with winning wines at select wineries. The number-one event in the valley, usually held in September (book accommodation way in advance). *www.barossagourmet.com*

Ø1

Courtesy of Skillogalee

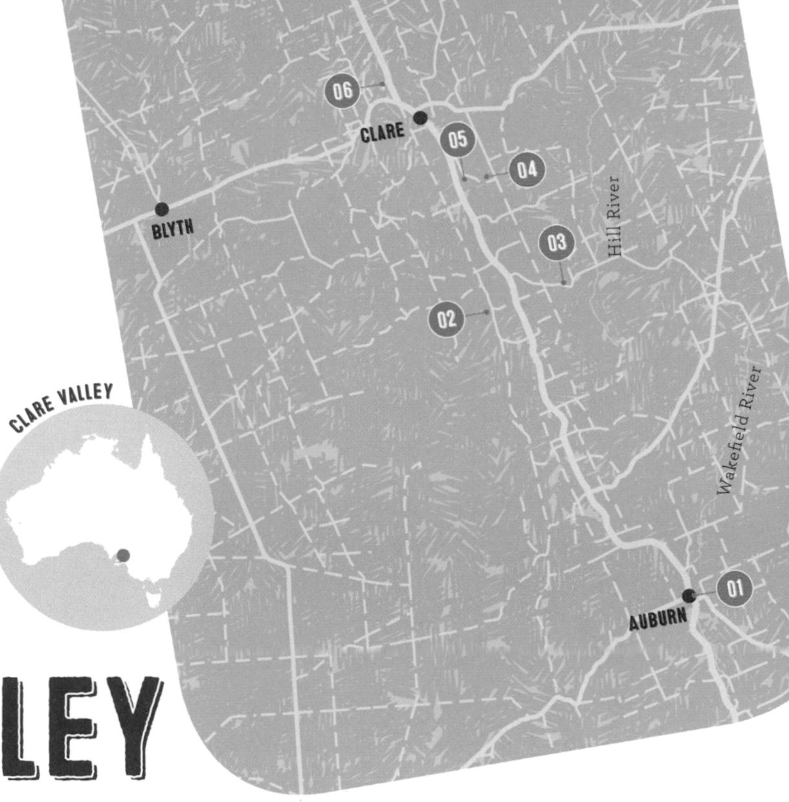

[South Australia]

CLARE VALLEY

Take the Riesling Trail through sleepy Clare Valley to meet friendly winemakers and sample some of Australia's most food-friendly wines.

Follow a back-road south out of a town called Clare – a left, a right, and a left under a canopy of blue-green gum trees – and a few minutes later you could be sipping from a glass of chilled Riesling on the porch of Skillogalee. Skillogalee is one of around 40, mainly family-run wineries in South Australia's Clare Valley, an Edenic plateau (not a valley) about two hours' drive north of Adelaide. Most of the wineries have cellar doors offering tastings and often platters of locally sourced produce, and the welcome at each is as warm as the Australian sun. Base yourself around the town of Clare and you'll be within easy reach of most cellar doors.

Clare, says Skillogalee owner Dave Palmer, is a well-kept secret. This is one reason why it makes the Wine Trails cut; unlike Barossa, the cellar doors don't have parking spaces for coaches. Another reason is that it's extremely pretty, with secluded wineries hiding down shady lanes. And the final reason is what those wineries make – some of the best Riesling in the world.

Riesling is a distinctive white wine most often associated with northern Europe (especially Alsace in France and Germany's Mosel Valley) but in Clare they've taken the grape, lost some of its sweetness and added a strong mineral edge. What ends up in your glass here is arguably the best possible companion for Asian food.

Most wine-tourers will be arriving from Adelaide – beyond Clare, the terrain gets increasingly rugged until you arrive in the Flinders Ranges and the start of the true Outback. Before you arrive in Clare you'll pass through the Barossa, now home to many of Australian wine's biggest and most historic names. Clare too is rich in heritage, with some century-old vineyards. But the place also seems to inspire an adventurous spirit in its winemakers – long may that continue.

GET THERE
Adelaide has the closest airport; Clare is a couple of hours' drive away, beyond Barossa Valley.

01 WINES BY KT

Kerri Thompson's a one-woman band, founding Wines by KT in 2006 after a career making wine in not only Clare Valley but also Tuscany, Beaujolais and McLaren Vale. As a Riesling evangelist, she has set up shop in the right place, occupying a small cellar door on the main street of Auburn in the south of Clare Valley. Her solo venture combines her experience with an experimental edge that allows her to produce the Pazza, an unfiltered, wild-fermented natural wine among more classic single-vineyard wines. It's an interesting place to begin your journey into Clare's world-class Rieslings.

www.winesbykt.com; tel 0419 855500; 20 Main Rd, Auburn; 11am-4pm Sat-Sun from Sep-Jan, outside these days only on the last weekend of the month

02 SKILLOGALEE

'We were city kids but always had a yen to do something in the country,' says David Palmer. So Dave and Diane Palmer bought Skillogalee, a vineyard with a cottage little-changed since it was built by a Cornish miner in 1851. As Barossa was being settled by Germanic people, so British, Irish and Polish settlers ventured further up to Clare; the Cornish came out to work in the mines.

When the Palmers took over the winery in 1989 they knew nothing about winemaking, admits David. 'A local said "just watch when your neighbour gets his tractor out and take yours out then", so that's how we learned.'

Today, son Dan is the winemaker, producing some of Clare's best wines, and daughter Nicola is the chef at the cellar door's cosy restaurant. Skillogalee's basket-pressed Shiraz, with a minty, acid edge, is more food-friendly than reds from Barossa, which tend to have higher alcohol levels. His very best wines are bottled under the Trevarrick label. The family wanted the vineyard to become sustainable so they plant cover crops to protect the soil, and the skins, seeds and stalks are composted and returned to the earth.

In their out-of-the-way location down an eucalypt-lined lane,

From top left: courtesy of Skillogalee; Tim Adams Wines; Jim Barry Wines; Skillogalee

'To make a product that gives people so much pleasure is a privilege.'

–David Palmer, Skillogalee

01 Skillogalee cellar door

02 Skillogalee vines

03 Skillogalee's David Palmer at work

04 Tom and Sam Barry of Jim Barry Wines

05 The view from Paulett Wines

06 Tim Adams wines

the Palmers are living the rural Australian idyll, with echidnas under the verandah, frogs in the pond and 'roos out back. 'At sunset,' says Dave, 'we take a bottle and some glasses up to the top of the hill and watch the sun set over the dry sheep and wheat country to the west.'
www.skillogalee.com.au; tel +61 08 8843 4311; Trevarrick Rd, Sevenhill; 10am-5pm daily

03 PAULETT WINES

It was Penfolds' head winemaker who recommended Neil and Alison Paulett start a winery in Clare Valley. 'It's a reliable region,' says Alison Paulett, 'the elevation brings hot days and cool nights, which slow the ripening and lend the Riesling its austere style.' Winemaker Neil's Polish Hill River Riesling has waves of citrus and a mineral backbone, helping it to age for 10 years or more. Their single-vineyard Andreas Shiraz, named after the property's first Polish owner, comes from 80-year-old vines and then spends more than two years in French oak barrels. 'The most important thing,' laughs Alison, 'is getting people to know where Clare is.' Their wines are spreading the word.
www.paulettwines.com.au; tel +61 08 8843 4328; Polish Hill River Rd, Clare, 10am-5pm daily

04 ADELINA

You shouldn't judge a wine by its bottle but Adelina has some of the best-looking labels in the business.

Courtesy of Paulett Wines

Adelina is the brainchild of New Zealand-born young gun winemaker Col McBryde and his wife Jennie Gardner: 'I studied oenology and viticulture at Adelaide University, Jennie was doing a PhD in yeast when we met,' he says.

Luckily, what's in Adelina's bottles lives up to the promise of its label. This is in part because the couple have access to one of the most historic vineyards in Australia, Wendouree, established in 1895. 'We're fortunate as young producers in an age-old industry to have the resources of 100-year-old Shiraz vines and 85-year old Grenache vines. For us it's more of a custodianship, to look after the vineyard, the soil and make sure what we're doing is sustainable.'

McBryde's tastes tend towards the more spartan, Old World styles and at Adelina, in the heart of a region known for its cool-climate Shiraz and well-honed Rieslings, McBryde and Gardner strived do things differently. 'If there are two regions that speak to us, they'd be Piedmont and Burgundy.' They started chasing, as McBryde puts it, 'something more medium-bodied with a certain femininity.' The results can be tasted (by appointment) in the Estate Shiraz, the Estate Grenache and in Adelina's Riesling, all made with grapes harvested from vines planted in the early 20th century.
www.adelina.com.au; tel 08-8842 1549; Lot 2, Wendouree Rd East, Clare; by appt only

05 TIM ADAMS WINES

Brett Schutz, a winemaker at Tim Adams, in the heart of Clare Valley, believes European makers of Riesling are adopting the Australian style, with lower sugar levels. In return, the Clare Valley is adopting an European idea: 'The essence of *terroir* is important here. No two areas of Clare are the same; there are microclimates so you can blend minerality from Watervale with fruitier grapes from the warmer north end of Clare.' The result is a brisk, dry, crisp Riesling, thanks to a fast 14-day fermentation. 'All Tim asks us to do is express the fruit through the wine.'
www.timadamswines.com.au; tel 08-8842 2429; Warenda Rd, Clare; 10.30am-5pm Mon-Fri, 11am-5pm Sat & Sun

06 JIM BARRY WINES

For some of Clare's most exciting wines, from its highest and oldest vineyards, head up to the far side of town. First planted in the 1960s, the Armagh vineyard, named after the green hills of Irish settlers' home county, makes world-class Shiraz wine. The Florita vineyard in Watervale, one of the area's oldest, produces the monstrously good Lodge Hill Riesling.
www.jimbarry.com; tel 08-8842 2261; 33 Craig Hill Road, Clare; 9am-5pm Mon-Fri, 9am-4pm Sat & Sun

ESSENTIAL INFORMATION

WHERE TO STAY

CLARE VALLEY MOTEL

The Clare Valley Motel is an affordable base for a weekend away among the vines. It has been renovated over recent years by owners Lee and Jan Stokes but retains the quaint vibe of a traditional country motel.
www.clarevalleymotel.com.au; tel 08-8842 2799; 74a Main North Road, Clare

SKILLOGALEE

An overnight stay at Skillogalee's cottage, perhaps after a home-cooked meal in the restaurant, allows you to wake up to breakfast in the peace and quiet of the vineyard. That's a win-win.
www.skillogalee.com.au; tel 08-8843 4311; Trevarrick Rd, Sevenhill

WHERE TO EAT

SEED

Newly germinated in Clare, Seed is an all-day eatery in an atmospheric old building. Fresh, healthy, regional cuisine is served, including platters for sharing. In the evening the wine bar is buzzing.
Tel 08-8842 2323; 308 Main North Rd, Clare

06

Courtesy of Tim Adams Wines

WHAT TO DO

Following the course of a disused railway line between Auburn and Clare, the fabulous Riesling Trail is 24km of traffic-free cycling trail. The gentle gradient means you can walk or push a pram along it easily. Take your time and explore the dozens of detours to cellar doors along the way. Bikes can be hired at either end of the route.
www.rieslingtrailbike-hire.com.au

Some three hours' drive beyond Clare, the Flinders Ranges National Park is a highlight of South Australia. Its saw-toothed ranges are home to native wildlife and, after rain, carpets of wild flowers. An 80-sq-km natural basin known as Wilpena Pound is the big-ticket drawcard. There's accommodation at the Wilpena Pound Resort.

CELEBRATIONS

Slurp previews of the latest wines from the local makers at the annual Clare Valley Gourmet Weekend in May. Around 20 wineries participate, with food and live music also on the menu.
www.clarevalley.com.au

BRAND'S LAIRA
COONAWARRA
01

Courtesy of Brand's Laira

[South Australia]

COONAWARRA

Make the pilgrimage to secluded Coonawarra to give thanks to its terra rossa for killer Cabernets and seductive Shiraz.

Coonawarra is a fairly remote place, 340km southeast of Adelaide and roughly halfway between Melbourne and Adelaide but positioned well off the Western Highway, the main road linking the two. Nevertheless, it's the main wine region of the Limestone Coast, the name given to this southeastern stretch between the flat, olive span of the lower Murray River and the Victorian border.

Coonawarra's wine story began in 1861 when a Scot named John Riddoch established the Coonawarra Fruit Growing Colony, choosing this spot close to the town of Penola on the advice of a fellow Scot, William Wilson, who had settled in the area several years earlier. Small landholders planted fruit trees and grapevines, and Riddoch built a winery (present-day Wynns) to vinify their grapes. The Depression of the late 19th century and Riddoch's untimely death sadly put paid to his dreams of prosperity for the region, but Coonawarra went on to flourish in the second half of the 20th century and is today synonymous with Cabernet.

The not-so-secret ingredient of its success is the unusual *terra rossa* (red earth) soil: a thin layer of red clay-loam with a deep limestone subsoil, the residue of eons of retreating coastlines. On the present coastline are the charming fishing towns of Robe and Beachport, and well-timed detours off the main roads will reward you with stunning lagoons, surf beaches and sequestered bays. What's below the road is even more amazing: a bizarre subterranean landscape of limestone caves, sinkholes and bottomless crater lakes – a broad, formerly volcanic area that's known as the Kanawinka Geopark. Another unmissable geological spectacle is the world heritage-listed Naracoorte Caves, a half-hour's drive north of the wineries on our trail, and well worth the trip.

GET THERE
Coonawara is halfway between Melbourne and Adelaide – the drive from Adelaide takes about 3.5hrs.

01 Topping up the glasses at Brand's Laira

02 Katnook cellar door

03 Highland cattle on Bellwether's land

04 Bellwether's sheep shed-turned-winery

01 PARKER COONAWARRA ESTATE

Soft, white Mount Gambier stone is the preferred building material in the southeast and many wineries make use of it, including Parker Estate's striking maturation cellar and cellar door. Erected in 2001, it stands in the Abbey vineyard which was planted by founder John Parker, just north of the Penola township in the southern half of the Coonawarra region.

Today, the property is owned by the Hesketh family's WD Wines and the 20-hectare vineyard is mainly given over to Cabernet Sauvignon, Merlot and Petit Verdot. The flagship wine is the famous First Growth Cabernet Sauvignon, a high-priced and rather pretentiously named wine that has greatly improved in recent vintages. It's brighter and more nuanced than ever, with a multitude of berry, spice and floral aromas.
www.parkercoonawarraestate.com.au; tel 08-8737 3525; 15688 Riddoch Hwy, Coonawarra; 10am–4pm daily

02 PATRICK OF COONAWARRA

One of Coonawarra's newer wineries, Patrick of Coonawarra was opened in 2004 by the late Patrick Tocaciu, a renowned winemaker. His eldest son Luke, a university-trained winemaker with international experience, is now at the helm, continuing family tradition at the same time as experimenting with other ventures: he's behind the refreshing cider, christened Applelation Cider, handmade at the winery from fresh apple juice. For another source of refreshment, take your pick from Patrick's Rieslings, which are among the region's finest.

The family owns 80 hectares of vines in Coonawarra and Wrattonbully, with their Home Block dedicated to Cabernet Sauvignon. At the cellar door, you can buy assorted wine paraphernalia, including Riedel glassware, books and decanters, as well as a case or two of wine and cider.
www.patrickofconnawarra; tel 08-8737 3687; cnr Riddoch Hwy and Ravenswood Ln, Coonawarra; 10am–5pm daily

From top left: courtesy of Katnook / Mike Annese / Blink Productions; Bellwether (2)

03 KATNOOK ESTATE

Katnook Estate takes its name from an indigenous word meaning 'fat land', a tribute to the rich resource of the terra rossa. It's a place steeped in history: the cellar door is a renovated limestone building from the 1860s from which the wine region's founder John Riddoch once ran his Coonawarra Fruit Growing Colony, and his former shearing shed served as the original winery. Katnook has twice won Australia's most famous wine award, the Jimmy Watson Trophy, in 1987 and 1998, as well as a double trophy at the International Wine & Spirit Competition in 2003. Ironically, neither of the Watsons went to the estate's finest wine, the flagship Cabernet Sauvignon named Odyssey, a wonderfully concentrated, decadently rich and complex wine.

Take a look at the soil pit near the cellar door, a hole in the ground which clearly shows the layered soil profile that helps make Coonawarra such a special wine-growing region. It's worth nothing that tastings are free here, even if you reach for the top-price Odyssey and Prodigy wines.

www.katnookestate.com.au; tel 08-8737 0300; Riddoch Hwy, Coonawarra; 10am–5pm Mon–Sat, 11am–5pm Sun

04 MAJELLA

Brian ('Prof') and Tony Lynn, proprietors of Majella, are fourth-generation Coonawarrans whose family started out as shopkeepers, moving into grazing and later into viticulture. Brian and Tony established the vineyards in 1968, initially selling the grapes on to other producers, but eventually bringing winemaker Bruce Gregory on board – he's stayed for every vintage since.

The Lynns now have about 60 hectares of vines, mainly Cabernet Sauvignon and Shiraz, and their own on-site winery. Their most famous wine is a classic Australian blend of Shiraz and Cabernet, the peppermint- and fruitcake-scented The Malleea. The winery and cellar door complex is housed in a bold, modern corrugated iron building designed by a local Mt Gambier architect.

www.majellawines.com.au; tel 08-8736 3055; Lynn Rd, Coonawarra; 10am–4.30pm daily

05 WYNNS COONAWARRA ESTATE

Wynns' name is synonymous with Coonawarra – there is no better wine producer in the region, thanks partly to its large holdings of mature vineyards on the best terra rossa soils. With Treasury Wine Estates as its owner, Wynns has the resources needed to invest in improving its vineyards,

05 Fresh from the kitchen at Bellwether

06 Inside Naracoorte Caves National Park

which it has done with great effect over the past 20 years. Revered for its flagship John Riddoch Cabernet Sauvignon and Michael Shiraz, it's the black label Cabernet Sauvignon with a lineage back to 1954 that is the most renowned. There are also good-value, widely available wines: a fragrant Riesling (one of the region's best), Chardonnay, white label Shiraz and red-stripe labelled Cabernet Shiraz Merlot are all very affordable.

The cellar door dates from 1896, when it was constucted by Penola pioneer John Riddoch, and serves up excellent cheese platters and wine by the glass to enjoy as you sink into deep armchairs and squishy sofas. Older vintages are also available to buy – and often to taste. If you're so inclined, you can try your hand at a spot of winemaking with the 'make your own blend' experience, and head home with your own personal version of Wynns' Cabernet Shiraz Merlot.

www.wynns.com.au; tel 08-8736 2225; 1 Memorial Dr, Coonawarra; 10am–5pm daily

06 BRAND'S LAIRA

Brand's is a sizeable owner of vineyards making first-rate wines. Started by the Brand family in 1966, it's now part of the even more sizeable Casella group which also owns Peter Lehmann and Yellowtail.

Visiting the winery you'll find some wines exclusive to cellar door customers, one of which is Stentiford's Shiraz, named after the man who planted the oldest block of Brand's vines, in 1893. Off to one side is a tiny, old stone building which is dubbed Eric's Cellar (after founder Eric Brand), lined with bins of ancient bottles, and where personalised tastings are conducted at its rough-hewn bench tables.

www.brandslaira.com.au; tel 08-8736 3260; 14860 Riddoch Hwy, Coonawarra; 9am–4.30pm Mon–Fri, 11am–4pm Sat–Sun

07 BELLWETHER

Seven kilometres north of Coonawarra village, Bellwether is one of the smallest producers in the region. Before buying the historic 1868 Glen Roy stone shearing shed – built by Chinese labourers en route from fishing port Robe to the Victorian goldfields – and transforming it into a winery, Sue Bell was chief winemaker at Hardys' Padthaway winery, since closed. She makes a classic Coonawarra Cabernet Sauvignon as well as wines from regions as far apart as Tasmania, Heathcote and the Riverland. But alongside these superb wines, Bell has used her wealth of experience and creative bent to hew something very special here – the cellar door includes a community kitchen, produce garden and camping ground, a paradise for kids with a tree house, trampoline and farm animals mooching about.

www.bellwetherwines.com.au; tel 0417 080 945; 14183 Riddoch Hwy, Coonawarra; 11am–5pm Thu–Mon

ESSENTIAL INFORMATION

WHERE TO STAY

GIRRAWEEN HOUSE

Run by Bruce Gregory, Majella's winemaker, and his wife, this comfortable and spacious B&B is right in the heart of the wine region. You're left to your own devices, with ample breakfast supplies provided and a shop, restaurant and a handful of wineries all within walking distance.
www.stayz.com.au; tel 08-8736 3220; 10 Helen Rd, Coonawarra

ALEXANDER CAMERON SUITES

Looking much less bleak now that some trees have matured around it, this newish motel over on the Mt Gambier side of town offers stylish rooms, well-tended gardens and rural Australian architectural stylings. It's named after Penola's founder, a wiry Scottish pastoralist: you can check out his statue next to the pub. A three-bedroom house is also available.
www.alexandercameronsuites.com.au; tel 08-8737 2200; 23 Church St, Penola

WHERE TO EAT

PIPERS OF PENOLA

A classy, intimate dining room tastefully constructed inside a 1908 Methodist church, with friendly staff and seasonal fare. The menu is studded with ingredients like truffled parsnip, mustard fruit and labneh (Lebanese yoghurt cheese) – serious gourmet indicators – and there's a great wine list with lots of local names. The prices are lofty, but so is the quality.
www.pipersofpenola.com.au; tel 08-8737 3999; 58 Riddoch St, Penola; 6pm–9pm Tue–Sat

WHAT TO DO

NARACOORTE CAVES NATIONAL PARK

While you're in the area, don't miss the World Heritage-listed Naracoorte Caves – 26 limestone caves including Alexandra Cave, Cathedral Cave and Victoria Fossil Cave, all with arresting stalactite and stalagmite formations. The discovery of an ancient fossilised marsupial raised palaeontological eyebrows around the world, and featured in the BBC's David Attenborough series *Life on Earth*.
www.environment.sa.gov.au/naracoorte; tel 08-8762 2340; 89 Wonambi Rd, Naracoorte; 9am–5pm daily

PENOLA

A friendly rural town, Penola is famous not only for being smack-bang in the middle of the Coonawarra wine region, but also for its association with the Sisters of St Joseph of the Sacred Heart, co-founded in 1687 by Australia's first saint, Mary MacKillop. You can drop in at the Mary MacKillop Interpretative Centre to find out more, and see the old stone schoolhouse where she taught.
www.mackilloppenola.org.au; tel 08-8737 2092; cnr Portland St and Petticoat Ln, Penola; 10am–4pm daily

CELEBRATIONS

COONAWARRA CABERNET CELEBRATIONS

A month-long Cabernet carnival, with tastings, dinners, showcase events and live music.
coonawarra.org/event/coonawarra-cabernet-celebrations

01

Courtesy of Bremerton / Dylan Minchenberg

[South Australia]

LANGHORNE CREEK

Mellow Malbec and full-bodied Cabernet Sauvignon reign supreme in this sometimes overlooked little pocket of South Australia, ripe for exploring on two wheels.

At the eastern reach of the Fleurieu Peninsula, tucked between the Adelaide Hills and Lake Alexandrina, Langhorne Creek is a somewhat under-appreciated wine region. Granted, it's a small place, lacking the glamour of McLaren Vale (and not quite so close to the big city), but there are other reasons why it hovers under the radar. The region's grape-growers historically sold most of their grapes to big wineries elsewhere, who often neglected to mention Langhorne Creek as the source. It therefore struggled to muster much of a public profile, unlike the Barossa or Coonawarra. Secondly, and no doubt related, there were only a handful of wineries – today, the region has gained recognition for cultivating new varietals and there are more than enough wineries with cellar doors to warrant a weekend trip.

Until recently, the most unusual feature of the wine region was an annual flood. By a system of weirs, gates and channels, the Bremer River waters would be diverted through the vineyards on the river flats, giving them a crude form of flood irrigation. This depended on a high river following good rains in the Adelaide Hills catchment – a relatively uncontrolled technique that is now frowned upon. Many of today's vineyards are at a distance from the floodplain and out of reach of the water anyway.

The natural fertility of the floodplains, cool maritime climate and moderating effects of winds moving across huge Lake Alexandrina together create conditions in which red varieties thrive. Cabernet Sauvignon is top dog and Shiraz and Merlot can also be very good, but it's full-bodied, plummy Malbec that has a special affinity. Of all Australian wine regions, Langhorne Creek is the one most likely to produce reds with pepperminty aromas, and this applies to all varieties.

GET THERE
Langhorne Creek is just under 1hr southeast of Adelaide by car.

01 ANGAS PLAINS ESTATE

Positioned on the delta of the Angas River just before it empties into Lake Alexandrina, this small vineyard and winery has won awards for its food, rustic dishes such as pumpkin soup, pies, pizzas and grazing platters served up at its cosy cellar door. Fortunately the wines, made by Coonawarra-based contract winemaker Peter Douglas, are also very good.

Owners Philip and Judy Cross enrich their soils with mulch provided by cover-crops grown between the vines. The wines are vinified in small batches to maximise the winemaker's control of style and quality.

PJ's Shiraz is the pick, with soft tannins and greater elegance than is usually found in this district – the 2014 is recommended. The Special Reserve wines, a Cabernet Sauvignon and a Shiraz, are a step up in concentration and structure, big wines with ripeness and balance. *www.angasplainswines.com.au; tel 08-8537 3159; 317 Angas Plains Rd; 11am–5pm Thu–Mon or by appt*

02 BREMERTON

Lucy and Rebecca Willson, marketing manager and chief winemaker respectively, are the first sisters in Australia to manage and operate a winery, and an excellent one it is. The wines are top quality, and many of them are surprisingly modestly priced, especially those with the Special Release, Tamblyn (a four-way Cabernet-led blend), Selkirk (Shiraz) and Coulthard (Cabernet Sauvignon) labels. Don't miss their flagship reds: the powerful, chocolatey Old Adam Shiraz and Walter's Reserve Cabernet. The BOV (Best Of Vintage) is a real showstopper, an intensely dense blackberry-and-licorice 50/50 Cabernet Shiraz.

The cellar door is housed in an airy restored 1860s stone barn, the walls bedecked with artworks by local artists. Tempting luncheon platters and gourmet pizzas are served here, and you can also stock up on other goodies like local produce, souvenirs and gifts.

From top left: courtesy of Lake Breeze; Bremerton; Lake Breeze

01 Bremerton's restored stone barn

02 The restaurant deck at Lake Breeze

03 Lucy and Rebecca Wilson of Bremerton

04 Lake Breeze

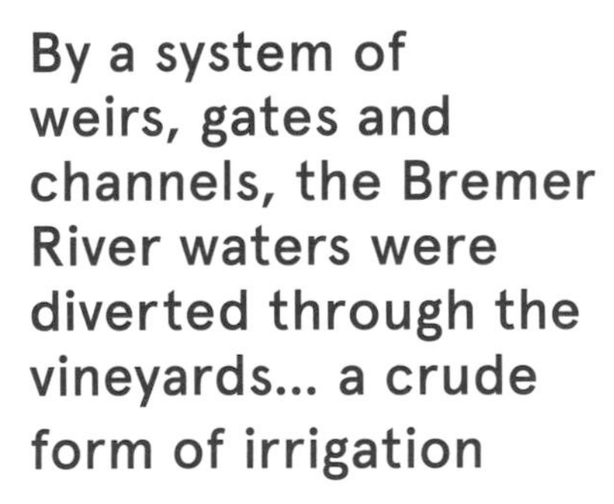

By a system of weirs, gates and channels, the Bremer River waters were diverted through the vineyards... a crude form of irrigation

www.bremerton.com.au; tel 08-8537 3093; Langhorne Creek Rd, Langhorne Creek; 10am–5pm daily

03 THE WINEHOUSE

Every wine region should have one of these: a central tasting facility where visitors can sample a range of local wines, and eat a tasty, freshly cooked meal in pleasant surroundings. This stone building in the middle of town is home to six producers who don't have any other cellar door: Ben Potts, Gipsie Jack, John's Blend, Heartland and Kimbolton. And Meechi craft beers: a lager and an ale brewed in Langhorne Creek. Meechi's partners include Ben Potts and Bremerton's Lucy Willson.

Ben is from one of the district's most distinguished wine families. He runs Gipsie Jack with former long-time Wolf Blass chief winemaker John Glaetzer. Glaetzer's own wine is the iconic John's Blend, a statuesque, oak-driven Cabernet Sauvignon that's been made for 39 years (as of the 2013 vintage). Heartland is the Langhorne Creek brand of high-profile Barossa winemaker Ben Glaetzer, a nephew of John's. And Kimbolton is a vineyard on land that was once part of Bleasdale. Apart from that, they have nothing in common!
www.thewinehouse.com.au; tel 08-8537 3441; 1509 Langhorne Creek Rd, Langhorne Creek; 10am–5pm daily

05 Sam Martin, sales manager at Bremerton

06 Pelicans at Coorong National Park

04 BLEASDALE

Founded by the Potts family in 1850, this is the region's elder statesman winery, celebrating 165 years of Potts family involvement just a few years ago. There's certainly a sense of history about the place – an old press with a 3.5 tonne red-gum lever makes an awe-inspiring centerpiece and the spacious cellar door is decorated with local artists' handiwork and historical memorabilia.

With talented winemaker Paul Hotker in charge – recently crowned 2018 Halliday Winemaker of the Year – the wines have never been better, and consistently reel in awards by way of recognition of this fact. Malbec is a speciality and there are at least three bottlings: Second Innings, Generations and the flagship, Double Take. Some of the wines are only available at the cellar door – which offers even more reason to visit.
www.bleasdale.com.au; tel 08-8537 4022; 1640 Langhorne Creek Rd, Langhorne Creek; 10am–5pm daily

05 LAKE BREEZE

One of the oldest established vineyards on the floodplain of the Bremer River, Lake Breeze boasts a beautiful location, lush, wide open spaces framed by statuesque old river red gums. The owners, the Follett family, have farmed in this area since 1880, grown grapes since the 1930s and made wine since 1987.

The cellar door is cool and spacious and lunches are served in the contemporary restaurant, which has a fine view from the upstairs deck. Winemaker Greg Follett's wines regularly land trophies in the wine shows, and his entry-level Shiraz Cabernet, Bernoota, is one of the best-value reds you'll find anywhere.
www.lakebreeze.com.au; tel 08-8537 3017; 319 Step Rd, Langhorne Creek; 10am–5pm daily

06 TEMPLE BRUER

Temple Bruer is a maverick winery, starkly individual in a region of broad-acre vineyards and big-company influence. It is small, self-sufficient and certified organic since 1995. The winery is also carbon-neutral, more environmentally aware than most, and describes itself as 'dedicated to producing 'wines that don't cost the earth'.

Happily, most of Temple Bruer's wines are modestly priced too, and while they don't offer conventional tastings, this is still a special place worth visiting. The slurpy 2017 Grenache Shiraz is raspberry-scented and gentle on the palate; the 2017 Pinot Noir is robust and minty and the 2017 Rosé is bright and cherry-like.
www.templebruer.com.au; tel 08-8537 0203; 689 Milang Rd, Angas Plains; 9.30am–4.30pm Mon–Fri

ESSENTIAL INFORMATION

WHERE TO STAY

BOATHOUSE RETREAT

Low-key and elegant Goolwa is an unassuming river port with a fantastic beach – not a bad choice for a base. Around the riverfront from downtown, the Boathouse is a photogenic, woody boat shed (minus the boat), with a sunny deck and private marina out front full of bobbing boats. It's a two-person affair, angled towards the romantically inclined. DIY breakfast goodies will be waiting in the fridge. *www.birksharbour.com.au; tel 08-8555 0338; 138 Liverpool Rd, Goolwa*

GASWORKS COTTAGES

Quaint and comfortable self-contained cottages, including a converted stables, in the heart of Strathalbyn. You'll have all manner of birds for company in the beautiful landscaped gardens, and a spa too. *www.gasworks-strathalbyn.com.au; tel 08-8563 4291; 12–14 South Terrace, Strathalbyn*

06

WHERE TO EAT

FLYING FISH CAFE

Sit down for a cafe breakfast and you'll be here all day – the views of Horseshoe Bay, a gorgeous orange-sand arc with gentle surf and good swimming, are sublime. Otherwise, grab some takeaway Coopers-battered flathead and chips and head for the sand.

At night things get classy, with à la carte mains focusing on independent SA producers. One of SA's must-visit foodie haunts. *www.flyingfishcafe.com.au; tel 08-8554 3504; 1 The Foreshore, Horseshoe Bay, Port Elliot; cafe 9am–4pm daily, restaurant noon–3pm daily, 6pm–8pm Fri–Sat*

THE OLFACTORY INN

A welcome boost to Strathalbyn's dining scene, this small restaurant has a regularly changing menu of generous plates laden with local produce. If decision-making powers have deserted you after a day's wine tasting, opt for the 'feed me' menu for two, a selction of the chef's specials that should satisfy everyone. *www.theolfactoryinn.com.au; tel 044 777 1750; 35 High St, Strathalbyn; lunch from noon, dinner from 6pm Thu–Sat, tapas 3pm–7pm Sun*

WHAT TO DO

Langhorne Creek itself is a tiny hamlet, but nearby Strathalbyn is a charming, heritage-listed historic town, with a high street full of antique shops.

The flat country of Langhorne Creek is perfect for exploring on two wheels. From Goolwa, you can take to the water with various tours, such as an eco-cruise on the Murray and into the Coorong National Park, including lunch and guided walks, or an all-day small-boat cruise with walks, bush tucker, seal spotting and digging for pipis (shellfish) on the beach. *www.coorongcruises.com.au; www.cruisethecoorong.com.au*

CELEBRATIONS

HANDPICKED FESTIVAL

Lake Breeze hosts this annual (Nov) festival of music and more – thousands descend for a day of live music, local food and wine and handmade goods by local makers. *handpickedfestival.com*

01

Courtesy of D'Arenberg

[South Australia]

MCLAREN VALE

Drift down from Adelaide for an easy day's cellar door-hopping and a taste of the Med, rounded off with a sundowner on the beach.

Just two years after the colony of South Australia was settled, John Reynell and Thomas Hardy planted the first grapevines in McLaren Vale in 1838. They couldn't have chosen a better spot – with its beautiful beaches of sparkling white sand, dramatic cliffs and gentle surf, and proximity to Adelaide, this is one of South Australia's favourite wine tourism destinations. There are over 80 cellar doors and more than a third of them offer local produce, ranging from high-end restaurants to simple platters.

With 30km of coastline, McLaren Vale has an extremely maritime climate which favours the so-called Mediterranean grape varieties, such as those of southern France, Italy and Spain, including Shiraz, Grenache, Mourvèdre, Montepulciano, Tempranillo, Sangiovese, Barbera and Nero d'Avola for reds; and Viognier, Roussanne, Marsanne, Fiano and Vermentino on the white side. In recent years the region has re-focused on what is does best: red grape varieties now predominate, accounting for about 85% of the vines. At the same time, many of the cooler-climate varieties that never truly suited the local conditions have been jettisoned. The maritime climate means there are fewer extremes of temperature – nights are warmer and days cooler than might be expected, resulting in red wines with notably soft tannins.

No Australian region has explored its geology more thoroughly, but then, few have a geology as interesting and varied. Detailed research has resulted in soil maps and identification of rock sub-strata, with the result that many wineries now produce separate sub-regional bottlings of some varieties, especially Shiraz. The best of these are allowed to use the description McLaren Vale Scarce Earth Selection. With such treasure below ground, it follows that McLaren Vale is also noted for its large number of organic vineyards.

GET THERE
McLaren Vale is only 40mins south of Adelaide. Car hire is available at Adelaide Airport.

01 The five-storey d'Arenberg Cube

02 Chapel Hill's cellar door, a former church

03 Loading the truck at Bekkers

04 Hugh Hamilton

01 BEKKERS

A highly qualified duo, viticulturist Toby Bekkers and his winemaker wife Emmanuelle earned their stripes working for other McLaren Vale wineries before setting up on their own in the high Seaview area in 2010. Production is very small – only about 700 cases a year – and the prices are unapologetically high but rest assured, the quality is stunning. They make a Syrah, Grenache and Syrah-Grenache blend, all elegantly packaged and all superb.

As a side project, Emmanuelle taps her contacts in her native France to make small volumes of premier cru Chablis Vaillons. Yes, the wines here are on the expensive side, but you can still taste for a modest $10 fee at their striking tasting room, with its floor-to-ceiling windows and expansive views.

www.bekkerswine.com; tel 0408 807 568; 212 Seaview Rd, McLaren Vale; 10am–4pm Thu–Sat or by appt $

02 CHAPEL HILL

Set in a high, hilly part of McLaren Vale, beside the spectacular Onkaparinga Gorge, this is an extra special stop on the trail. The cellar door is an old, deconsecrated stone church, and there's also a function centre, accommodation and a kitchen where popular cooking classes are held. Every corner of the property enjoys lovely vistas across rolling, vine-bedecked hills. Winemaker Michael Fragos produces a superb array of wines, from the flagship Road Block and Gorge Block Shirazes down to remarkably affordable, regionally typical, character-filled hearty reds of various styles, including Grenache and Mourvèdre.

www.chapelhillwine.com.au; tel 08-8323 8429; cnr Chapel Hill Rd and Chaffeys Rd, McLaren Vale; 11am–5pm daily

03 CORIOLE

Coriole is family-run estate in a picture-perfect location. An 1860s ironstone cottage houses the cellar door, with visitors spilling out into the beautiful garden to enjoy regional tasting platters of homegrown kalamata olives, homemade breads and Adelaide Hill's Woodside cheeses.

Coriole is a pioneer of Italian varieties: Sangiovese, Fiano, Nero d'Avola, Barbera and others are specialities. Owner Mark Lloyd

has led the way with several Mediterranean grapes, the first being Sangiovese in 1987, and his latest obsessions are Fiano and Picpoul. The Fiano makes a delicate, refreshing, dry white suitable for serving as an aperitif or with lighter seafood and fish dishes. Coriole's standard-bearer is Lloyd Reserve Shiraz, a powerful, chocolatey red made from the oldest vines on the property, planted in 1919.

The flourishing garden provides fresh ingredients for the lunch menu in the adjoining restaurant, which is in a converted, vine-covered courtyard with soothing views over the Coriole vineyards and rolling countryside. The garden also serves as a picturesque venue for opera, theatre and poetry readings, as part of a busy events calendar.

www.coriole.com; tel 08-8323 8305; Chaffeys Rd, McLaren Vale; 10am–5pm Mon–Fri, 11am–5pm Sat–Sun

04 KAY BROTHERS AMERY

With the Kay family history stretching back to 1890, the past looms unsurprisingly large here – the style is proudly traditional and the very old vines at the heart of the 22-hectare vineyard set the tone for the whole experience. McLaren Vale's oldest winery has one of the best cellar door locations of the region, at the crest of a hill 5km outside the township.

Reds and fortified wines are the strongpoint, with the crowning glory Block 6 Shiraz: a lush, concentrated wine made from vines over 120 years old. Pack a picnic, borrow some glasses and stretch out on the lawns in front of the cellar door while you savour a historic drop or two. Alongside regular exhibitions by local artists, the meticulous diaries kept by the Kays from 1891 are on display. You can even buy their book, *Kay Brothers: The First 125 Years*.

www.kaybrothersamerywines.com; tel 08-8323 8201; 57 Kays Rd, McLaren Vale; 9am–5pm Mon–Fri, 11am–5pm Sat–Sun

05 D'ARENBERG

Atop a hillside with terrific views, the zany, colourfully dressed Chester Osborn holds court at 'd'Arry's', a unique family winery. The five-storey d'Arenberg Cube – a geometric glass structure, reminiscent of a Rubik's cube touched down among the vines – is the latest innovation: a cellar door, restaurant, wine bar and general wine spectacular that sets the bar higher for the whole district. A fee of $10 gains you entry to five levels of oenophilic experiences (there's no additional fee for cellar door tastings, but you do have to cough up if you fancy a helicopter ride or eight-course degustation menu).

The range of wines is vast and extraordinary, each one with a quirky name and a story to go with it – the Dead Arm Shiraz and Broken Fishplate Sauvignon Blanc are our favourites. The first refers to a fungal disease of old vines, which results in drastically reduced crops of very concentrated grapes; a fishplate is a malfunction-prone

05 Tasting sessions at d'Arenberg

06 SC Pannell's grounds

part of the grape-collecting apparatus of a mechanical harvester. These wine names have become increasingly bizarre and unpronounceable with time – a drop of The Cenosilicaphobic Cat, anyone? Nobody produces more old-vine, single vineyard Shiraz bottlings, some of them under the Scarce Earth banner.
www.darenberg.com.au; tel 08-8329 4888; Osborn Rd, McLaren Vale; 10am–5pm daily

06 SC PANNELL

Stephen Pannell distinguished himself as chief red winemaker at Hardys McLaren Vale, and knows the area intimately. He also has a nose for great wine, an instinct that led him and his wife Fiona to buy two outstanding old vineyards plus an established function centre which they have refurbished to house their winery, cellar door, restaurant and wedding venue.

The brand is only 14 years old but already highly regarded, helped no doubt by Pannell and his wines winning many top awards, including Winemaker of the Year in 2015. Italian and Mediterranean varieties are a speciality, including one of Australia's best Nebbiolos.
www.pannell.com.au; tel 08-8323 8000; 60 Olivers Rd, McLaren Vale; 11am–5pm daily

HUGH HAMILTON

Hugh Hamilton is a fifth-generation member of one of South Australia's most famous wine families, but he casts himself as a maverick, with wines labelled The Oddball, The Scallywag, The Scoundrel and The Ratbag. His Black Sheep wine club offers some quirky wines including Saperavi, a densely concentrated red wine from both McLaren Vale and Georgia (Hugh travels to the former Soviet state for the harvest), plus three majestic McLaren Vale sub-regional Shirazes labelled Black Blood I, II and III.

The cellar door is suitably unique: a polygonal raised platform among the vines with 270-degree views and all sorts of interactive extras (think soil samples, fabric swatches...) to help you engage with the vineyard and the wines, which are served up with matching cheese platters.
www.hughhamiltonwines.com.au; tel 08-8323 8689; 94 McMurtrie Rd, McLaren Vale; 11am–5pm daily

WIRRA WIRRA

Wirra Wirra's charismatic founder, Greg Trott, prioritises play over corporate polish – be it hurling watermelons from a replica medieval catapult or installing a boundary fence of massive red gum slabs, nicknamed Woodhenge (also the name of one of the vineyards, all of which are biodynamically managed). The wines are serious business though: RSW Shiraz and The Angelus Cabernet are standouts but there are plenty of affordable bottles, such as the famous Church Block blend.

Harry's Deli provides coffee and light foods with an emphasis on South Australian produce. Or you can create your own DIY feast at the barbecue area.
www.wirrawirra.com; tel 08-8323 8414; McMurtrie Rd, McLaren Vale; 10am–5pm Mon–Sat, 11am–5pm Sun

Courtesy of D'Arenberg

ESSENTIAL INFORMATION

WHERE TO STAY

BETHANY CHAPEL

Rest in peace in this lovely split-level conversion of an 1854 Wesleyan chapel, with honey-coloured floorboards, a sunny rear deck and wide views across the vines (and the old cemetery). Terrific value for your own private, self-contained church (worship your complimentary bottle of Wirra Wirra on arrival). *www.bethanychapelbnb.com; tel 0416 342 470; 219 Strout Rd, McLaren Vale*

MCLAREN EYE

Super-luxe hillside architectural splendour with an outlook from here to eternity. McLaren Eye has everything you need for a decadent stay – and every room has a view, even the bathroom (slip into the fancy two-person bath). In Kangarilla, 13km from McLaren Vale township. Two-night minimum. *www.mclareneye.com.au; tel 08-8383 7122; 36a Peters Creek Rd, Kangarilla*

WHERE TO EAT

BLESSED CHEESE

The staff at this blessed cafe crank out great coffee, croissants, wraps, salads, tarts, burgers, cheese platters, massive cakes and funky sausage rolls. The menu changes every couple of days, always with an emphasis on local produce. *www.blessedcheese.com.au; tel 08-8323 7958; 150 Main Rd, McLaren Vale; 8am–4pm Mon–Fri, to 5pm Sat, 9am–4pm Sun*

SALOPIAN INN

This old vine-covered inn has been here since 1851. Its latest incarnation features super Mod Oz offerings with an Asian twist: launch into the Berkshire pork buns or blue swimmer crab and prawn dumplings, with a bottle of something local which you can hand-select from the cellar. *www.salopian.com.au; tel 08-8323 8769; cnr Main and McMurtrie Rds, McLaren Vale; noon–3.30pm daily, 6pm–late Thu–Sat*

WHAT TO DO

McLaren Vale is an energetic, utilitarian town that's not much to look at, but it has some great places to eat and of course it offers easy access to all of our selected cellar doors.

If this leaves you with a thirst for beer, head for family-run Goodieson Brewery, where pale ale, pilsner, wheat beer and brown ale are brewed, plus brilliant seasonal beers. Sip a few on the sunny terrace. *www.goodiesonbrewery.com.au*

CELEBRATIONS

SEA & VINES FESTIVAL

It seems like most of Adelaide buses down to the annual Sea & Vines Festival over the June long weekend. Local wineries cook up seafood, splash wine around and host live bands. *www.seaandvines.com.au*

06

01

Courtesy of Puddleduck / Sarah Ryan

[Tasmania]

COAL RIVER VALLEY

From A-list producers to family-focused cellar doors and new restaurants, the Coal River Valley is keeping step with the rise in wine tourism.

Just a short drive northeast out of Hobart, crossing the lofty Tasman Bridge, brings you to the centre of Tasmania's fastest-growing wine region, the Coal River Valley. Some operations here are sophisticated affairs with gourmet restaurants, others are small, family-owned vineyards with cellar doors open by appointment. While it's tempting to combine a visit to the Coal with a dip into nearby Derwent Valley wineries, there are enough cellar doors here to warrant a dedicated visit. In fact, this region has the largest concentration of vineyards in southern Tasmania.

Tasmania's most important grape variety, Pinot Noir, finds itself at home in the Coal River Valley where the mild climate provides near-perfect ripening conditions, although differentiation in climate and soil add interest and variety to the wines. A case in point: the Pooley family finds its Richmond vineyard Butcher's Hill ripens two to three weeks earlier than Cooinda Vale, upriver near Campania at the top of the valley. Domaine A, also at Campania, is one of the few places in Tasmania where Cabernet Sauvignon ripens with any consistency: while the nights are colder, the days are hotter.

Hobart is a good base – a vibrant harbour town, with plenty to fill your downtime between wine trails. The Gasworks Cellar Door bottle shop stocks more than 300 wines from 81 Tasmanian producers, including those that don't open to the public, like renowned Tolpuddle, plus spirits from the island's distilleries. Closer to the Coal River Valley, Richmond and Cambridge are quieter places to stay.

Full of 19th-century buildings, Richmond is arguably Tasmania's premier historic town, although businesses err on the 'kitsch colonial' side of tourism. That said, it's picturesque and convenient for the airport.

GET THERE
Coal River Valley is a short drive from Hobart. Fly to Hobart from Sydney or Melbourne, or travel by car ferry (9-11 hrs).

Courtesy of Domaine A / Jon Jarvela (2); Frogmore Creek / Ewen Bell

01 POOLEY WINES

A visit to this 1830s sandstone building near Richmond reveals one of the most heartwarming stories in Tasmanian wine. The family are Tasmania's only third-generation wine business: Denis and Margaret Pooley, grandparents of the current generation Matt (vineyards) and Anna (winemaker), planted the first vines at Cooinda Vale, overlooking the Coal River, in 1985. The impressive Margaret, whose name is enshrined on the Margaret Pooley Tribute Reserve Riesling, continued working well into her nineties.

The business expanded in 2005 with the purchase of a second property, Belmont, the old stables being reclaimed as the new cellar door. Here the Pooleys planted another vineyard, Butcher's Hill, whose cracking, black, dolorite-based clay soils produce richer, more powerful Pinots, contrasting with the elegant wines, lifted with a fine acid line, from Cooinda Vale's sandy loam soils. Both vineyards are fully credited as environmentally sustainable – the only vineyards in Tasmania to earn this status, so far.

The set up is supremely family friendly, and you can enjoy games, pizzas (served at weekends) and cheese platters with your wine.
www.pooleywines.com.au; tel 03-6260 2895; 1431 Richmond Rd, Richmond; 10am–5pm daily

02 FROGMORE CREEK

Frogmore Creek pulls off that old-new trick – traditional, sustainable farming methods inform the vineyard management, as sheep graze between the vines; while in the restaurant, modern tastes are embraced with adventurous dishes using mainly Tasmanian produce. There are more innovative menus to try at Frogmore's other restaurants, The Lounge and Atmosphere, both in Hobart, the latter offering a 'hidden' menu appealing to all the senses.

The cellar door overlooks the Mt Pleasant Observatory and affords sweeping views across the fields and down to the Pittwater estuary. Upstairs, check out Flawed History, an in-floor jigsaw by celebrated local artist Tom Samek which tells the story of Tasmanian wine, before sampling Frogmore's own

01 A feathered resident at Puddleduck

02 Domaine A's bunker-like building

03 Domaine A gateway

04 Locally sourced fare at Frogmore Creek

Pinot Noir finds itself quite at home here, although differentiation in the climate and soil add welcome interest and variety to the wines

contributions – French-born winemaker Alain Rousseau crafts several ranges which start with the affordably priced 42 Degrees South. Try the Chardonnay, Pinot Noir and sticky botrytis Riesling. *www.frogmorecreek.com.au; tel 03-6248 5844; 20 Denholms Rd, Cambridge; 10am–5pm daily*

03 RIVERSDALE ESTATE

One of the newer cellar doors and restaurants in the region, but with some of the oldest vines, Riversdale has hit the ground running and is already a major drawcard for wine tourists. Overlooking the Pittwater estuary, the vineyard has been producing its own superb wines since 2008 – its Crater Chardonnay is the most awarded in Tasmania. The restaurant, The French Bistro, is a more recent addition, and an elegant high tea can be had at The Orangery Conservatory.

A more unusual extra, the Peter Rabbit Garden, makes Riversdale Estate a no-brainer for families with young children. This is the only such garden in the southern hemisphere, endorsed by the estate of Beatrix Potter. All the familiar characters are there, set amid carefully reimagined grounds. *www.riversdaleestate.com.au; tel 03-6248 5555; 222 Denholms Rd, Cambridge; 10am–5pm daily*

04 COAL VALLEY VINEYARD

Pinot Noir is the star of the show at Coal Valley, a small, 5-hectare, sustainably cultivated vineyard, but

05 The pretty Domaine A estate

06 Russell Falls in Mt Field National Park

an unusual sideline is a red made from Tempranillo, the famous Spanish grape that's rarely found in Tasmania. That said, the vineyard's 2017 Riesling won an elite gold medal (with a score of 96 points) at the 2017 Canberra International Riesling Challenge.

There's an informal restaurant which opens daily for lunch and specialises in house-smoked meats. In fine weather, nab a table on the terrace and soak up the glorious views across the Coal River Valley and Pittwater, as at Riversdale Estate and Frogmore Creek.
www.coalvalley.com.au; tel 03-6248 5367; 257 Richmond Rd, Cambridge; 11am–5pm daily (closed July)

05 PUDDLEDUCK VINEYARD

Puddleduck is an antidote to any winery that takes itself too seriously. Stuck for inspiration, once Jackie and Darren Brown settled on their vineyard's name they really ran with the theme: from the logo and the resident ducks on the lake to the gift shop crammed with ducky paraphernalia. It all adds up to a family-friendly venue, with carbon-neutral status and good wines to boot. Opt for the Riesling, Pinot Noir or 'Bubbleduck' sparkling white.

Snacks and platters are available but the 'reverse BYO' policy means you can bring food to enjoy outside, as long as your accompanying drinks are Puddleduck.
www.puddleduckvineyard.com.au; tel 03-6260 2301; 992 Richmond Rd, Richmond; 10am–5pm daily

06 PRESSING MATTERS

Pressing Matters is a no-apologies Riesling specialist, owned by Hobart barrister Greg Melick who's a devotee of Mosel and Burgundy. Pinot Noir is also produced, but surrender to the Riesling, graded by sweetness level from super-dry (R0) to sweet (R169). Though not open regularly, it's straightforward to make a cellar door appointment via the website, just don't expect to turn up hankering after Chardonnay.
www.pressingmatters.com.au; tel 03-6268 1947; 665 Middle Tea Tree Rd, Tea Tree; by appt

07 DOMAINE A

Domaine A, with its sub-label Stoney Vineyard, is one of Tasmania's most famous wineries, and the oldest in the Coal River Valley – it was established in 1973, and bought by Moorilla Estate in 2018. Its superb, estate-grown and made wines were distributed around the world by the owners, Swiss immigrants Peter and Ruth Althaus, for 29 years.

Domaine A wines, which enjoy the 'outstanding' ranking in Langton's Classification of Australian Wine and have critics in raptures, are on the expensive side but the Stoney range is more pocket-friendly. The cellar door, winery and barrel room share the one concrete bunker-like building, and you can see the barrels of quietly maturing Cabernet from the tasting room. It's a place of pilgrimage for serious wine geeks.
www.domaine-a.com.au; tel 03-6260 4174; 105 Tea Tree Rd, Campania; 10am–4pm Mon–Fri

ESSENTIAL INFORMATION

WHERE TO STAY

DAISY BANK COTTAGES

A rural delight: two spotless, stylish self-contained units (one with spa) in a converted 1840s sandstone barn on a working sheep farm. There are loft bedrooms, views of the Richmond rooftops and plenty of bucolic distractions for kids and adults alike nearby – from golf and natural parks to a maze and a gaol. The surrounding farmland has interpretative walks and soaring birds of prey. Breakfast stuff is provided on your first morning. This is one that's hard to beat. *www.daisybankcottages.com.au; tel 03-6260 2390; 78 Middle Tea Tree Rd, Richmond*

BIG4 HOBART AIRPORT TOURIST PARK

Filling a long-vacant void in the Hobart tourism sector is this newish caravan park near Hobart Airport – big, clean and grassy with excellent cabins, caravans and camping options, and perfectly located if

you've got an early flight. *www.hobartairporttouristpark.com.au; tel 03-6248 4551; 2 Flight St, Cambridge*

WHERE TO EAT

COAL RIVER FARM

A snappy piece of hillside architecture, Coal River Farm is a family-friendly spot to try some artisan cheese, chocolate, or grab some breakfast or lunch in the bistro – perhaps some smoked wallaby with white bean mash and spicy tomato and capsicum sauce. You can also pick strawberries, feed the goats and collect eggs from the chooks. *www.coalriverfarm.com.au; tel 1300 455 215; 634 Richmond Rd, Cambridge; 9am–5pm daily*

RICHMOND BAKERY

Come for takeaway pies, pastries, sandwiches, croissants, muffins and cakes, or munch on them in the courtyard. Their version of the Tasmanian classic curried scallop pie more than passes muster. If the main street is empty, chances are everyone is in here. *Tel 03-6260 2628; 50 Bridge St, off Edward St, Richmond; 7.30am–6pm*

WHAT TO DO

MT FIELD NATIONAL PARK

Mt Field, 80km northwest of Hobart and 7lm beyond Westerway, was declared a national park in 1916. It is famed for its alpine moorlands, lakes, rainforest, impressive waterfalls, walks, skiing and rampant wildlife. Don't miss the magnificently tiered, 45m-high Russell Falls, an easy 20min return amble from behind the visitor centre. The park is an accessible day trip from Hobart, or you can bunk down overnight. Either way, things can get mighty chilly here so wrap up warm!

SULLIVANS COVE WHISKY

It doesn't look much from the outside, but this tin shed near the turn-off to Richmond has managed to produce the best single malt whisky in the world, as adjudged at the 2014 World Whiskies Awards. And now there are a dozen distillers around Tasmania... Tours run on the hour; booking advised. *www.sullivanscove.com; tel 03-6248 5399; 1/10 Lamb Pl, Cambridge; 10am-4pm Mon-Fri*

01

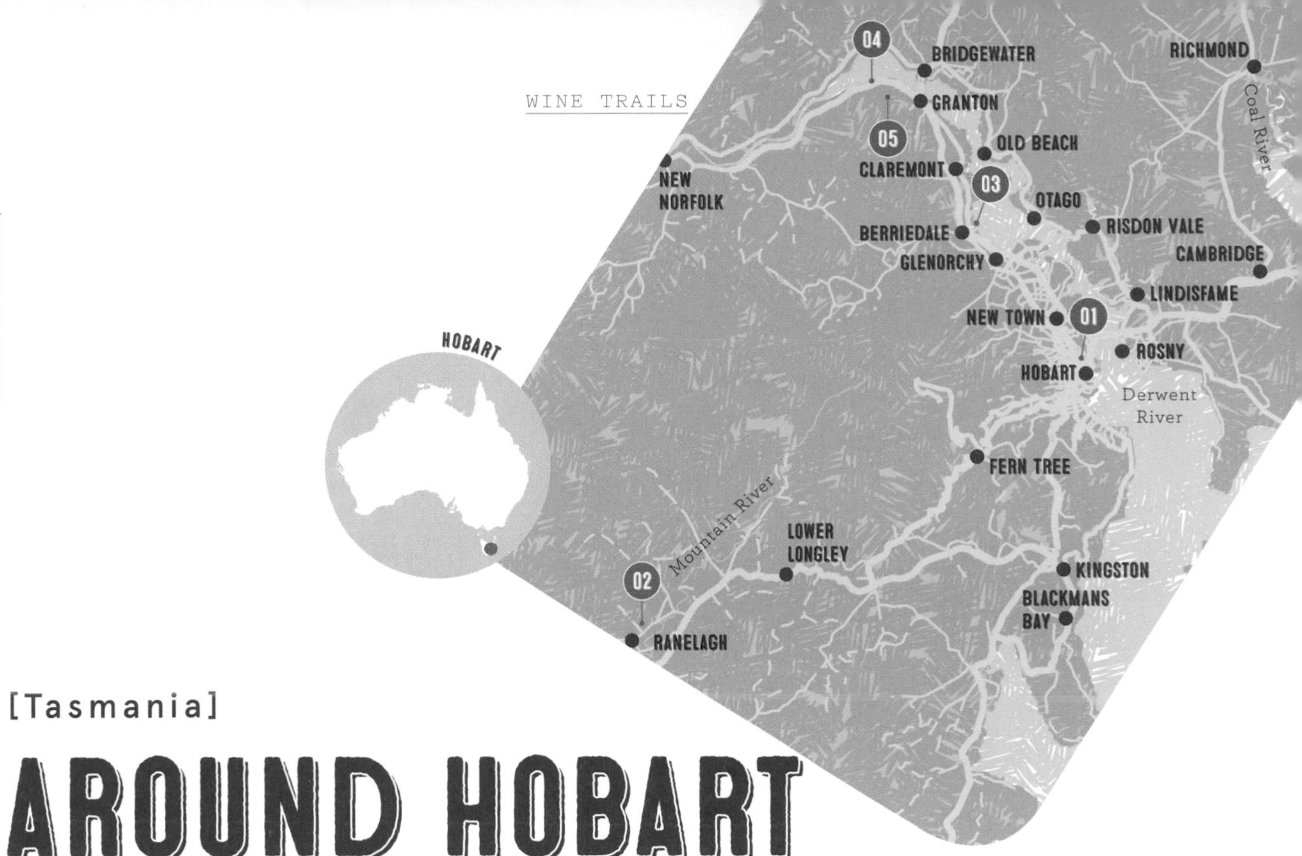

[Tasmania]

AROUND HOBART

Toast the buzz of the cosmopolitan state capital with a glass or two of exemplary cool-climate wine, produced a stone's throw from the city limits.

Australia's second-oldest city and southernmost capital, Hobart dapples the foothills of Mt Wellington, angling down to the slate-grey Derwent River. The town's rich cache of colonial architecture and natural charms are complemented by innovative festivals, eclectic markets and world-class food and drink experiences. It's the ideal base for winery touring in the Huon Valley, less than an hour to the south, and the Upper Derwent Valley, a half-hour's drive northwest.

Hobart is a harbour town, a port city, where the world rushes in on the tide and ebbs away again, bringing with it influences from afar and leaving the locals buzzing with global zeitgeist. Or so the theory goes. These days, Hobart's waterfront precinct is certainly abuzz, with old pubs alongside new craft-beer bars, restaurants and cafes, museums, festivals, ferries, accommodation... all washed with sea-salty charm. The Museum of Old and New Art (MONA), with its amazing subterranean spaces and subversive, saucy, sometimes hilarious displays, has brought new vigour to the state since opening in 2011. All in all, there are few more pleasant towns in Australia to find yourself on a sunny afternoon.

The wine region's climate, the coolest of all Tasmania's, is not without its challenges – the Huon Valley, in particular, has to contend with severe frosts in the spring. However, the long and slow growing season combined with rich soils results in delectable wines, from stunning Pinot Noir to delicate Chardonnay, refined Riesling and fine sparklings. All of these find their natural companions – cheese, fish and seafood – in plentiful supply from the island's artisan food producers and growers, not to mention Hobart's blossoming dining scene and gourmet extravaganzas.

GET THERE
Direct flights to Hobart from Melbourne and Sydney daily. The airport is a 30min taxi or bus ride from town.

01 GLAETZER-DIXON FAMILY WINEMAKERS

Winemaker-owner Nick Glaetzer 'emigrated' to cool-climate Tasmania from his distinguished winemaking family's Barossa Valley base in 2005. Having previously made use of other people's wineries, Nick and his wife Sally decided to set up shop themselves, recently transforming an old ice works on the edge of Hobart's CBD into their cellar door and winery. It's a slick, modern space – a far cry from the more common rustic setting – with wines poured at an altar-like light-box table.

A Barossan cannot help but make Shiraz, no matter where he is, and Nick's is called Mon Père as a tribute to his winemaker dad, Colin. His reserve Shiraz, this time named after his mother Judith, is one of the island's most expensive bottles at $220 a pop. Happily, there's also (affordable) Riesling and Pinot Noir. *www.gdfwinemakers.com; tel 04-1785 2287; 93 Brooker Ave, Hobart; 11am–5pm Sat–Sun and by appt*

02 HOME HILL

Tiny, sleepy Huon Valley district is home to this standout winery with a massive reputation, especially for its Pinot Noir, and a top restaurant. Apples used to be the main crop here, until farmer Terry Bennett turned his hand to grapes and gradually allowed a hobby to morph into a full-time, award-winning occupation. You can still stock up on apples and honey in the area, which has the coolest climate of all Tasmania's wine regions. From the car park beside the vineyard, check out the unusual lyre trellis system, which is high-maintenance but also well-suited to the soil and climate.

Home Hill wines win trophies with metronomic regularity for its Pinot Noirs under the Estate, Kelly's Reserve and Landslide labels. Demand is high and quantities low – your only chance of tasting the feted 2015 Kelly's Reserve Pinot Noir is with dinner in the winery restaurant, so there's your excuse. *www.homehillwines.com.au; tel 03-6264 1200; 38 Nairn St, Ranelagh; 10am–5pm daily*

03 MOORILLA

No visit to Tasmania is complete

01 Start your tour in Hobart

02 Moorilla's modern cellar door

03-04 The delights of Stefano Lubiana

05 Founders Monique and Steve Lubiana

The long and slow growing season combined with rich soils results in delectable wines, from stunning Pinot Noir to fine sparklings

06 Home Hill vineyards in Huon Valley

without a pilgrimage to Moorilla. Few venues manage to combine a vineyard and winery, museum, micro-brewery, fine-dining restaurant, beer bar and luxury cabin accommodation – all built on a stunning promontory in the Derwent River estuary – let alone with such verve. Moorilla has quite a backstory (it was established in 1958) but for the last decade has been home to Tasmanian entrepreneur and art collector David Walsh, who has masterminded its reinvention and also owns MONA, the Museum of Old and New Art, now the biggest single attraction in the state. Take the MONA ferry from Hobart's Constitution Dock to max the experience. The wines, crafted by Canadian-born Conor van der Reest, are suitably excellent.
moorilla.com.au; tel 03-6277 9960; 655 Main Rd, Berriedale; 9.30am–5pm Wed–Mon

04 DERWENT ESTATE

The Hanigan family have been farming here on the banks of the Derwent River, upstream from Hobart, since 1913. While the last century has seen vegetables, poppies and seed crops sown, since 1992 the focus has been on grapes (give or take the odd sheep). The vineyard is farmed with 'integrated pest management', so no pesticides or insecticides are used.

The family built their own winery in 2014 and employed winemaker John Schuts, who already had plenty of experience working with their fruit at Winemaking Tasmania. The usual varieties – Riesling, Chardonnay, Pinot Gris and Pinot Noir – are grown, the standout wines being a late-harvest Riesling, reserve Chardonnay and a premium Pinot Noir named Calcaire, made from grapes grown on the shallowest limestone layers.
derwentestate.com.au; tel 03-6263 5802; 329 Lyell Hwy, Granton; 11am–4pm daily

05 STEFANO LUBIANA

Almost next door to Derwent Estate is Steve and Monique Lubiana's burgeoning business, where the revamped cellar door has lately sprouted a restaurant offering a daily changing menu of Italian-style fare, in keeping with Steve's ancestry.

High-quality vintage, non-vintage and late-disgorged sparkling wines, produced entirely on the premises, are a speciality. The vineyards are biodynamically run, as is the vegetable and herb garden which supplies the Osteria restaurant. Meats are local, seafood is wild-caught, they bake their own bread and harvest their own honey – you get the (very noble, very tasty) idea. Next step for the Lubianas is working on their recent purchase of the established Panorama vineyard in the Huon Valley.
www.slw.com.au; tel 03-6263 7457; 60 Rowbottoms Rd, Granton; 11am–4pm Wed–Sun

ESSENTIAL INFORMATION

WHERE TO STAY

ASTOR PRIVATE HOTEL

A rambling downtown 1920s charmer, the Astor retains much of its character: stained-glass windows, old furniture, lofty ceilings and the irrepressible Tildy at the helm. Older-style rooms have shared facilities, which are plentiful, while the more recently refurbished are en suite. *www.astorprivatehotel.com.au; tel 03-6234 6611; 157 Macquarie St, Hobart*

HENRY JONES ART HOTEL

Super-swish HJs is a beacon of sophistication. In the restored waterfront Henry Jones IXL jam factory, with remnant bits of jam-making machinery and huge timber beams, it oozes class but is far from snooty (this is Hobart, not Sydney). Modern art enlivens the walls, while facilities and distractions (bar, restaurant, cafe) are world class. *www.thehenryjones.com; tel 03-6210 7700; 25 Hunter St, Hobart*

WHERE TO EAT

FRANKLIN

In a lofty industrial space (the former Hobart Mercury newspaper printing room – the papers would roll straight out the front window), Franklin is all concrete, steel beams, cowhide and curtains. Ignore the cheesy Eric Clapton soundtrack and have a drink at the bar, or settle in for a creative Mod-Oz meal cooked in the central kitchen. *www.franklinhhobart.com.au; tel 03-6234 3375; 30 Argyle St, Hobart; 8.30am–late Tue–Sat*

GINGER BROWN

When a food business is this well run, the mood infects the entire room: happy staff, happy customers and happy vibes. Try the slow-cooked lamb panini with cornichons and hummus, or the signature kimchi pancake. Very kid- and cyclist-friendly, and the coffee is the best in South Hobart. Last orders 3pm. *tel 03-6223 3531; 464 Macquarie St, South Hobart; 7.30am–4pm Mon–Fri, 8.30am–4pm Sat–Sun*

WHAT TO DO

SALAMANCA PLACE, HOBART

This picturesque row of three-and four-storey sandstone warehouses is a classic example of Australian architecture. Restorations work began in the 1970s and these days Salamanca hosts myriad restaurants, cafes, bars and shops, and an unmissable Saturday morning market. *www.salamanca.com.au*

MONA

Twelve kilometres north of Hobart's city centre, MONA occupies a saucepan-shaped peninsula jutting into the Derwent River. Arrayed across three underground levels, abutting a sheer rock face, the $75-milion museum has been described by philanthropist owner David Walsh as 'a subversive adult Disneyland'. Ancient antiquities are showcased next to contemporary works: sexy, provocative, disturbing and deeply engaging. Don't miss it.

To get here catch the MR-1 ferry or MONA Roma shuttle bus from Hobart's Brooke Street Pier. *www.mona.net.au; tel 03-6277 9900; 655 Main Rd, Berriedale; 10am-6pm daily Jan, 10am-6pm Wed–Mon Feb–Apr & Dec, 10am–5pm Wed–Mon May–Nov*

CELEBRATIONS

MONA hosts two annual extravaganzas, FOMO and MOFO, that share the museum's avant-garde take on art and culture.

TASTE OF TASMANIA

On either side of New Year's Eve, this week-long harbourside event is a celebration of Tassie's gastronomic prowess. The seafood, wines and cheeses are predictably fab, or branch out into mushrooms, truffles, raspberries... Stalls are a who's who of the Hobart restaurant scene and there's live music, too. *www.thetasteoftasmania.com.au*

Courtesy of Bay of Fires

[Tasmania]

PIPERS RIVER

Discover the mirror image of northern France, with fine wines to match,in the picturesque northern reaches of the apple isle.

Neighbouring the Tamar Valley wine region, and slightly cooler given its proximity to the Bass Strait, Pipers River was the site Dr Andrew Pirie settled on after exhaustive research, much of which fed into his doctoral thesis on viticulture. He was after a place that closely matched the cool-climate terroir of northern France. Pirie's planting of Pipers Brook Vineyard in 1974 signalled the birth of the modern industry, and a host of other vineyards followed, adding a new dimension to the rolling hills of sheep-dotted pasture and eucalypt forests of this pretty part of northern Tasmania.

Pirie was the first to realise that high humidity – rare in Australian vineyards – would be important if he was to emulate the wines of Burgundy and Champagne. Ocean breezes, relatively stable maximum temperatures and a long ripening season combine to yield fruit that retains a delicate bouquet and lingering sharpness, ideal for first-rate cool-climate wines. Nearly 40 years later Pirie is still hard at work in the area, making fine bubbly at his diminutive Apogee vineyard.

Riesling was the first variety to put Pipers River on the wine map, soon joined by Chardonnay, Pinot Noir and later, Pinot Gris. High-quality sparkling wine, made by the traditional bottle-fermentation method, is important here, with several high-profile producers such as Jansz and Clover Hill. Even boutique wineries, including Delamere, Apogee and Sinapius, make fine sparklings.

Several mainland wine companies have outposts in the region. Familiar names include Accolade with its Bay of Fires and House of Arras brands, Yalumba (Jansz and Dalrymple) and Taltarni (Clover Hill). With about 10 wineries open for visits, within an hour's drive of Launceston, Pipers is a rewarding day trip.

GET THERE
Pipers River is an easy day trip, one hour's drive north of Launceston.

01 PIPERS BROOK VINEYARD

Pipers Brook is the vineyard that triggered the stampede to plant vines in the region in the 1980s. First planted by Dr Andrew Pirie in 1974, it's now part of the Belgian-owned Kreglinger group, which also makes wine in Mount Benson, South Australia. Here's your chance to taste the wines that put Tasmania on the map: long-lived Riesling, spicy Gewürztraminer, highly structured Pinot Noir and complex sparkling wine. The large vineyard holdings of 200 hectares supply an array of wines under the Pipers Brook Vineyard and very affordable Ninth Island labels.

The cellar door offers simple cheese platters to accompany tastings, and visitors are invited to take a self-guided tour of the vineyard. There is a second cellar door, the Strathlynn Wine & Function Centre, at the company's Tamar Valley vineyard in Rosevears. *www.kreglingerwineestates.com; tel 03-6382 7527; 1216 Pipers Brook Rd, Pipers Brook; 10am-5pm daily*

02 JANSZ

Owned by Hill-Smith Family Vineyards of Yalumba in the Barossa Valley, and named after explorer Abel Jansz Tasman, Jansz is the only dedicated sparkling wine producer in Tasmania. The well-established range encompasses vintage and non-vintage, rosé, Blanc de Blancs and late disgorged (vintage wine released following extra maturation time). After the French term *méthode champenoise* was banned in Australia, Jansz fell back on its Aussie sense of humour and retorted with *méthode Tasmanoise*. Jansz, after all, was the first sparkling wine in Tasmania produced by the traditional method, in collaboration with Louis Roederer. The Jansz Interpretive Centre, much more than a cellar door, is an engaging educational experience. *www.jansz.com.au; tel 03-6382 7066; 1216B Pipers Brook Rd, Pipers Brook; 10am-4.30pm daily*

03 DALRYMPLE

Vigneron Peter Caldwell is a devotee of Pinot Noir, resigned to its challenges – it's not so much that Pinot is hard to grow, more

From top left: courtesy of Delamere; Pipers Brook; Bay of Fires

01 Bay Of Fires

02 Harvesting at Delamere

03 Tasting rooms at Pipers Brook

04 Bay Of Fires' cellar door

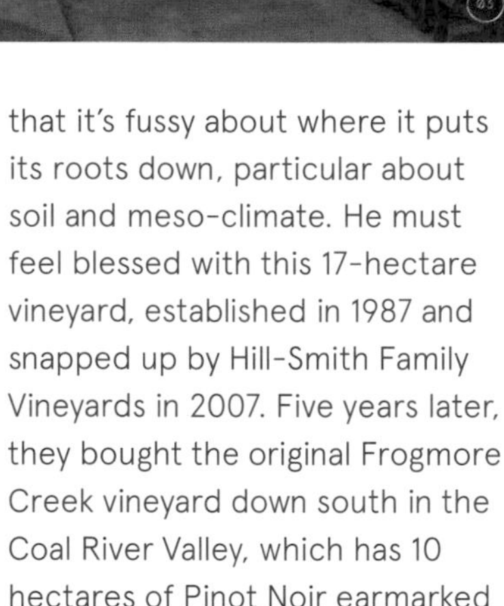

that it's fussy about where it puts its roots down, particular about soil and meso-climate. He must feel blessed with this 17-hectare vineyard, established in 1987 and snapped up by Hill-Smith Family Vineyards in 2007. Five years later, they bought the original Frogmore Creek vineyard down south in the Coal River Valley, which has 10 hectares of Pinot Noir earmarked for Dalrymple. The wines are made at sister property Jansz.

There's no cellar door but tastings can be arranged by emailing 48 hours in advance. You can take a self-guided virtual tour too, with the recorded words of Caldwell. *www.dalrymplevineyards.com.au; tel 03-6382 7229; 1337 Pipers Brook Rd, Pipers Brook; by appt only*

04 SINAPIUS

Sustainability is the catchphrase at Sinapius. Low yields from the close-spaced, unirrigated vineyard and traditional, artisan winemaking are employed to create these single-vineyard wines. With this approach, the owners hope to truly express the vineyard's unique position and character, its terroir. The small 4-hectare vineyard manages to accommodate Grüner Veltliner, Gewürztraminer, Pinot Blanc and Gamay as well as the more predictable Pinot Noir, Chardonnay, Pinot Gris and Riesling. It's located on a pretty site close to Pipers Brook and just 5km from the sea. *sinapius.com.au; tel 04-1734 1764; 4232 Bridport Rd, Pipers Brook; 12pm–5pm Thu–Mon (closed July)*

05 DELAMERE

Established by the Richardson family back in 1983, Fran Austin and her husband Shane Holloway, both qualified winemakers, have been owner-operators since 2007. They've taken Delamere to the next level, with a beautifully packaged range of sparkling wines which embraces vintage and non-vintage, rosé and Blanc de Blancs, all made by the traditional Champagne method. As winemaker/manager at Bay of Fires for 10 years, Fran built up plenty of experience before going it alone. She was voted young winemaker of the year in 2005 and was selected as a Len Evans Scholar in '09 (wine professionals vie for the twelve places at this

05 Barrel tasting at Pipers Brook

06 On the vine at Bay Of Fires

prestigious wine school).

The unstuffy cellar door is set within the winery, with lovely surrounding gardens. Delamere don't provide food but they invite you to bring your own and they'll provide a 'glass of godliness'. *www.delamerevineyards.com.au; tel 03-6382 7190; 4238 Bridport Rd, Pipers Brook; 10am–5pm daily*

06 BAY OF FIRES

Bay of Fires is named after an incredibly beautiful stretch of Tasmania's east coast, itself christened by Captain Tobias Furneaux in 1773 when he noticed a number of fires along the coast, evidence of Aboriginal communities. At the winery, Tasmanian-born Penny Jones, who has experience of winemaking in several Australian wine regions and has travelled widely in Europe and the USA in pursuit of winemaking know-how, crafts exceptionally successful Pinot Noirs, which layer black cherry, oak and tannin to superb effect. She has helped Bay of Fires become one of Tasmania's headline wineries, but she's not done it alone. Bay of Fires has a sister brand, House of Arras, dedicated to traditional Champagne-style sparkling wine and helmed by Ed Carr. *www.bayoffireswines.com.au; tel 03-6382 7622; 40 Baxters Rd, Pipers River; 11am–4pm Mon–Fri, 10am–4pm Sat–Sun*

07 CLOVER HILL

Victorian winery Taltarni established Clover Hill in 1986 to produce sparkling wine, and that remains the focus. The cuvées utilise all three of the classic Champagne varieties – Pinot Noir, Pinot Meunier and Chardonnay – with magnificent, refined results.

Clover Hill has only recently opened up its cellar door, the newest in the region, to daily visitors. The building is unique, shaped like a clover leaf and with walls of rammed earth. In addition to quaffing the region's finest fizz, you can branch out to try their small range of still wines, Idiom Wines. *www.cloverhillwines.com.au; tel 03-6395 6114; 60 Clover Hill Rd, Lebrina; 10am–4.30pm daily*

08 APOGEE

Dr Andrew Pirie is one of the heroes of Tasmanian wine. After 30 years at Pipers Brook Vineyard, which he founded, and a brief stint at Tamar Ridge, Pirie re-established himself at a new vineyard at Lebrina, not far from Pipers Brook. High altitude (by Tasmanian standards) gives a very cool climate well-suited to the delicate sparkling wines that are Pirie's aim. He has already released some superb sparkling Pinot Noir-Chardonnay bubblies, including a rosé, in tiny volumes, and there's also a still Pinot Gris. Tiny is the operative word – the vineyard will remain limited to 2 hectares, the average size of a holding in Champagne. Pirie is testing his theory that small size helps deliver top quality – that perfect vineyard management is a natural limit on scale. *www.apogeetasmania.com; tel 03-6395 6358; 1083 Golconda Rd, Lebrina; 11.30am–4.30pm Wed–Sun*

ESSENTIAL INFORMATION

WHERE TO STAY

JENSENS BED & BREAKFAST

If only all B&Bs could be like this. Occupying a handsome Federation-style house surrounded by apple trees and a manicured garden, Jensens has a gracious communal lounge with open fire, two stylishly presented en-suite rooms and a large verandah with distinctive rotunda and spectacular river views. Helpful host Carol cooks her guests a full breakfast in the morning. Beauty Point makes a good base for the Tamar Valley or Pipers River trails. *www.jensensbedandbreakfast.com.au; tel 0410 615 678; 77 Flinders St, Beauty Point*

TWO FOUR TWO

Launceston's best self-catering accommodation, super-stylish Two Four Two is on the Charles St cafe strip, making a perfect base for a city sojourn or a wine-tasting long weekend. Two double studios and an apartment sleeping up to four feature fully equipped kitchens with coffee machines, spacious bathrooms and comfortable bed sheathed in quality linen. *www.twofourtwo.com.au; tel 03-6331 9242; 242 Charles St, Launceston*

WHERE TO EAT

RIVER CAFE

On sunny days at the River Cafe the windows fold right back and the water feels so close you could touch it. The menu tempts with all-day breakfasts, gourmet panini, pasta and a delectable array of local seafood – try the signature seafood platter with a glass of local wine. Takeaway pizzas, too. *tel 03-6383 4099; 225 Flinders St, Beauty Point; 9am–4pm, till 9pm Dec & Jan school holidays*

GEORGE TOWN SEAFOODS PTY LTD

Not far west of the Pipers River region, George Town is a rewarding stop for history buffs and has pleasant beaches, but it's this local favourite that reels us in. Super-fresh fish 'n' chips, seafood wraps, prawns and scallops mean this place – predominantly a wholesaler – is regularly packed, but you can opt for takeaway and then crack open a bottle of bubbly alongside. *www.georgetownseafoods.com.au; tel 03-6382 4183; 38–44 Franklin St, George Town; 11am–2pm Mon–Fri*

06

WHAT TO DO

You'll find plenty of distractions in Launceston itself – this is a city where art and design are highly valued, where locals embrace the outdoors and where food and coffee culture thrives. Entrance is free at both the Queen Victoria Museum and Queen Victoria Art Gallery – the Museum's planetarium is perennially popular. At magnificent Cataract Gorge, the bushland, cliffs and ice-cold South Esk River feel a million miles from town. At First Basin there's a free outdoor swimming pool (Nov to Mar), the world's longest single-span chairlift and Victorian-era gardens. Elsewhere, there are walking and cycling tracks as well as lookouts. The whole shebang is impressively floodlit at night. *www.qvmag.tas.gov.au; www.launcestoncataractgorge.com.au*

01

Courtesy of Holm Oak / Chris Crerar

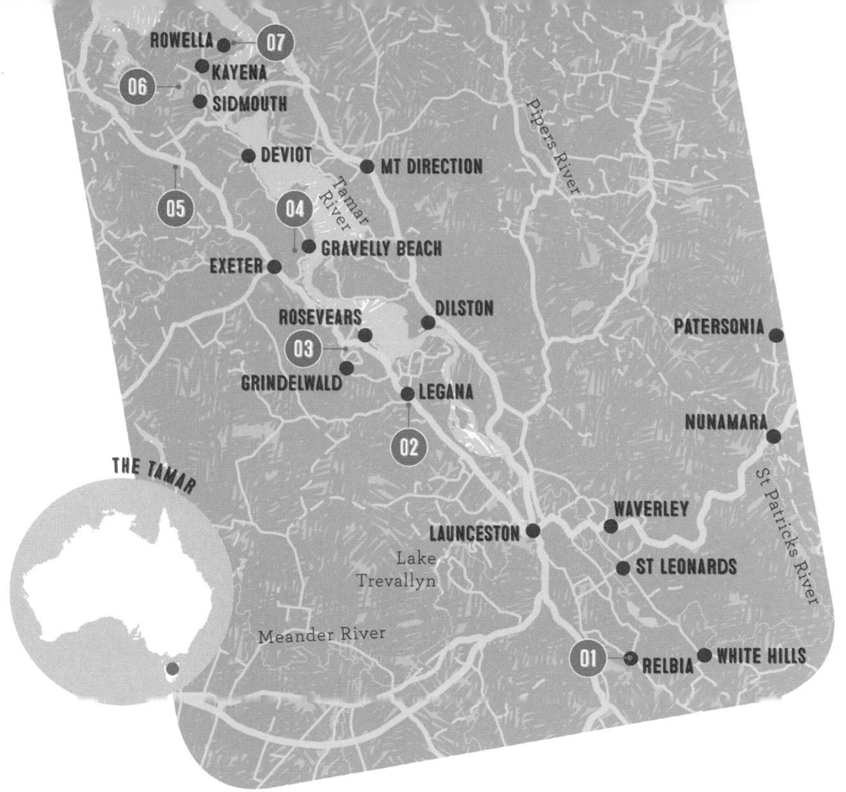

[Tasmania]

THE TAMAR

Encounter devilishly delicious Pinot Noir and outstanding local produce in the north of Tasmania on a road trip along the Tamar River.

A wine made with Pinot Noir grapes seems to inspire rapture like no other can. People describe good Burgundy in almost mystical terms. In the cult wine film *Sideways* (is this the only cult wine film?), Miles attempts to explain his love of Pinot Noir: 'It's thin-skinned, temperamental, ripens early… needs constant care and attention… and it can only grow in these really specific, little, tucked-away corners of the world.' And one of those tucked-away places is the Tamar Valley (and the Piper River region next door) in northern Tasmania, which shares a similar climate to the famed Côte d'Or in Burgundy.

If you can tear yourself away from the other attractions of Tasmania – staggeringly beautiful beaches, multiday hikes through pristine wilderness, a one-of-a-kind art gallery – a weekend beside the Tamar River will introduce you to some of the world's finest Pinot Noirs and some deliciously moreish local produce; northern Tasmania is Australia's orchard, where farmers markets are a regular feature of weekend life. The island's food scene is the match of its wine – try fresh seafood with the Tamar's white wines and its lamb with the Pinot Noirs.

The origins of Tasmanian wine lie in a vineyard just east of Launceston which was once called La Provence and is now known as Providence. It was planted with Pinot Noir and Chardonnay in 1956 by Jean Miguet, the son of a winemaking family. By the 1990s, wines from this part of northern Tasmania were winning international medals.

Starting the tour further up the Tamar River, in tiny Relbia, means that you finish close to the Southern Ocean, for a contemplative walk along a deserted beach. 'Haunting and brilliant and thrilling and subtle…' is how Miles describes Pinot Noir in *Sideways*; it's a description that also applies to Tasmania.

GET THERE

Launceston airport, 30 mins taxi or bus ride from the city, is served by most Australian cities. There's a ferry from Melbourne.

01 JOSEF CHROMY

This landmark winery is led by one of Australian wine's more remarkable characters. Having survived 11 years of Nazi and Soviet occupation, a penniless 19-year-old left his Czech village and made his way to Australia. Over the next 40 years he built up a fortune in the butchery trade and poured the proceeds of his company's stock market float into the nascent Tasmanian wine industry, establishing Tamar Ridge in 1994 and investing in what is now Bay of Fires. Now in his 80s, Josef Chromy has hardly slowed down but it's winemaker Jeremy Dineen who has the task of creating Chromy's eponymous wines. 'My winemaking is mostly influenced by the site,' says Jeremy. 'Just as a person displays their heritage by accent, great wines should reveal their origins by the unique characteristics of their vineyard.' He's got a geographic advantage in nurturing Chromy's Pinot Noir vines: 'Our southerly latitude gives us the cool climate and long ripening season required by Pinot Noir. Being an island, the ocean has a huge moderating effect on Tasmania's climate so we don't get extremes of heat or cold.'

Jeremy Dineen has seen Tasmanian wine evolve over recent years. Not only is there more first-class fruit being grown, but a new generation of younger winemakers has the determination to produce distinctive, expressive wines.

So, what inspires Jeremy's own winemaking? 'Some of the amazing single vineyards of the Mosel. And Tom Waits.'

www.josefchromy.com.au; tel 03-6335 8700; 370 Relbia Rd, Relbia; 10am-5pm daily $

02 VÉLO WINES

Cycling and wine have long been bedfellows. Indeed, in the earliest days of the Tour de France, riders would raid cafes and bars at the foot of mountains, carrying out bottles with which to fortify themselves for the tough climb ahead. Sadly, by the time that Australian Olympic cyclist Micheal Wilson had turned professional that practice had stopped. He's now surrendered the saddle, and

From top left: courtesy of Moores Hill / Chris Crerar; Josef Chromy / Rob Burnett (2)

01 Bringing in the grapes at Holm Oak

02 Cellar door at Moores Hill

03 Kicking back at Josef Chromy

04 Josef Chromy tastings

winemaking responsibilities, at boutique-sized Vélo Wines – the new owners are keeping the name but revamping the cellar door, and hosting the excellent on-site restaurant, Timbre Kitchen. Standout wines include old-vine Cabernet Sauvignon (from some of the island's oldest Cabernet vines, planted in 1966 by Graham Wiltshire) and late-disgorged sparkling wines.
www.velowines.com.au; tel 0418 130 067; 755 West Tamar Hwy, Legana; 10am–4pm daily

03 TAMAR RIDGE

Follow the blue-and-yellow signs of the Tamar Valley Wine Route to Tamar Ridge, where you can take a break and unpack a picnic on a lawn overlooking the river as it broadens. This is one of the region's larger cellar doors and was purchased from Dr Andrew Pirie, the man behind Tasmania's most successful wine brands, by the big business Brown Brothers. In 1994, Pirie entered a Tasmanian Chardonnay in the blind-tasting International Wine Challenge – and came away with the Best White Wine trophy. Pirie is still involved with Brown Brothers and produces a range of excellent sparkling wines, but his legacy at Tamar Ridge is white wine, including a straw-coloured, botrytis-affected Riesling dessert wine and a peachy Chardonnay.
www.brownbrothers.com.au; tel 03-6330 0300; 1a Waldhorn Dr, Rosevears; 10am–5pm daily

04 STONEY RISE

Former cricketer Joe Holyman and his wife Lou preside over this small winery, just a 20min walk from the Tamar's shore. Since hanging up his wicket-keeping gloves, Joe worked in wineries in Portugal and France before returning home to restore Stoney Rise. Their 4.2 hectares include some of the rare Austrian white grape, Grüner Veltliner, as well as the more predictable Pinot Noir and Chardonnay. They have begun using biodynamic preparations in order to improve the health of their soil, and have given up spraying herbicides for the same reason. They make two tiers of wine, the entry-level Stoney Rise label and also Pinot Noir under the Holyman label, made from grapes

05 The evening draws in at Josef Chromy

06 Holm Oak views

from a single parcel of vines. The Holyman Pinot Noir is aged in oak barriques, which makes for a wine with plenty of depth and fruit. Try it in the cellar door, which overlooks the Tamar as it nears the ocean. *www.stoneyrise.com; tel 03-6394 3678; 96 Hendersons Ln, Gravelly Beach; 11am–5pm Thu–Mon, closed Jul–Sep*

05 MOORES HILL

Moores Hill recently amalgamated with fellow West Tamar vineyard Native Point, the two owner families – the Allports and the Highs – pooling resources to build a new winery and cellar door at Moores Hill and a bottling plant at Native Point. The result is Tasmania's first off-grid winery, its 108 solar panels providing 100% of its electricity needs. There's also an electric vehicle-charging station, useful if you're looking for that sort of juice.

Going green seems to be top priority: Viticulturalist Sheena High is moving towards a more sustainable way of managing the vineyard – which comprises Chardonnay, Pinot Noir and Riesling, as well as small patches of Cabernet and Merlot – using preventative methods of controlling vine diseases and minimising chemical intervention way. The sparkling Blanc de Blancs is especially recommended. *www.mooreshill.com.au; tel 03-6394 7649; 3343 W Tamar Hwy, Sidmouth; 10am–5pm daily*

06 GOATY HILL

'Wine is not a job for us, it's our passion.' So say the owners of Goaty Hill, a small vineyard at Kayena with – like almost all of the nearby vineyards, admittedly – wonderful views across the Tamar River and its valley. Some grapes are sold on while most are sent for winemaking at Josef Chromy Wines, a short distance south in Relbia. The cellar door is a tranquil, scenic place to chill out over a glass of the excellent Maia vintage sparkling wine, or an outstanding Pinot Noir, and a gourmet platter or selection of local cheeses. *www.goatyhill.com; tel 1300 819 997; 530 Auburn Rd, Kayena; 11am–5pm daily*

07 HOLM OAK

Winemaker Rebecca Duffy and her husband Tim, a viticulturist, head up a friendly and intimate venture, named after a grove of well-established English holm oak trees originally planted to make tennis racquets, long before the days of carbon fibre. The wood didn't quite meet requirements, but the fertile soils have proved more than capable of producing winning wines – the estate-grown Pinot Noir is named The Wizard after the racquet used by Australian Wimbledon champion Jack Crawford.

The wines (and cider) are all very good and quite idiosyncratic – indeed the Duffys would like to be known for down-to-earth, not super-polished but authentic wines. The cellar door sells local goodies so you can compose your own picnic to enjoy on the grounds, overlooking lush orchards and vineyards. *www.holmoakvineyards.com.au; tel 03-6394 7577; 11 West Bay Rd, Rowella; 11am–5pm daily*

ESSENTIAL INFORMATION

WHERE TO STAY

RED FEATHER INN
At the ocean-end of the Tamar Valley, on the east side of the river, Red Feather Inn is one of Tasmania's best boutique hotels and also offers dinner and even cookery classes. The accommodation is in a series of historic sandstone buildings. *www.redfeatherinn.com.au; tel 03-6393 6506; 42 Main St, Hadspen*

KURRAJONG HOUSE
Owned by a Scottish-Australian couple, this well-run B&B in a handsome 1887 house near Windmill Hill Reserve offers three rooms in the main house and a self-contained cottage in the garden. Angling for a mature clientele (over 21s only), it is made exceptional through attention to detail – fresh flowers, fresh milk for in-room tea, homemade jam with breakfast. *www.kurrajonghouse.com.au; tel 03-6331 6655; Cnr High & Adelaide Sts, Launceston*

WHERE TO EAT

STILLWATER
Stillwater is set in a stylishly renovated 1840s flour mill beside the Tamar in Launceston. It serves laidback breakfasts, relaxed lunches – and then puts on the ritz for dinner, with delectable seafood, meat and vegetarian dishes. *www.stillwater.net.au; tel 03-6331 4153; 2 Bridge Rd, Ritchie's Flour Mill, Launceston; opening times vary, check website*

INGLESIDE BAKERY CAFE
Sit in the flowery walled courtyard or under the high ceiling inside this former council chambers (1867), where fresh-baked aromas waft from the wood oven. Expect delicious pies and pasties, a hefty ploughman's lunch and all manner of sweet treats, including Devonshire teas. *tel 03-6391 8682; 4 Russell St, Evandale; 8.30am–4.30pm Mon–Fri, to 4pm Sat, to 3.30pm Sun*

WHAT TO DO

A terrain of undulating emerald hills covered with vineyards, orchards and stands of native forest, the Tamar Valley should be explored at a leisurely pace. On the Tamar River's eastern bank is Launceston's ocean port, Bell Bay, near George Town. The western bank is home to a string of laid-back country hamlets that are popular weekend and summer escapes for Launcestonians. The Batman Bridge unites the two shores hear Deviot.

It's worth making a trip to Evandale, south of Launceston. Walk down the main street and you'll feel like you've time-warped back a century – precisely why the entire town is National Trust-listed. Allow a few hours so you can admire its historic streetscapes, and browse a few boutiques. And if you visit on a Sunday, don't miss the Evandale Market.

06

CELEBRATIONS

In Launceston, Festivale is an annual summer party celebrating Tasmanian food, wine, beer and music, taking over the historic City Park for three days on the second weekend of February. It's a chance to try some of food-obsessed Tasmania's local produce. *www.festivale.com.au*

01

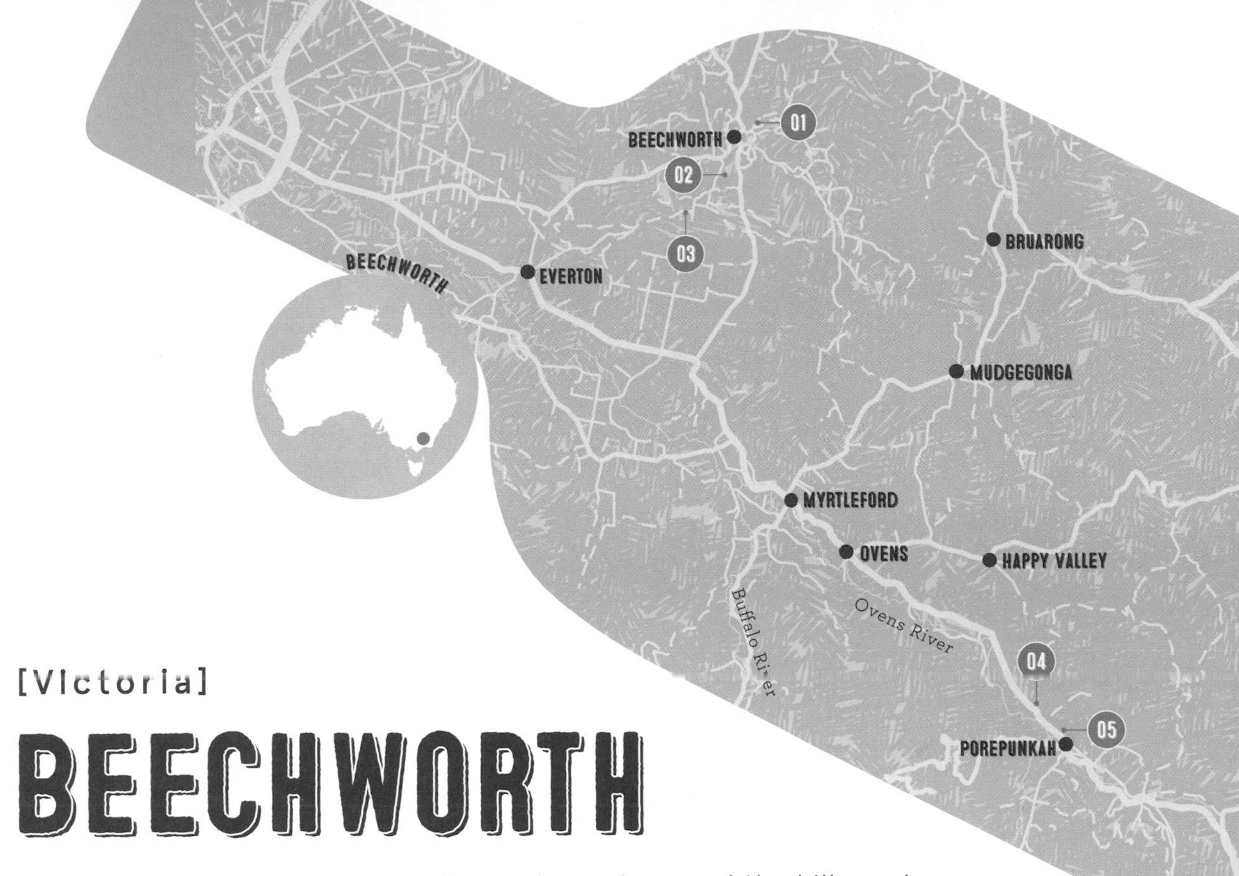

[Victoria]

BEECHWORTH

Explore this up-and-coming wine region set around the hills and rivers of Northeast Victoria by bicycle or car.

Beechworth is blessed not only with one of the best preserved 19th-century town centres in Australia but also mineral-rich hills that once yielded gold to hardy prospectors. The gold may be gone (or is it?) but the soils of this plateau now generate another form of treasure - some of the most interesting wines in Victoria. More than 400 million years ago, volcanic activity shoved this region between 300m and 800m above the surrounding plain. The geology, the altitude and the aspect have combined to create ideal conditions for a wide range of grapes, grown by around 30 wine-making families.

Few Victorian towns can beat handsome Beechworth for a weekend away: there's an abundance of great places to eat and drink, plus historic buildings that played in part in the Ned Kelly story. But this is a slightly different trail in that it doesn't stay in one region but is instead based along the Murray to the Mountains Rail Trail (or the Great Alpine Rd from Beechworth to Bright for drivers), the gateway to Australia's alpine region. Several wineries cluster around the town of Bright and this traffic-free trail links the two bases.

If you're a fit cyclist you can cover the largely flat 60km between them in a day or two, staying along the route. Or you can hire a bike in Beechworth and in Bright to explore each town and skip the ride between the two bases by driving. Or just use a car throughout. Do not underestimate the cycling if you're not a regular rider. Saddle soreness is more likely to be a factor than exhaustion. There is an added incentive: this trail is bookended by a pair of brilliant breweries in Beechworth and Bright, so there's more than one way to quench your thirst in this region.

GET THERE
Beechworth is a 3hr drive northeast of Melbourne via the Hume Freeway. Base yourself in Beechworth and Bright.

Courtesy of Ringer Reef Winery / Fletcher Photography

01 SORRENBERG

'We were serious from the start,' says Jan Morey, owner of Sorrenberg with husband Barry. 'We looked at a lot of places, including Tasmania, but we knew Beechworth and Barry had worked at Brown Brothers and Giaconda.' Giaconda is a famed winery on the outskirts of Beechworth and Sorrenberg is today approaching the same level of regard. Their first vintage was in 1990 and back then it was harder to sell Beechworth wines when there were just a handful of wineries. As Beechworth has developed, so has Sorrenberg. They now make a Cabernet Sauvignon, an outstanding example of Beechworth Chardonnay, a Sauvignon Blanc and probably the best Gamay in Australia: 'The Gamay was planted because a university project identified Beechworth as the closest region to compare with Beaujolais in France,' explains Jan. 'These days Barry doesn't rely on science but trusts his palate. He lines up the samples in the winery and gets everybody's opinion.' Together with trusting their instincts, Sorrenberg also trusts the soil and the process of making great wine - they're a certified biodynamic winery and use only natural yeast.

The vines are planted on some of the highest land around Beechworth (they're actually located along the road to the town's mountain bike park). From this north side of Beechworth, cross the town to the next winery, where you can join the rail trail.
www.sorrenberg.com; tel 03 5728 2278; 49 Alma Rd, Beechworth; visits by appointment only

02 PENNYWEIGHT WINERY

The dirt track up to Pennyweight curves around the crown of a hill striped with vines before ending at a large, rustic tin-roofed cellar door that is surrounded by roses and overgrown by giant eucalyptus trees. It's wild, natural and beautiful - much like the wine. Elizabeth and Stephen Morris - related to the Rutherglen Morris wine family - planted vines here, at 600m above sea level, in 1977 and made their first wine in 1983. 'We came here because it's cooler,'

From top left: courtesy of Baarmutha; Robin Barton; Pennyweight Winery

01 Ringer Reef Winery amid rolling hills

02 Baarmutha's distinctive cellar door

03 Beechworth's Victorian architecture

04 Ripe for the picking at Pennyweight Winery

says Elizabeth. They don't believe in watering their vines or using chemicals in the vineyard – their grapes are biodynamic and organic. 'Our opinion was that chemicals were bad for you; we wanted to live in harmony rather than control nature.' So they used natural tricks, such as planting in arcs not straight lines to conserve water and cultivating the vines with fava beans to add nitrogen. The natural approach continues in the winery with all wines aged in oak not steel.

You can taste the quality in Pennyweight's table wines: try the melon-accented Chardonnay and the excellent Bordeaux-style Cabernet blend with its red fruit and chocolate aromas. An added reason to stop at Pennyweight is the range of fortified wines, made with grapes from their vineyard in Rutherglen. They produce three sherries, including Woody's Amontillado, which averages eight years in solero. But the stand-out is the incredible 'Gold' white port, best served slightly chilled. Visitors are welcome to bring picnics up to Pennyweight. It's hard to tear yourself away but the rail trail runs past the winery so hop on your bike and continue.
www.pennyweight.com.au; tel 03 5728 1747; 13 Pennyweight Lane, Beechworth; 10am-5pm daily

03 BAARMUTHA WINES

A few minutes down the road from Pennyweight, Baarmutha is an interesting contrast, being a new winery. Vinny and Sharon Webb planted their vines in 2006, deciding to focus on just two grapes – Chardonnay and Shiraz – and do them justice. The small cellar door has a homespun charm and visitors can also book a one-hour tasting with Vinny in his Chardonnay 'cave': a shipping container artfully insulated with shot-blasted concrete and covered with dirt. The mining trolley that acts as a table in the cave is a reference to the region's gold-mining history. 'We come in here for a bit of a taste of three years of chardonnay,' says Vinny. 'The first is straight from the barrel from the most recent harvest, then with one year ageing and then from the bottle. It's always interesting: you'll find some sweetness from the first

05 The Ringer Reef Winery vineyard

year's barrel before it gets rounded off.' The DIY attitude extends to the wine-making. 'We don't use pesticides and only weed by hand,' says Vinny. 'You keep a lot of control of the process.' Vinny uses a basket press and open vats to allow wild yeasts to work their magic; the wines go into French oak barrels - unfiltered - and then straight underground. 'I believe some of the best Chardonnay outside France comes from Beechworth,' he adds. 'We get long sunny days, sitting on a tabletop at 500m. It's always 3-4 degrees cooler and with a gentle breeze.' With the breeze at your back, it's time to head onward. The stop is about 50km southeast on the Murray to the Mountains Rail Trail - if that sounds a lot, it's possible to stop overnight halfway in Myrtleford. Drivers simply need to follow the Great Alpine Rd.

www.baarmuthawines.com.au; tel 03-5728 2704; 1184 Diffey Rd, Beechworth; 4-7pm Mon-Fri, 12-6pm Sat-Sun

04 FEATHERTOP WINERY

'Mt Feathertop influences the local climate, hence the name,' explains Naomi Armstrong at the cellar door of this large, family-owned winery overlooking the Murray to the Mountains Rail Trail. Mt Feathertop, one of the highest peaks in the alpine region, looms behind the town of Bright and makes a tempting challenge for hikers. Founding and growing the winery has been challenge enough for owners Kel and Janelle Boynton. They've been in business more than 20 years, surviving fire and frost, and now focus on delivering approachable, food-friendly wines. They rely on nature for irrigation and do everything by hand: picking, pruning and making.

Kel Boynton discovered his love for winemaking while working at winery in Alsace, France on one of his many overseas trips. The climate can be similarly cool here and Boynton has planted more than 20 grape varieties, although the Sauvignon Blanc is a stand-out. *www.feathertopwinery.com.au; tel 03-5756 2356; 6619 Great Alpine Rd, Porepunkah; 11am-late Fri-Sun*

05 RINGER REEF WINERY

It's the view that grabs your attention on arriving at Ringer Reef. In the distance rise the mountains of Mount Buffalo National Park, first explored by European explorers in 1824 who named it for the bovine outline, but the area was long known to Aboriginal people, who would catch bogong moths for food. Ringer Reef was founded by Bruce and Annie Holm in 2005 but son Mark and his wife Julie manage it today. They make a range of Italian-style red and white wines, aided by research trips to Italy. The Pinot-Chardonnay sparkling wine, made from grapes grown at the vineyard, is a zesty start to any tasting. The cellar door is just 6km from Bright so it's easy to reach by bicycle from the town. *www.ringerreef.com.au; tel 03 5756 2805; 6835 Great Alpine Rd, Porepunkah; 12-5pm daily*

Courtesy of Ringer Reef Winery

ESSENTIAL INFORMATION

WHERE TO STAY

ARMOUR MOTOR INN
This family-run motel is a great value option in the centre of Beechworth, with clean, tidy rooms and friendly service. It's a short walk to the town's best pubs, restaurants and ice cream parlour or around Lake Sambell for a sunset stroll.
www.armourmotorinn.com.au; tel 03-5728 1466

BRIGHT ON TRACK
For smart, spacious and very clean rooms, Bright on Track motel, on the right as you enter the town, is a good choice. The rail trail passes the entrance and is a quick route into town, or walk along the Ovens River (watch out for platypus at dusk).
www.brightontrack.com.au; tel 03-5750 1421

WHERE TO EAT

Beechworth abounds with dining options, from the high-end restaurants The Provenance, The Ox and Hound, and The Press Room Wine Bar to such pubs as The Empire Hotel and The Commercial Hotel serving food that's a cut above. But one of our favourite spots to eat is a brewery.

BRIDGE ROAD BREWERS
Ben Kraus' Beechworth brewery is almost as well known for its pizzas as its beer - both are extremely good and make perfect companions. The seasonal specials board is always worth checking carefully. You'll need reservations at weekends.
www.bridgeroadbrewers.com.au; tel 03-5728 2703; 50 Ford St; food served 12-3pm daily, 5.30-8.30pm Wed-Sun

BRIGHT BREWERY
At the opposite end of this wine trail, Bright's brewery is a highlight of the town, set beside the river from which it draws its water. There are always new and exciting beers to try, accompanying a basic menu of pub food.
www.brightbrewery.com.au; tel 03-5755 1301; 121 Great Alpine Rd; 11am-late daily

TOMAHAWKS
Great burgers have come to Bright, thanks to this smart new venue. It's a short menu, including a wagyu cheeseburger, Cajun pulled pork shoulder or a roast pumpkin fritter with eggplant kasundi and mint yogurt. Southern fried chicken or Korean sticky fried chicken satisfies those who don't fancy buns.
www.tomahawksbright.com.au; tel 03-5750 1113; 15 Camp St; 12pm-late Wed-Sun

WHAT TO DO

MURRAY TO THE MOUNTAINS RAIL TRAIL
This sealed and largely traffic-free cycle path runs from Wangaratta to Bright, with an uphill detour to Beechworth, covering about 100km in total. It's all clearly signposted and there are regular places to stop and refuel along the way. Most people take a couple of days or more, though experienced riders can manage it in a day. Autumn is a spectacular time of year, with the changing colour of the leaves. Keen cyclists can also go mountain biking on off-road trails at Beechworth and Bright.
www.visitvictoria.com

MOUNT BUFFALO NATIONAL PARK
Hikers are spoiled for choice in this region. The waterfall-threaded slopes of this national park are laced with trails. Really fit cyclists can pedal the 20km up to 'The Horns' or the Mt Buffalo Chalet.
www.parkweb.vic.gov.au

CELEBRATIONS

SPRING TASTING
This annual exhibition of Beechworth wines is a great opportunity to taste wines from around 30 local producers, including such names as Giaconda, Savaterre and Sorrenberg for a bargain fee of $35 (and you can keep the Riedel glass). It takes place on a Saturday in November in Beechworth's Memorial Hall on historic Ford St.
www.beechworth-vineyards.com.au.

01

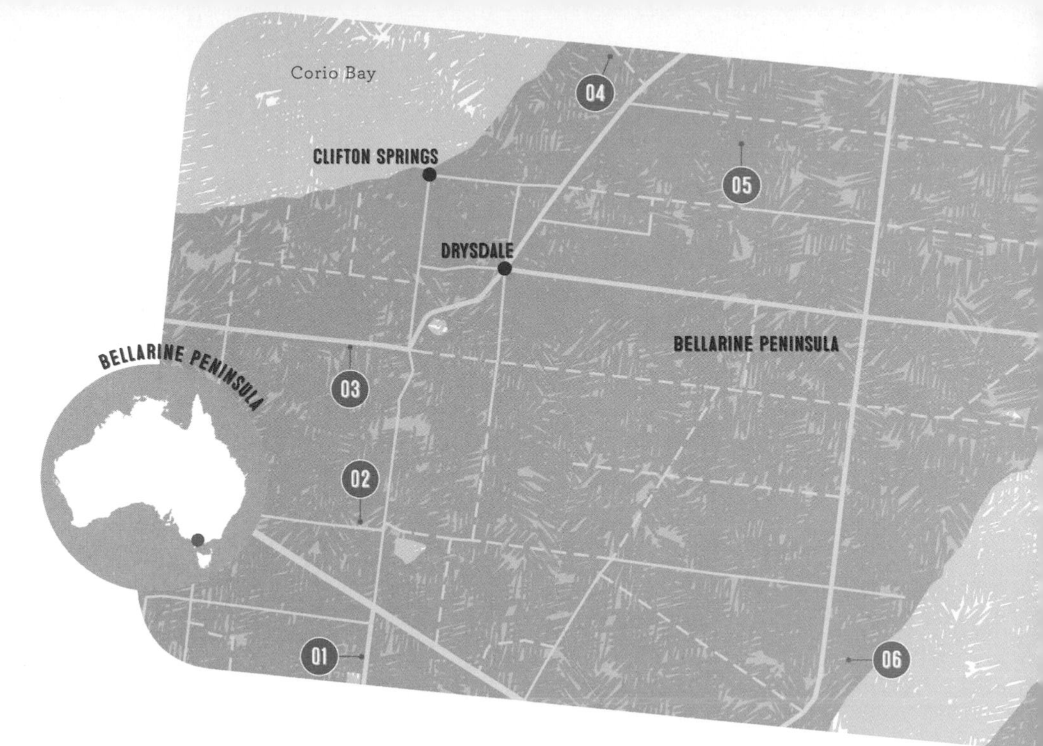

[Victoria]

BELLARINE PENINSULA

Get ready for sandy feet, sea views and some of Australia's best boutique cool-climate wines in this historic grape-growing region on the coast.

Asked to rate the country's wine regions, most minds conjure images of the top-rate wineries in South Australia's Barossa Valley, the emerald-green hills of Victoria's Yarra Valley, the sun-drenched vineyards of Margaret River in Western Australia or New South Wales' acclaimed Hunter Valley. But there's a spot on Victoria's coastline punching well above its weight, with award-winning wines attracting a huge amount of interest – Geelong & the Bellarine Peninsula. While the peninsula has always drawn holidaymakers for its stunning beaches, the Bellarine is now making waves, not just in the water, but also among oenophiles seeking fine wines paired with gourmet local produce.

A comfortable drive from Melbourne in Victoria's southwest, this area was the largest grape-growing region in Victoria's gold rush era in the mid-19th century when Swiss settlers established vineyards. The discovery of the pest phylloxera in the late 1800s, however, meant all of the vines had to be dug up. After a hiatus, the wine region was built from the ground up again in the 1980s and has bounced back in the last couple of decades with a clutch of wineries delivering some excellent fruit-driven cool-climate drops influenced by the coastal environment. The combination of the soil, moderate rainfall and the environment gives the region a terroir often likened to France's Burgundy and Bordeaux. The Bellarine Peninsula delivers excellent Pinot Noir, Chardonnay and spicy Shiraz, with Pinot Gris turning heads of late.

Geelong, Victoria's second largest city, is a 25min drive from the Bellarine Peninsula wineries and makes a great base for exploration. The once industrial city has been transformed to offer plenty of enticing restaurants and wine bars where you can sample the best wine and produce from the region.

GET THERE
Geelong is an hour from Melbourne by car or train. A ferry from Melbourne's Docklands to Portarlington on the Bellarine takes 90mins.

01 OAKDENE

Tasting the award-winning wines produced at this boutique winery will turn your world upside down, quite literally. The cellar door is as quirky as they come, located in an 'Upside Down House' – a timber A-frame barn where the roof sits against the ground as if it's been blown over in a gale (or knocked back a little too much wine, perhaps?). The grounds are dotted with eclectic sculptures and art objects, though the offbeat vibe possibly belies the high quality of the wines produced here. Oakdene specialises in cool-climate wines of the region, with varietals including Chardonnay, Pinot Noir, Shiraz, Sauvignon Blanc, Merlot and Pinot Gris. 'Our single vineyard wines are made from our own unique vineyard, and express both site and vintage each year,' says general manager Steven Paul. Their Pinot Noir and Chardonnay both won awards at the 2017 Geelong Wine Show.

www.oakdene.com.au; tel 03-5256 3886; 255 Grubb Rd, Wallington; 10am–4pm daily

02 MCGLASHANS WALLINGTON ESTATE

Winemaker Robin Brockett (from nearby Scotchman's Hill) produces the wine for McGlashans using French oak and maturing for 12 months prior to bottling. Taste his premium cool-climate wines, including the standout Pinot Noir and Chardonnay, at the rustic cellar door alongside exceptional food, such as wild-caught abalone and fresh seafood platters – you can tell the winery is run by a local diver. The cellar door is decked out in automotive and maritime memorabilia and a collection of classic cars is on display.

mcglashans.com.au; tel 03-5250 5760; 225 Swan Bay Rd, Wallington; 11am–5pm Sat & Sun, daily in January

03 LEURA PARK ESTATE

Leura Park has gone from strength to strength since its first vines were planted in 1995, becoming an acclaimed producer of maritime cool-climate wines. Darren Burke is the primary winemaker and attributes the quality of his wines

From top left: courtesy of Scotchman's Hill / Pete James; Oakdene / Brad Hill; Scothman's Hill

01 Port Lonsdale lighthouse

02 The cellar door at Scotchman's Hill

03 Oakdene's offbeat tasting room

04 Enjoying Toast to the Coast at Scotchman's Hill

'What makes our wine unique is what we don't put in, we let the unique characteristics of the region be represented.'

–Kim Dema, Basils Farm

to 'the use of ambient (wild) yeast commonly employed providing the wines with an extra layer of complexity and verve. This theme of respecting the fruit is supported by subtle use of only the very best French oak barrels for barrel-matured wines'. The stellar line-up of Leura Park wines includes sparkling Pinot Chardonnay, Sauvignon Blanc, Riesling, Pinot Gris, Chardonnay, Rosé, Pinot Noir and Shiraz. The Block 1 Reserve Chardonnay is crafted to age in bottle and is consistently rated one of the top 20 in Australia.

Ninety-minute segway tours around the vines are available (AU$80), which include a glass of wine and a tasting platter or pizza.

leuraparkestate.com.au; tel 03-5253 3180; 1400 Portarlington Rd, Curlewis; 10am–5pm Thu–Sun, daily in January

04 JACK RABBIT

With such sweeping water views from the alfresco deck here, you might be satisfied with a $5 cask wine, but thankfully you don't have to stoop that low. Jack Rabbit's experienced winemaker, Nyall Condo, was one of ten finalists in the Wine Society 'Young Winemaker of the Year' Awards 2012 and approaches his craft with minimal intervention and creative use of oak to produce some terrific results. Pair an elegant Chardonnay with a bowl of local Portarlington mussels in the cafe, or take it up a notch

05 Sampling the reds on Basils Farm

06 Aerial view of Barwon Heads

in the contemporary Jack Rabbit restaurant. Extend this trail with a stop in at Terindah Estate next door to sample their rival bay views and excellent Pinot Noir.
www.jackrabbitvineyard.com.au; tel 03-5251 2223; 85 McAdams Ln, Bellarine; 10am–5pm daily

05 SCOTCHMAN'S HILL

The oldest winery on the Bellarine Peninsula, with the first vines being planted in 1982 on the extinct volcano of Mt Bellarine, Scotchman's Hill is a classy operation. The main varietals grown in the vineyard are Sauvignon Blanc, Chardonnay, Pinot Noir and Shiraz, along with the recently planted Pinot Gris. Chief winemaker Robin Brockett explains: 'Our wines are made with pride, passion and heart. Meticulous viticulture and minimal intervention winemaking are at the heart of our ethos. We love to let the fruit drive the result.' And those results are garnering plenty of recognition and awards: their 2016 Scotchman's Hill Chardonnay scored 97 points in James Halliday's 2017 Wine Companion and the winery was also rated among Halliday's Top 100 Wineries for 2018. Don't miss tasting one of their knockout Shirazes.

A new cellar door opened up in 2017 with a cosy atmosphere, leafy alfresco area and views out across the water to the Melbourne city skyline. The eagerly awaited restaurant is set to open in 2018.
www.scotchmans.com.au; tel 03-5251 3176; 190 Scotchmans Rd, Drysdale; 10am–4.30pm daily

06 BASILS FARM

Like most wineries on the peninsula, Basils Farm takes full advantage of its location with endless views across Swan Bay. Take a stroll through the veggie gardens and plonk down on the lawn under a parasol, or grab a table in the cafe to sample the range of artisanal wines. General Manager Kim Dema explains the appeal of their drops, 'What makes our wine unique is what we don't put in, we let the unique characteristics of the region be represented in the wine. Minimal intervention starts in the vineyard and is continued via our winemaker Ray Nadeson, who is strongly guided by our artisan winemaking principles, incorporating wild fermentation with natural yeasts, and using no artificial additions or enhancers.'

Try a wine flight – where three half glasses are matched with a tasting platter – to appreciate the range, which includes Rosé, Chardonnay, Pinot Noir, Shiraz, Sauvignon Blanc, and Pinot Gris starting from the 2018 vintage.
www.basilsfarm.com.au; tel 03-5258 4280; 43–53 Nye Road, Swan Bay; 11am–4pm Mon–Fri (closed Tue), 11am–5pm Sat & Sun

ESSENTIAL INFORMATION

WHERE TO STAY

DEVLIN APARTMENTS

Choose from a range of themed boutique apartments at this former tech school and heritage-listed building dating from 1926. The chic 'New Yorker' loft apartment has beautiful arched windows while fans of Scandi-chic will enjoy the 'Modernist'. The location's great too; it's an easy stroll to some of the city's best dining options and a couple of intimate wine bars. *www.devlinapartments.com.au; tel 03-5222 1560; 312 Moorabool St, Geelong*

ATHELSTANE HOUSE

Queenscliff is a historic maritime city in the heart of the Bellarine Peninsula and this 1860s house is a lovely place to rest your head after one too many glasses of wine. As Queenscliff's oldest guesthouse, the decor is a perfect fusion of period details and mod cons, such as iPod docks and spa baths, and all rooms, some with French windows, feature bright original artworks. *athelstane.com.au; tel 03-5258 1024; 4 Hobson St, Queenscliff*

06

WHERE TO EAT

IGNI

The hottest ticket in town, IGNI has gastronomes from all over Victoria suddenly putting a trip to Geelong top of their weekend getaways list. This stylish yet unpretentious restaurant was awarded Regional Restaurant of the Year in 2018 by *Gourmet Traveller.* You'll need to book ahead (online only) to sample either the five- or eight-course menu, with dishes using a mix of European cuisine and indigenous and foraged ingredients. *www.restaurantigni.com; tel 03-5222 2266; Ryan Pl, Geelong; Thu dinner, Fri–Sat lunch & dinner, Sun lunch*

WHAT TO DO

Be sure to take in some of the Geelong sights before heading out to the wineries. Art lovers will enjoy the excellent collection of Australian art at the Geelong Art Gallery. For more contemporary works, check out what's showing at Boom Gallery in a red-brick old wool mill building near the Barwon River. The Narana Aboriginal Culture Centre in nearby Grovedale has a gallery with Victoria's largest collection of indigenous art as well as fascinating insights into Aboriginal culture.

The Bellarine beckons with beautiful beaches and quaint, laidback coastal towns. Stroll the streetscape of 19th-century buildings in historic Queenscliff and take a guided tour of Fort Queenscliff, explore the lighthouse at Point Lonsdale, take a long walk along the stunning stretch of beach at Ocean Grove, and grab your board for a surf at Barwon Heads' Thirteenth Beach.

CELEBRATIONS

TOAST TO THE COAST

Geelong & the Bellarine celebrate their bounty of wine and produce at the annual Toast to the Coast, held over the first weekend in November. It takes place at wineries all over the region and there is a shuttle bus that operates so no need for a designated driver. Cheers to that. *winegeelong.com.au/toast-to-the-coast*

01

Courtesy of Jasper Hill / Catherine Black

[Victoria]

HEATHCOTE

With ancient soils, open spaces and old-school country hospitality, Heathcote is one of the wine world's great hidden treasures.

It may still be building momentum but there's a buzz about Heathcote, luring winemakers to the region and wine lovers to their wines. Powered by a second generation of young guns who have taken the reins of family businesses, the future is looking very bright. More wineries are opening their doors to visitors to share what makes this place so special – what lies just beneath the surface.

That's what caught the eye of Ron Laughton as he was driving through the area back in the '70s. He noticed a roadside cutting that exposed a layer of soil which, upon further investigation, was identified as being rather fertile, and old. Pre-dinosaur old. In fact, 550 million years old and from the Cambrian era. This decomposed granite soil is what has lured viticulturalists and winemakers to the region in pursuit of a particular style of Shiraz, one celebrated for its fine balance of intensity and elegance.

As far as official classification goes, Heathcote is a relatively young region but wines have been made here since the gold rush days, with a few vines remaining which date back to 1891. It's humble too. You won't find opulent cellar doors with chef-hatted fine-dining restaurants, art galleries or sculpture gardens. What you will find – a reminder of what makes Heathcote so unique – will be caked on the back of your car by the end of the day. The dusty, red dirt roads that lead to cellar doors and farm sheds in Heathcote represent the lifeblood of this region, the soil.

Stretching approximately 100km from end to end, you could cover most of this ground in a couple of days. But you don't want to rush it – the people you'll meet, the experiences you'll have and the wines you'll drink deserve time. After all, they've been over 500 million years in the making.

GET THERE
Heathcote is a 1.5hr drive from Melbourne and half an hour from Bendigo.

01 MERINDOC

Merindoc is the one of the first wineries you come to as you approach from Lancefield at the southern tip of Heathcote. The Shelmerdine family have been growing grapes for three generations and converted their old machinery shed into a cellar door in 2006. It's now home to the tasting bar and bistro and is one of the only cellar doors with a restaurant. Produce is sourced locally including lamb, fruit and veggies from the property, and pork from neighbouring McIvor Farm. Staff are passionate about the region, service is friendly and the tables outside have beautiful views of the granite hills.

Merindoc's wines demonstrate the effects of the local meso-climates and the impact of a slight temperature change from north to south.

The Willoughby Bridge vineyard wines are sourced from Colbinabbin in the north and highlight the bigger style of reds that it's famous for – the Sangiovese and Nebbiolo are great examples. Here at the cellar door there are 40 acres under vine and the cooler climate and granite soils produce a lighter, more crisp style, the Riesling being a highlight.

www.merindoc.com.au; tel 03-5433 5188; 2905 Lancefield-Tooborak Rd, Tooborak; 10am-4pm Fri, noon-5pm Sat-Sun, by appt Mon

02 SANGUINE

Like most wineries in Heathcote, Sanguine is all about family – established by Tony and Linda Hunter in the late '90s, it's one of the bigger wineries and cellar doors and now involves the couple's children, Mark and Jodi, as well as extended family. You may well meet one of them in the barrel room which doubles as the cellar door. There's no mistaking the fact you're in a working winery.

Sanguine's 'Inception' Shiraz is available to taste out of large glasses which give the bold style room to move – this wine alone is worth the visit. Tempranillo is another variety that thrives on the estate. Wines are available to buy by the glass or bottle, which you

From top left: courtesy of Jasper Hill / Catherine Black; Tellurian (2)

01 Ron Laughton and daughter Emily at Jasper Hill

02 The pair among the vines

03 A feast at Tellurian

04 Chief winemaker Tobias at Tellurian

05 Live music at Sanguine

06 Summer tastings outdoors at Sanguine

The dusty, red dirt roads that lead to cellar doors and farm sheds in Heathcote represent the lifeblood of this region – the soil

can take outside onto the lawn or to one of the shaded tables to swig with a BYO picnic.
www.sanguinewines.com.au; tel 03-5433 3111; 77 Shurans Ln, Heathcote; 10am–5pm Sat–Sun

03 JASPER HILL

Just beyond the town of Heathcote on the Northern Highway you'll see a sign pointing to Jasper Hill. There were no such signs back in the early '70s when Ron Laughton was driving through, though there was something that caught his attention – that aforesaid roadside cutting with no apparent rock strata, just plenty of grass growing out of it. Something out of the ordinary that Ron, Elva and their family have since turned into something altogether extraordinary.

Regarded by many as icons and pioneers of the region, the family planted the first vineyards in 1975 with the first vintage produced in 1982. As a food scientist and chemist, Ron saw the problem that chemicals cause to the environment and was passionate about producing pure, unadulterated wine. Vineyards are dry-grown and organic with a minimal intervention philosophy.

Jasper Hill wines are testament to the terroir and rather than display medals won (of which there are many), it's a geological map of the region that has pride of place on the wall. The Shiraz vineyards, or paddocks, are named after daughters Emily and Georgia who

are now involved in the business themselves.

Each vintage sells out quickly so it's a rare privilege to taste these wines at the cellar door, a beautiful building open by appointment only – which makes sense, as this is the kind of place that merits more than just a quick sip; it deserves time.
www.jasperhill.com.au; tel 03-5433 2528; 88 Drummonds Ln, Heathcote; by appt

04 TELLURIAN

Travelling north, keep an eye out for the Toolleen pub – it's where you'll turn off for Tellurian. The foothills of the Mt Camel Range provide a stunning backdrop to the vineyards, as well as all-important shelter for the vines. The name Tellurian means 'of the earth' – here, it's decomposed greenstone rock and limestone that is the source of nutrients for the award-winning wines.

The cellar door is a relatively new building, with the tasting room boasting sweeping views. Family or friends are likely to be behind the tasting bench so get chatting and ask questions – they're a font of knowledge. Interesting varieties to try here include Fiano, Marsanne and Nero d'Avola. Of course there's exemplary Shiraz too.
www.tellurianwines.com.au; tel 0431 004 766; 408 Tranter Rd, Toolleen; 11am–4.30pm Sat–Sun

05 HEATHCOTE II

It's a tricky one to type into Google maps – is it 2, two or II? You can see it from the Tellurian cellar door, but that doesn't help much either. Persevere, using the Toolleen pub as a reference, and you'll find Heathcote II a few kilometres further on, just off the Cornella–Toollen road. The name refers to the two owners, Peter and Lionel, who've poured their passion into this place.

Rocks from the property were collected by hand and feature on the exterior of the cellar door and winery – a small building that wouldn't look out of place in the Mexican desert. The bold, rich, terracotta colour of these rocks is something of a clue to the style of wines made here. Tasting takes place around a barrel – it's nothing fancy and it doesn't need to be, as the wines deserve all the attention. They all spend a significant time in oak and are released after further bottle ageing – the Grenache is a real highlight.
www.heathcote2.com; tel 03-5433 6292; 290 Cornella–Toolleen Rd, Toolleen; 11am–5pm Sat–Sun

Courtesy of Sanguine / Graham Hosking; Sanguine / James Lauritz

ESSENTIAL INFORMATION

WHERE TO STAY

THE CELLARS AT HEATHCOTE II

These self-contained villas are ideal if you want to make a weekend of it. Guests will find the fridge stocked with free-range eggs from the farm next door and a bottle of vintage champagne. The staggered positioning of each villa affords privacy and the view overlooking the vineyards and Mt Camel range is spectacular. The real highlight, however, is the cylindrical, temperature- and humidity-controlled cellar in each room, fully stocked with wines from around the world. *www.thecellars.heathcote2.com; tel 03-5433 6292; 290 Cornella–Toolleen Rd, Toolleen*

WHERE TO EAT

HEATHCOTE HARVEST

Heathcote Harvest has a small dining room and a deli for takeaway produce making it the place to fill a picnic basket if you're opting to BYO. Fresh produce and pork, including lip-smacking bacon, is sourced from the owner's working farm. *www.heathcoteharvest.com.au; tel 0466 542 329; 32 Tuscan Ct, Heathcote; 11am–4pm Fri–Sun, Sat dinner by reservation*

HEATHCOTE WINE HUB

In town, Fodder (on the High Street) does good, wholesome breakfasts and lunches and The Heathcote Wine Hub stocks everything you'll need for the weekend. It also features a comprehensive selection of wines from the region to taste or purchase by the glass from one of the three enomatic machines. *www.heathcotewinehub.com.au; tel 03-5433 2204; 105 High St, Heathcote; 8.30am–5pm daily*

WHAT TO DO

HEATHCOTE

Heathcote's main street features beautiful buildings from the late 1800s and is worth a stroll – keep an eye out for the Mechanics' Institute, the Old Gaol, Commercial Bank and Old Courthouse. A few minutes' walk from the Visitor Centre is the Powder Magazine which was used to store explosives back in the mining days. You can see the impact of gold-mining on the landscape at the Pink Cliffs Reserve which is only a few kilometres away.

O'KEEFE RAIL TRAIL

If you're feeling a little more adventurous hire a bike and ride along the O'Keefe Rail Trail, which runs for some 50km from Heathcote to Lake Weeroona at Bendigo, with a pit stop at the Axedale Tavern along the way. Or hike up Mt Ida for great views of the McIvor Ranges, vineyards and Graytown National Park – take a picnic, some water and a bottle of wine. *www.railtrails.org.au*

CELEBRATIONS

The Heathcote Food and Wine festival takes over the showgrounds in early October each year and draws crowds from all over the country to taste new vintage releases paired with local produce and entertainment. *www.heathcotewinegrowers.com.au/festival*

01

Courtesy of Red Feet

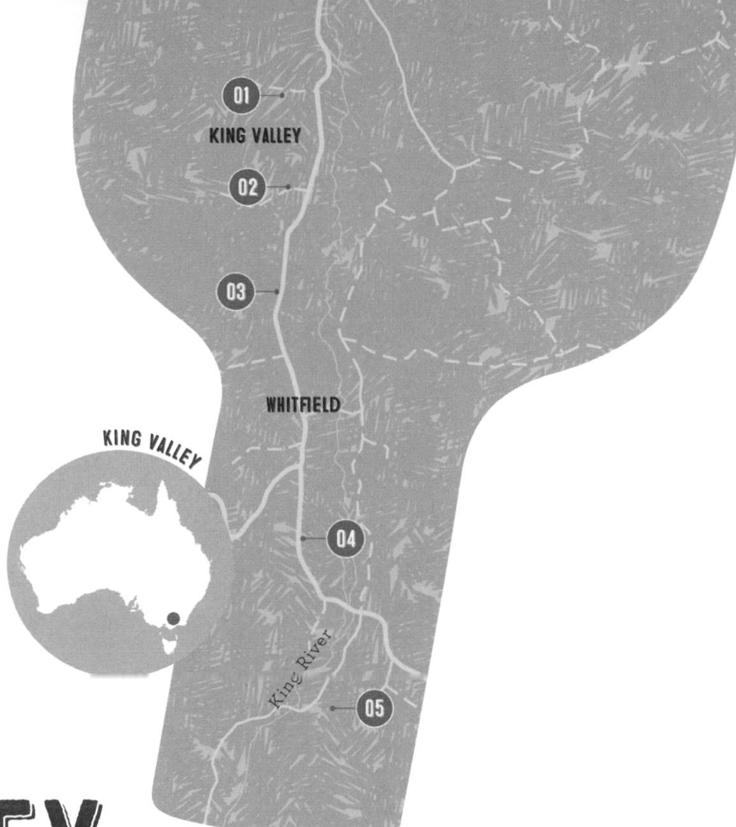

[Victoria]

KING VALLEY

Follow the Prosecco Road through gorgeous scenery in this Italian-influenced wine region.

The broad King Valley lies along the Whitfield to Wangaratta road about three hours' drive northeast of Melbourne. It's a peaceful part of Victoria: the road runs parallel to the burbling King River, which feeds Lake William Hovell at the southern end of the region. In the distance are the snowcapped mountains of Australia's alpine region, while forested hills, once the haunt of 19th-century bushrangers such as Harry Powers, surround the valley. It's a fun drive from Melbourne if you take the upland country roads via Mansfield rather than the freeway.

The story of farming here starts not with wine but tobacco. In the 1850s and '60s, the Chinese had started cultivated tobacco in Northeast Victoria to meet demand from incomers drawn by the gold rush. By the 1950s, Italian-born farmers had taken over tobacco production but, as we know, the times were changing and by the early 1980s some of the Italian tobacco growing families – names such as Corsini of La Cantina and Pizzini – had switched to growing grapes, focusing initially on the varieties from back home with which they were most familiar: Sangiovese, Nebbiolo and what is now known as Glera, used to make prosecco. The distinctively Italian flavour of King Valley has remained ever since.

This trail concentrates on the southern portion of the Prosecco Road, starting halfway along King Valley and heading south towards Melbourne. At the north of the valley are a couple of big names in Australian wine, Sam Miranda and Brown Brothers (for whom many of the Italian families first grew grapes) but this compact itinerary, can be completed in one day and crowned with bottle of chilled Riesling at Lake William Hovell for a swim and a sundowner.

GET THERE

The King Valley is a 3hr drive north from Melbourne, the closest international gateway, and about 5hrs from Canberra.

01 RED FEET

Begin the day by taking a gravel track off the C521, the valley's main road. It leads up to Red Feet's cellar door and one of the warmest welcomes in the valley. Red Feet was started in 2008 by winemaker Damian Star (previously at Hardys) with sister and business brain Megan but their cellar door only opened in October 2017. It has been worth the wait. Although they're one of the smallest wineries in the valley by tonnage, they have some of the biggest views from their glass-sided cellar door across the valley to the Black Range mountains. Like many of the region's wineries, Red Feet grows a wide variety of grapes, which makes for a more interesting experience. Damien started with plantings of Sangiovese and the Spanish grape Tempranillo - 'a bit controversial with the Italian families,' says Megan. If there's time in the season, Damien may give tutorials in the differences between clones of Sangiovese: comparing wine from three varieties of Sangiovese straight from the barrel: even to an average palate it's obvious that all three produce very different flavours from the same soils. Clearly there's more to the winemaker's art than meets the eye. 'You learn so much as you go along,' says Megan. Red Feet also has a cool-climate Shiraz. 'I want to make the best wine that I can but I want it to be approachable,' says Damien. *www.redfeet.com.au; tel 03-5729 3535; 49 Cemetery Lane; 10am-5pm Thu-Mon*

02 LA CANTINA

Continuing south, the next stop is also off to the right: La Cantina, owned by the Corsinis, one of the King Valley's original Italian families. Appropriately enough, tastings take place in the chapel-like cellar door because these unfiltered and unpredictable wines merit a certain amount of reverence.

If you're lucky you'll find patriarch Gino Corsini behind the counter. The family, from Lucca in Tuscany, has been in the King Valley for about 50 years, originally as tobacco growers. 'I was born in wine,' says Gino. 'I started on it when I was three years old. My father and grandfather made wine in Tuscany.' When the Corsinis came to the King Valley they planted grapes for their

From top left: courtesy of Red Feet; © Robin Barton; courtesy of Chrismont

01 Red Feet by name...

02 Collecting grapes at Red Feet

03 Old tobacco sheds at Pizzini

04 On the terrace at Chrismont

own personal wine, as was usual in Italy, but it remained a hobby until Gino's daughter got married. 'She wanted to serve my wine at the wedding but I didn't think it was good enough,' says Gino. 'She won that argument. A couple of her friends loved it and it spread by word of mouth. I thought then that I had better get a licence and build a cellar door.' They planted more vines and opened the cellar door in 1997. All their wines are biodynamic and preservative-free, which may account for the hangover-free response at the wedding party. Surprisingly, they use more than the expected Italian varietals of Sangiovese (the home of which is Tuscany) and Pinot Grigio. There are Cabernet, Shiraz and Merlot blends, but the wine Gino is most proud of is the Saperavi, a grape that's new to Australia but represents the very birth of winemaking being from Georgia. At 15% ABV it's a monster with tons of body but still smooth. *www.lacantinakingvalley.com.au; tel 03-5729 3615; 54 Honey's Lane; 10am-5pm daily*

03 GRACEBROOK

If it's time for a food break, stop at Gracebrook, a larger winery on the same side of the main road. David Maples, the owner, has been making wine here for 15 years but the cellar door itself dates back to 1870 when it was a stables; all the original features, including the stringybark, red gum and yellow box timbers remain. That history is acknowledged in The Stables Riesling, a deliciously aged example (try the 2008 if there's any left) with sweet-but-tart marmalade notes. Grapes are grown at three vineyards around the valley: a block of Chardonnay, a block of Shiraz and a block of Cabernet Sauvignon directly in front of the cellar door

Behind are fields with goats, pigs, quails and chickens: some are destined for the kitchen because the ingredients for the restaurant's modern Australian menu - featuring mains such as quail with local hazelnut salad - are home-grown or locally sourced. Eat under the shade of an umbrella on the terrace. *www.gracebrook.com.au; tel 03-5729 3562; 4446 Wangaratta-Whitfield Rd, 10am-5pm daily*

05 Relaxing in the Red Feet gardens

06 The vista from the Powers lookout

04 PIZZINI

The Pizzini family has long been at the heart of the King Valley. They were also 1950s tobacco farmers - check out the row of original drying kilns out front - but turned to wine so successfully that the cellar door has won national awards. Part of the reason for that is the variety of things to do here: there are games to play in the beautiful gardens and Katrina Pizzini's A Tavola! cooking school where you can learn to make pasta, risotto and gnocchi.

The variety is also reflect in the wines: Alfredo Pizzini has planted a number of unusual Italian grapes that go into many of their wines. Pizzini's Lana range references the family's Italian history: Alfredo's father, Roberto, met his mother Rosetta in the Italian town of Lana. The Lana Il Nostro Gallo is a savoury, earthy blend of Sangiovese, Canaiolo and Colorino, made using more traditional winemaking techniques. That's adventurous attitude is taken a step further with Pizzini's fresh-tasting Verdicchio white, which is made with wild yeasts. But it was Sangiovese and Nebbiolo that were first planted in the red, iron-rich soils here. A stream runs through the Nebbiolo vineyard so in a dry year they can choose which side to cultivate. The Coronamiento (at $135 a bottle) is a memorable mouthful of deep red fruits, spice and layers of leather and spearmint flavours.

www.pizzini.com.au; tel 03-5729 8278; 175 King Valley Rd, Whitfield; 10am-5pm daily

05 CHRISMONT

Finally, at the foot of the King Valley, stands the amazing modernist cellar door of Chrismont. The award-winning galleried building opened in 2015 and looks up the valley to the Black Ranges. Owners Arnie and Jo Pizzini (yes, first cousins) represent the whole of Italy with their wines: tall, blue-eyed Arnie is from the Trento region of Italy's mountainous north and Jo is from Sicily. So, you'll find wine made from Sicily's white Fiano grape for example. The Barbera grape (from Piedmont) is a mainstay of Chrismont and produces a tangy red with acidity, plum and blackberry flavours perfect for quaffing with a pizza. Food at Chrismont's restaurant is classic home-style Italian cooking with dishes such as burrata, fig and prosciutto salad or risotto con funghi. Chrismont is the last stop of this King Valley wine trail but there are still new wine experiences to be had here: as Arnie says: 'Everybody has something different to offer, just as well because everybody has a different palate.' Chrismont is also at the start of the road that leads to Lake William Hovell, so we can recommend continuing onward for a few more minutes and ending the day at the waterside, listening to the birdsong.

www.chrismont.com.au; tel-03 5729 8220; 251 Upper King River Rd, Cheshunt; 10am-5pm daily

ESSENTIAL INFORMATION

WHERE TO STAY

Several wineries offer upscale accommodation, including Chrismont, Dal Zotto and Pizzini (at the Mountain View Hotel in Whitfield).

CASA LUNA

This B&B near Whitfield makes a cosy base for discovering the wines of the King Valley with the advantage of enjoying great meals at home - it's a member of the Slow Food movement founded in Italy that prizes local and seasonal ingredients. *www.casaluna.com.au; tel 03-5726 7650*

06

WHERE TO EAT

King Valley, which borders the Milawa Gourmet Region at its north end, is surrounded by world-class food producers. You can drop into many of them to pick up supplies for a picnic. Look out for bread and cheese from Milawa, more cheese from King Valley Dairy, and some of the sweetest walnuts you'll ever taste.

THE WHITTY CAFE

Whitfield stands at the junction of the Mansfield and Wangaratta roads, midway along the trail. The Whitty Cafe does good home-made focaccia sandwiches and burgers for $18. *Tel 03-5729 8388; 4905 Wangaratta-Whitfield Rd*

DAL ZOTTO

In addition to the wineries serving food mentioned so far, Dal Zotto is a fixture on Prosecco Road with a popular trattoria. The airy restaurant serves classic Italian dishes – pasta, gnocchi and antipasto platters – with views over the vines around the property. *www.dalzotto.com.au; tel 03-5729 8321*

WHAT TO DO

POWERS LOOKOUT SCENIC RESERVE

Bushranger Harry Powers, who mentored local outlaw Ned Kelly, had a camp in the hills south of Whitfield with incredible views along the King Valley from which to spy on any approaching police troopers. *www.parkweb.vic.gov.au*

CELEBRATIONS

LA DOLCE VITA

This annual festival of food and wine takes place every November and is the highlight of the King Valley calendar. All the big name wineries participate and shuttles are laid on to help visitors get from one to the next. Guest chefs cook special menus and provide masterclasses. Live music and kids' entertainment is also provided. *www.winesoftheking-valley.com.au*

01

[Victoria]

MACEDON RANGES

Follow the weekending Melbourne tastemakers seeking out sophisticated food, invigorating spa retreats and some of the country's best cool-climate wines.

The southern end of the Great Dividing Range runs like a spine down the Macedon Ranges region, with vineyards draped out either side. Many are small, family-owned concerns, dating back half a century or so – vines were planted in the late 19th century but it wasn't until the late 1960s that viticulture really started to take hold in the area. At between 300 and 700m above sea level and with a median January average temperature of around 18°C (64°F), this is true cool-climate wine. The fertile, volcanic soil and long ripening times – with harvest sometimes as late as May – allow complex flavours and aromatics to develop, resulting in a diverse range of light- to medium-bodied wines.

Pinot Noir, Chardonnay and Riesling thrive here and are much sought after for their crisp acidity and purity. But the list of wines produced by the 40 or so wineries here also takes in Shiraz, Merlot, Sauvignon Blanc, Gewürtzraminer, Cabernet Franc and other less familiar varieties, such as Lagrein.

There are some well-established cellar doors with purpose-built tasting rooms, but it's the smaller places which are the most endearing – and often run by the owners who double up as viticulturist-winemaker-cellar door manager. It's being welcomed at these family-owned businesses and treated like a guest that makes touring this region such a pleasure.

Towns and villages which flourished in the gold rush, such as Kyneton, Gisborne and Castlemaine, are now popular haunts for Melburnians, many of whom have been so charmed they've ditched big city life altogether. Incoming (and longstanding resident) artists and tree-changers have brought with them inner-city style, bars and live music venues – you'll find creative and foodie hubs that provide the perfect base for leisurely vineyard explorations.

GET THERE
Macedon is an easy 1hr drive from Melbourne. The train journey from Southern Cross Station to Kyneton takes just over an hour.

01 GISBORNE PEAK

Barbara Nixon is a proud and passionate spokesperson for wine tourism in Macedon while her husband Bob tends to let his work in the vineyard do the talking – they were among the first to plant vineyards in the region back in 1978, starting with a single acre, which has since developed into a formidable business. Barbara used to host wine tours to the Yarra Valley before establishing the cellar door and restaurant here in 2000; Bob confesses, 'It was a hobby that got out of control.'

The hobby is now a busy operation with 13.5 acres under vine, a packed restaurant and four self-contained cabins. With the two pizza ovens firing all weekend and Barbara greeting regulars by name and with hugs, it feels like visiting family. Wine tasting here is similarly relaxed, with the emphasis on finding a style you like rather than studying tech specs – though the Pinot Noir is often a highlight. *www.gisbornepeakwines.com.au; tel 03-5428 2228; 69 Short Rd, Gisborne South; 11am–4pm Mon–Fri; 11am–5pm Sat–Sun*

02 HANGING ROCK WINERY & VINEYARD

Invitations to a barbecue at the Ellis family's farm must be like gold dust – not only do they produce award-winning, grass-fed beef but their sparkling wine and Pinot are some of the best in the land. But if you're not on the list, seek consolation in the two fridges at the cellar door – one filled with wine, the other with beef for you to take home and cook for yourself.

The elevation and aspect of the winery afford one of the best views of Mt Macedon and Hanging Rock, with the main Jim Jim vineyard in the foreground. The family have been growing grapes here since they bought the property back in 1982. Most of the wines are made from estate vineyards but they also source fruit from Bendigo and Shiraz from family vineyards in Heathcote. If you're lucky, The Macedon NV Cuvee and the NV LD ('late disgorged', the process of removing the sediment after fermentation) Cuvee will both be

From top left: courtesy of Hanging Rock / James Lauritz (2); Granite Hills

01 Autumn colours in Macedon

02 The grounds of Hanging Rock Winery

03 Farm chickens at Hanging Rock

04 Vines at Granite Hills

'We want people to feel at home here. We don't bombard you with wine speak but we can answer questions. We want people to feel welcome'

Jenifer Kolkka, Curly Flat

available to taste. To find out what makes these sparkling wines so rich, creamy and complex just ask one of the Ellis family members who'll most likely be on bar duty. *www.hangingrock.com.au; tel 03-5427 0542; 88 Jim Rd, Newham; 10am–5pm daily*

03 PARAMOOR

Driving up the dirt road that leads to Paramoor feels like entering one of those old 'pioneer world' theme parks that you'd visit on a school excursion – featuring old wooden buildings with a slight lean, rusty machinery, horse-drawn carriages, dusty saddles and a guy on a tractor waving enthusiastically as you pass. That guy on the tractor will most likely be Will, waving from the vineyard. Formerly managing director of Kodak Australasia, Dr Will Fraser and his wife Kathy moved here and planted vines in 2003 as a retirement venture. Will embarked on further studies in wine technology and worked with a local winemaker for the first few years – now in his mid-70s, he's still out there tending to the vines and producing brilliant wine.

While reminders of its past life as a working Clydesdale farm remain, Paramoor's focus is now firmly on wine, with each bottle named after members of the family. The Joan Picton (Will's mum) Pinot Noir is delicious and the 'Doris' Riesling demonstrates the suitability of the variety to this cool-climate region. Come along on the first Sunday of

05 Llew Knight of Granite Hills

06 Hike up to Hanging Rock

the month when they stoke up the wood-fired oven for pizzas, but be sure to book ahead.
www.paramoor.com.au; tel 03-5427 1057; 439 Three Chain Rd, Carlsruhe; 10am–5pm Mon & Fri–Sun, or by appt ✂

04 COBAW RIDGE

With dreams of a self-sufficient life, living off the land but still within reach of Melbourne, Alan and Nelly Cooper built up this place by hand from the very first mud brick. When it came to planting vines, they experimented with Shiraz and Cabernet initially, the latter eventually replaced by a more suitable, albeit lesser-known variety called Lagrein in 1994, which represented the first commercial plantings in Australia of this red grape from Italy's northeast.

All wines are estate grown, made and bottled at this beautiful site bordering the Cobaw State Forest. These are certified organic and biodynamic producers with an intimate connection to the rhythms and cycles of nature. Talking about the cosmos, the land, Pinot and philosophy with Nelly at the cellar door, it's almost as though you can taste the moon and the stars in these ethereal wines.
www.cobawridge.com.au; tel 03-5423 5227; 31 Perc Boyers Ln, East Pastoria; 10am–5pm Mon & Thurs–Fri, 12pm–5.30pm Sat–Sun

05 GRANITE HILLS

Gordon and Heather Knight were teetotal sheep farmers before plummeting wool prices prompted them to decide to plant wine grapes at this site, 550m above sea level. Forty-two consecutive vintages of estate-grown Riesling later, their decision was clearly a good one.

A new generation has brought fresh ideas and they're now diversifying, producing Grüner Veltliner and Pinot Blanc to supplement staples Chardonnay, Merlot, Cabernet Sauvignon, Cabernet Franc and Shiraz.

Granite Hills plays an important role in the history of the Macedon Ranges, with the region's oldest plantings, and is worth a visit for the award-winning Riesling alone.
www.granitehills.com.au; tel 03-5423 7273; 1481 Burke and Wills Track, Baynton; 11am–6pm daily

06 CURLY FLAT

It's a cute name inspired by a Michael Leunig cartoon, reflecting founders Phillip Moraghan and Jenifer Kolkka's aim to create serious wine while not taking themselves too seriously. Pointing to the well-worn couch in their welcoming, spacious Vintage Hall tasting room, Jeni explains, 'We want people to feel at home here, we don't bombard you with wine speak but we can answer questions, we want people to feel welcome.'

Located on the eastern edge of the Macedon Ranges wine region, on land that produces excellent Pinot Noir and Chardonnay, Curly Flat is all about those two grapes, as well as Pinot Gris. They will typically have a couple of vintages available to taste, providing an insight into how well these wines evolve over time.

In winter the open fires glow, encouraging passing wine tasters to linger. And with plans to upgrade a guest bedroom into luxury accommodation, you may well be able to hole up for the weekend.
www.curlyflat.com; tel 03-5429 1956; 263 Collivers Rd, Lancefield; noon–5pm Sat–Sun, weekdays by appointment ✂

ESSENTIAL INFORMATION

WHERE TO STAY

Gourmet escapes and weekend getaways are the region's speciality, with a range of spas, cottages and B&Bs. Flop House offers a portfolio of super-cute cottages in and around Kyneton, as well as providing information on the region and suggested activities to help you make the most of your visit. *www.flophouse.com.au; tel 0438 160 671; 1/58-60 Piper St, Kyneton*

WHERE TO EAT

THE PARKLAND

Kyneton is the ideal base for exploring the Macedon Ranges, and its historic Piper Street showcases some of the region's best eateries, making it popular with Melbourne foodies. The Parkland, a new incarnation of the well-loved Mr Carsisi, nails the brief when it comes to serving local produce in a relaxed setting. *www.theparkland kyneton.com; tel 03-5422 3769; 37c Piper St; lunch from noon daily, dinner from 5.30pm Fri–Tues*

BANKS FINE WINES / PIPER STREET FOOD CO

If there are wineries you missed or you just need to replenish supplies, head to Banks Fine Wines which stocks the best selection of Macedon Ranges wine. For picnic provisions, Piper Street Food Co will sort you out – their pork pies are legendary. *www.banksfinewine.com.au; tel 03-5422 6682; 134 Mollison St; 10am–7pm Tues–Sat, noon–5pm Sun; www.piperstfoodco.com; tel 03-5422 3553; 89 Piper St; 9am–5pm Mon–Fri, 9am–2pm Sat*

SOURCE DINING

Once of central Victoria's best restaurants, this fine place has a menu that changes with the seasons and dish descriptions that read like a culinary short story about regional produce and carefully conceived taste combinations. *www.sourcedining.com.au; tel 03-5422 2039; 72 Piper St, Kyneton; noon–2.30pm & 6–9pm Thu–Sat, noon–2.30pm Sun*

WHAT TO DO

Hanging Rock, made famous by the spooky Joan Lindsay novel (and subsequent film by Peter Weir) *Picnic at Hanging Rock*, is an ancient and captivating place. The volcanic rock formations are the sacred site of the traditional owners, the Wurundjeri people, but you're welcome to clamber up the rocks along the 20min path. From the summit there are views to Mt Macedon and the surrounding countryside.

Lancefield, Woodend, Riddells Creek and Kyneton all have weekend farmers' markets and there are plenty of art galleries in the region to explore.

West of here, Daylesford and Hepburn Springs form the 'spa centre of Victoria'. Set among the scenic hills, lakes and forests of the Central Highlands, it's a fabulous year-round destination where you can soak away your troubles and sip wine by the fireside. *www.visitvictoria.com/regions/Daylesford-and-the-Macedon-Ranges*

04

CELEBRATIONS

The annual Budburst festival is a celebration of all things food and wine, with over 30 wineries participating and many restaurants hosting long lunches and dinners. It takes place over a weekend in November. *www.macedonranges wineandfoodfest.com.au*

01

[Victoria]

MORNINGTON PENINSULA

Hightail it out of Victoria's state capital for a weekend among the vines and lanes of this peninsula, and enjoy revitalising beach walks, great wines and local dining.

The Mornington Peninsula has long played an important role in Melbourne society. It's a place where wealthy wine enthusiasts – Melbourne's great and good – have sunk more than a few thousand dollars into their dream project, with the reasonable expectation of seeing the most pleasing results in the bottle rather than on the balance sheet.

Since the revival of the Peninsula's vineyards in the mid-1970s (grapes were first planted here in the 19th century) the 25-mile tendril of land has seen more than 50 cellar doors open, luring weekending cityfolk down the Nepean Highway. The Peninsula is relatively developed along the northwest coast but becomes wilder the further south you go, until you reach the Mornington Peninsula National Park. But along the central ridge around Red Hill, where many of the wineries are located, it is almost quaint in places, with twisty lanes, charming village corners and green valleys.

GET THERE
Melbourne is the closest city; the Mornington Peninsula is an easy 1hr drive south.

Pinot Noir's spiritual home might be Burgundy, but it has settled very happily here on the other side of the world. Australia's only wine-growing region with a truly maritime climate, the Mornington Peninsula's Pinot Noir grapes love the cool sea breezes that prolong its ripening cycle, increasing flavour. Characteristics of the Peninsula's Pinot include a transcendent scent – earthy, spicy yet, fruity – that seems to flick a pleasure switch deep within the brain, and a lighter body than Pinots from elsewhere in the New World. Few other grapes are as memorable. Chardonnay is just as distinctive a wine on the peninsula, with a delicacy not found elsewhere; only a few wineries have the know-how to get the best from this partnership. When you've tasted enough wines for the day, drive down to the east coast and watch the sun set from one of the forest-backed beaches.

01 Cape Schank

02 Ten Minutes by Tractor

03 An aerial view of Stonier

04 Stonier's wines

01 ELDRIDGE ESTATE

High on a hill just outside Red Hill, David Lloyd, the winemaker and owner of Eldridge Estate winery, has been chasing the perfect Pinot Noir since taking over the small vineyard in 1995. To that end, he has planted three different Burgundian varieties of the grape and produces examples of each. Note the care he takes over them: bunches are de-stemmed but berries left whole; pressed with an air bag press; fermented naturally without yeast; aged in French oak. The result is a fine example of Mornington Peninsula Pinot – dark cherry fruit but savoury – that demonstrates how food-friendly a grape Pinot Noir can be. It's always interesting visiting Eldridge Estate and one must-try wine is Lloyd's PTG, his take on Burgundy's Passe-Tout-Grain blend of Pinot Noir and Gamay, a light, quaffable wine that is bright but earthy simultaneously. Compare it with the pure Pinots on the terrace overlooking the vineyard. Mornington Peninsula vineyards are usually a bit higher and a couple of degrees cooler than average, and there's no frost as it's close to the sea. The cooler the climate, the longer the grapes take to ripen and build flavour.

Lloyd's expertise is also applied to Chardonnay and the Wendy Chardonnay, a tribute to David's wife, who died in 2014, is, as he says, 'the best Chardonnay I can make from the estate in any one year.'

www.eldridge-estate.com.au; tel 0414 758960; 120 Arthurs Seat Rd; 12-4pm Mon-Fri, 11am-5pm Sat-Sun

02 MONTALTO

Montalto is a winery that succeeds in covering all the bases: world-class wines, great food, and paths that lure visitors deep into the vineyard. But what makes Montalto a must-visit cellar door is its Chardonnay. Once described by James Halliday as 'power and grace personified', it's as enjoyable an example of the grape as you'll find. Picked from Montalto's main north-facing vineyard and from the plot behind the cellar door, the wine, despite its scarcity, has earned accolades from all over the world.

Montalto is owned by the Mitchell family, and the vineyard dates back 20 years, although the modern cellar door only opened in 2001. 'While we see ourselves as a winery, our philosophy is to be a destination to draw people to the Mornington Peninsula,' says John Mitchell. 'No matter where people are in the world, when they drink our wines we want them to remember the whole experience.'

To that end, the Mitchells have an olive grove with 1500 trees (you can taste the olive oil in the cellar door), four locations around the valley set aside for summer picnics, a restaurant supplied by herb and vegetable gardens, and an orchard. Afterwards, there are sculptures sprinkled around the vineyards to discover and a wetland walking trail. As John Mitchell says, the Mornington Peninsula offers more than wine, though, in Montalto's case, they're not doing too badly on that front either.
www.montalto.com.au; tel 03-5989 8412; 33 Shoreham Rd, Red Hill South; 11am–5pm daily

03 STONIER

Geraldine McFaul, winemaker at Stonier since 2003, has earned a reputation for producing some of the Mornington Peninsula's most expressive Pinot Noirs, wines with a rock-solid sense of place. Stonier is one of the first wave of vineyards on the peninsula, with its Chardonnay vines dating from 1978 and the Pinot Noir vines from 1982. But it is perhaps Geraldine McFaul's research trips to Burgundy that influence Stonier's Pinots the most. She produces just Chardonnay and Pinot Noir in three categories, ranging from blends from the younger vineyards to bottles from single vineyards, a dedication to *terroir* derived from Burgundy. Stonier's distinctive, airy cellar door, designed by Melbourne architect Daryl Jackson, is the perfect venue for these ambitious wines.

Bunches are counted in late December, when some may be pruned (fewer bunches concentrate the vine's energies and flavour). 'That's when our viticulturalist starts getting stressed about ordering barrels - at $1200 to $1500 each - and we all take bets on how much will be produced,' says cellar door manager Noella. Stonier is right on the east coast of the peninsula and the cool conditions suit Chardonnay too: 'Warmer areas produce bigger, buttery chards,' explains Noella. Look for a mineral edge instead in Stonier's Chardonnay, which is as refreshing as a walk on the beach across the road. 'But if you prefer Pinots,' adds Noella, 'go and try Nat White's at Main Ridge'.
www.stonier.com.au; tel 03-5989 8300; 2 Thompsons Lane, Merricks; 11am–5pm daily

04 MAIN RIDGE ESTATE

The rutted, pot-holed dirt track leading to Nat White's cellar door (as well as the tasting fee and signs warning off coach parties) seems designed to deter casual quaffers. It's an impression not dispelled by the tall, bespectacled figure of Nat White himself behind the countertop. Reserved and scholarly, the former engineer looks like there's nothing he'd rather do than close up the cellar door and get back to his grapes. But that's perfectly understandable, given that his vines were the first to be planted during the Peninsula's revival in the mid-1970s and produce some of the most fascinating wines from Red Hill's volcanic soils. 'We were the first winery on the Mornington Peninsula,' he says, over a tasting of his Half Acre Pinot Noir, 'so we planted several varieties to see what would take. We grow enough to produce 1200 cases of Pinot Noir and Chardonnay and we've kept on enough Merlot for a barrel a year and some Pinot Meunier.'

After a roadtrip through France in the 1970s, Nat and his wife Rosalie returned to Australia unable to forget about the Pinot Noirs of Burgundy. They planted the first vines at Main Ridge in 1975 and crushed their first grapes in 1980, aiming to replicate the lighter, fruitier Pinot Noirs of Burgundy. 'I find the Mornington Peninsula's cooler climate produces less tannic Pinots,' he explains. Nat produces two Pinots from the same sloping

05 Nat White of Main Ridge Estate

06 Barrel testing at Stonier

plot: the Half-Acre is picked from vines rooted in shallow soil, while the Acre comes from deeper soil. Treated identically in all other respects, including an 18-month sojourn in French oak barriques, the smaller berries from the Half-Acre make for a noticeably more intense mouthful. Lessons in wine-making don't come more comprehensible. It's no wonder that Nat White lets his wine speak for itself.
www.mre.com.au; tel 03-5989 2686; 80 William Road, Red Hill; 12–4pm Mon–Fri, 12–5pm Sat–Sun

05 TEN MINUTES BY TRACTOR

With its jazz soundtrack and a modern, minimalist interior, Ten Minutes By Tractor is one of the most chic cellar doors on the Mornington Peninsula. Wine is produced from three vineyards, all, you guessed it, ten minutes from each other by tractor. Owner Martin Spedding, who has run TMBT since 2004 alongside mentor Richard McIntyre, believes the region is coming of age now since the first vines were planted in the 1970s: 'Of the 60 or 70 wine producers here, a great majority of them are producing fantastic wine.'

This includes TMBT, where top-of-the-range wines go for $60 a bottle. 'These are small-yielding vineyards and the wines are expensive as a result.'

With a deck overlooking a valley and a small plot of vines, the cellar door restaurant offers food tailored to the estate's wines. 'Pinot Noir is better with food than some of Australia's heavier reds,' says Martin. 'The types of foods we're now eating in Australia – a fusion of Asian and Mediterranean flavours – is food with delicate layers of flavours. People are looking for wines that complement not dominate food.'
www. tenminutesbytractor.com.au; tel 03-5989 6080; 1333 Mornington–Flinders Rd, Main Ridge; 10am–5pm daily

06 RED HILL ESTATE

Wooden crates are still scattered around the old sorting shed at Red Hill Estate, on the road back to Shoreham, but the space around them has evolved into the tasting room of this 20-year old vineyard. Out the back, Max's Restaurant has views over green countryside all the way down to the sea and Phillip Island. Chef Max Paganoni selects local produce – strawberries from Sunny Ridge, cheese from Red Hill's own artisan cheesery – for his Italian-influenced menus. On summer weekends you can expect at least one wedding to be taking place in the gardens.

Back in the cellar door, Red Hill's wines are no less enjoyable. Concentrating on Chardonnay and Pinot Noir, Red HIll winemakers use traditional techniques, including wild yeasts and smaller bunches of berries to up the skin-to-flesh ratio. The result is a complex, earthy Classic Release Pinot Noir and a Chardonnay that is less big and brassy than you may find elsewhere. Both are designed to cellar for a long time; up to 15 years in the case of the Pinot.
www.redhillestate.com.au; tel 03-5989 2838; 53 Shoreham Rd, Red Hill South; 11am–5pm daily

Courtesy of Main Ridge Estate; Stonier

WHERE TO STAY

CAPE SCHANK RESORT

Although you can stay in Cape Schank's actual lighthouse (see below), this RACV resort has a bit more space. It overlooks wild Bass Strait. *www.racv.com.au; Trent Jones Drive, Cape Schanck*

WHERE TO EAT

RED HILL BREWERY

Red Hill's brewery grows its own hops, and brews enough European-inspired ales – from strong Belgian-style lagers and German pilsners to English stouts and bitters – to keep beer-curious wine-tourers refreshed. The English, Belgian and German theme continues with Ploughman's platters and *waterzooi*, the Belgian fish stew. *www.redhillbrewery.com.au; tel +61 03 5989 2959; 88 Shoreham Road, Red Hill South*

PORTSEA HOTEL

At the very tip of the peninsula, Portsea's hotel serves good pub grub, with views on the side. *www.portseahotel.com.au; tel +61 03 5984 2213; 3746 Point Nepean Rd, Portsea*

WHAT TO DO

Pack your hiking shoes for the one-hour bush walk to Bushranger's Bay, at the south-east tip of the peninsula. It's an untamed place, rich in wildlife, from the frogs croaking under the tea trees to the kangaroos bounding along the beach at sunset. Look south to see the Cape Schanck lightstation, which dates from 1859 and houses a small museum and self-catering accommodation. *www.parkweb.vic.gov.au; tel 03 5988 6184*

CELEBRATIONS

The biennial Pinot Noir Celebration (February), sees winemakers from all over the world converge on the Mornington Peninsula to sniff each other's Pinots and swap pruning tips. Later in the year the Winter Wine Weekend (June) is an opportunity to meet the producers, attend seminars and taste wine; accommodation gets booked early up for both occasions. *www.mpva.com.au/events*

01

courtesy of Mt Avoca / Simon Hughes

[Victoria]

THE PYRENEES

Follow the gold diggers out west to unearth savoury Cabernet Sauvignon, sublime Shiraz and some very approachable Chardonnay in this highly-regarded region.

Within two or three hours' drive of Melbourne, wine-tourers are spoiled for choice. But if you enjoy tasting elegant cool-climate Shiraz and some of Australia's best Cabernet Sauvignon outside of Margaret River, meeting passionate wine makers and exploring handsome gold-era towns, add the Pyrenees, out west, to your wishlist.

Driving into the Pyrenees is a little different to some other Victorian regions: the landscape is more open, with undulating, sun-baked hills, and the distances between towns are greater. But it's a treat when you do reach a town like Beaufort or Avoca because the heritage of the region is visible in the handsome architecture. Gold was mined in these hills and money flowed back through Ballarat, Bendigo and Castlemaine.

The region's wine history is equally resonant. Renowned Rhône winemaker Michel Chapoutier has said that Victoria is 'like a second France' thanks to the age and diversity of its soils and the Pyrenees is one region where there is a sense of terroir - that special relationship between the land and the wine - can be discerned.

Visiting some of the long-standing wineries here, such as Blue Pyrenees or Dalwhinnie, is like having a history and geography lesson, but one improved by sips from glasses of really very good Shiraz, Cabernet Sauvignon and Chardonnay.

But about that French name... it is nothing to do with wine. The region was named by Sir Thomas Mitchell, a Scottish soldier turned surveyor, who was reminded of the European Pyrenees by the chunky ranges on his 1836 exploration along the Murray. He also named the Grampians and in turn was commemorated by having a cockatoo, a highway, a river and a small species of hopping mouse named after him.

GET THERE
Avoca is about a 2hr drive from Melbourne (and the nearest airport) along the Western Freeway.

01 MT AVOCA

This winery, set down a dusty track bordering wooded hills, was founded by the Barry family more than 40 years ago (borrow a bike to explore further). However, it's not the family's only claim to fame: ancestor Sir Redmond was the judge who sentenced Victoria's legendary bushranger Ned Kelly to death. It was a divisive decision but feelings are much less equivocal about the Barry family's wine: it's excellent.

Mt Avoca is an organic winery (sheep graze between the rows of vines) and for their premium Estate Range winemaker David uses organic grapes grown in front of the cellar door. A Shiraz showdown sees the deep, rich 'Malakoff' Shiraz, made from grapes harvested from the steep-sided Malakoff vineyard face-off against the Old Vine Shiraz, which is made from grapes picked from vines planted in 1971 before being aged in oak barrels for two years. The Old Vine Shiraz has the hint of mint and savoury blackcurrant flavours characteristic of the region: perfect with roast lamb.

One of the best aspects of tasting wine at a cellar door is the chance that there might be some rare bottles open – at Mt Avoca these could be the limited release Nebbiolo and Sangiovese wines, which exhibit some of the winery's Northern Italian influences.

www.mountavoca.com; tel 03-5465 3282; Moates Lane, Avoca; 12-5pm Mon-Fri, 11.30am-4pm Sat-Sun (11.30am-3.30pm in winter)

02 BLUE PYRENEES

Continue your wine tour where winemaking in the Pyrenees began. During WWII, royalties from Rémy Martin's Australian distributor kept the French company afloat. In the early 1960s Rémy Martin came to Australia to find land on which to plant vines. Being French, they believed gravel soils were best, so they acquired gold-mining maps of Australia that showed soil types. Over these they laid a climate chart and looked for where ideal soils and climate met: the Pyrenees. 'Blue Pyrenees was the first vineyard in the region,' says chief winemaker Andrew Koerner, 'It's got mean, gravel soils like Bordeaux.'

The European connection continued with the climate:

01 Examining the fruit at Mt Avoca

02 An aerial view of Blue Pyrenees

03 Pouring Blue Pyrenees' Vintage Brut

04 Mt Avoca winery

'Victoria's climate is cooler, creating elegant wines in line with Europe. Warm days and cool nights in the Pyrenees lock in the flavours,' says Andrew.

As one of the region's largest wineries, with slopes facing in every direction, they're able to grow a large number of grape varieties and make the widest range of wines, including some great sparkling red and white wines: 'We took a sparkling Shiraz to a French wine show,' recalls David. 'You can't do that', they said. Yes, we can. It's Australia, there are no rules!'

The most popular wine is the Bone Dry Rose – nicknamed 'bro'se by Koerner due to the large number of men drinking it. But the definitive Blue Pyrenees wine is the Estate blend of Cabernet, Malbec and Merlot, a tribute to the winery's Bordeaux and their French heritage. Koerner explains what to look for in a top-notch Cabernet: 'Cassis has got to be there in spades and it needs to finish strongly on the tannins'. The Estate is about the art of blending, looking for a long, intense finish. 'It spends two years in barrels and two years in the bottle,' says David. 'The plum in the middle is the merlot. And the zing is the Malbec.' Blue Pyrenees hosts masterclasses three or four times a year, with vertical tastings for 20 to 30 people during which more of wine's secrets are revealed. *www.bluepyrenees.com.au; tel 03-5465 1111; Vinoca Rd, Avoca; 11am-5pm daily*

03 SUMMERFIELD

Some of Victoria's finest Shiraz is crafted by this family-run winery set on the road out of Avoca. Founded by farmer Ian Summerfield in 1970, when he planted some Shiraz vines, Summerfield wine is now made by son Mark, who focuses his energies on getting the best from the older blocks of vines. The Reserve Shiraz is a powerful example, using some whole bunches for extra complexity and spice. The Sahsah Shiraz also uses some of the 1970s vines and is aged in French oak for 18 months. Taste both at the small cellar door plus some good Cabernets. *www.summerfieldwines.com; tel 03-5467 2264; 5967 Stawell-Avoca Rd, Moonambel; 10am-5pm Mon-Sat, 10am-3pm Sun*

Ø5 Dalwhinnie's famed vineyard blocks

Ø6 You are now entering The Pyrenees

04 DALWHINNIE

'Wine is about accessibility, you should have fun with it.' So says ebullient David Jones, the co-owner of Dalwhinnie and its winemaker. 'You drink it with your besties, your family, and have a laugh.' It's an appealing sentiment and all but guarantees you'll have a good time at this cellar door. But David Jones' charm belies an extremely serious approach to fine wine that comes from three generations of family working the soil, with his father Ewan Jones, an architect, having bought the land and planted vines in 1973: 'I grew up drinking great Bordeaux and Burgundy and I thought 'I want more!' The location is beautiful: the 40-year-old vineyards are draped over the contours of slopes backed by eucalyptus forest, best viewed from the deck of the modern cellar door that overlooks the valley. From here, David points out the three vineyard blocks that have built Dalwhinnie's stellar reputation, each stemming from a Shiraz cutting from three famous vineyards. The Pinnacle block uses cuttings from Torbreck in the Barossa Valley and now produces about 150 cases; Southwest Rocks used a cutting from a vineyard called Bests, and Eagle was planted in 1977 and, when the stars align, now ranks as one of Australia's iconic wines. As is done in Burgundy, grapes from each of these blocks are used for Dalwhinnie's single-block and the difference between these three expressions of Shiraz is a revelation. 'We're looking for tannin, structure, power and finesse,' says David. Occasionally, he will host a vineyard walk, stopping and tasting wine at each block (fee $70). But, true to his word, there are also highly accessible Chardonnays, Cabernets and Shiraz wines in the Moonambel and Mesa ranges.

www.dalwhinnie.com.au; tel 03-5467 2388; 448 Taltarni Rd, Moonambel; 10am-5pm daily

05 SALLY'S PADDOCK

Ask local winemakers for tips on where else to visit and they'll always offer personal favourites (or mates). But one name was on everybody's tongue in the Pyrenees: Sally's Paddock. Founded by Neill and Sally Robb in 1973, the warm red-brick winery on top of a hill outside Redbank, is a stunning spot to toast the end of your trip. And if you time your visit cleverly you may catch some live music on Sundays.

Neill and their winemaking daughter Sasha use small hand-picked crops of non-irrigated vines to craft their Cabernet Sauvignon, Shiraz, Cabernet Franc, Merlot, Pinot Noir and Malbec. The Sally's Paddock range uses grapes from a single vineyard, basket-pressed and brought to life with wild yeast - you don't get much more of a taste of a place than these wines.

www.sallyspaddock.com.au; tel 03-5467 7255; 1926 Sunraysia Hwy, Redbank; 9am-5pm Mon-Sat, 10am-5pm Sun

ESSENTIAL INFORMATION

WHERE TO STAY

Many of the wineries in the Pyrenees offer accommodation, including Mt Avoca (three self-contained eco-lodges), Summerfield, Dalwhinnie (the Eagles Nest deluxe apartment) and Sally's Paddock (a self-contained mud-brick cottage). Most of the wineries are located around Avoca and Moonambel. Several rural B&B options pepper the region if you don't want to rent an entire property. The Avoca Hotel (see Where to Eat) is the top option in Avoca but there are also a couple of motels.

AVOCA MOTEL

This motel has 12 tidy units at the north end of town, where they are surrounded by gardens. There's a BBQ area, breakfast and plenty of parking space.
www.avocamotelvictoria.com.au; tel 03-5465 3464; 159 High St, Avoca

WHERE TO EAT

Several wineries, including Blue Pyrenees and Sally's Paddock, offer lunches so it can make sense to eat at one of them. Alternatively, Avoca Hotel is the star attraction in the region.

AVOCA HOTEL

Alison Chapman and Ian Urquhart's beautifully restored High Street pub offers seriously good food, open fires in the winter, and warm hospitality. They use local suppliers wherever possible for dishes such as Western Plains rolled pork lion with rhubarb, mushrooms, sweet herbs and crackling.
www.theavocahotel.com.au; tel 03-5465 3018; 115 High St, Avoca

MOONAMBEL GENERAL STORE

If you're peckish while on the road, the general store in Moonambel sells homemade pies, pastries and cakes to eat in or take away.
Tel 03-5467 2225; 29 Brooke St, Moonambel

WHAT TO DO

GRAMPIANS NATIONAL PARK

Continue 90min west to reach some of the best hiking in the state at the Grampians National Park. Trails for all abilities weave through the boulders and cliffs of this park, including the new Grampians Peak Trail, stretching 144km from Mt Zero to Mt Abrupt. Gather maps and advice from the visitor centre in Halls Gap.
www.parkweb.vic.gov.au

ANTIQUES HUNTING

The antiques stores and second-hand shops of the gold region's towns can be a treasure trove of items ranging from the newly retro to actually historic.

CELEBRATIONS

GRAMPIANS GRAPE ESCAPE

This wine and good festival takes place a 100km drive west of the Pyrenees around the town of Halls Gap in the Grampians National Park. Local wineries and food producers showcase their wares over a weekend of live music, cooking classes and kids' entertainment. It's usually scheduled for early May.
www.grampians-grapeescape.com.au

PYRENEES UNEARTHED

An April wine and food festival in Avoca with music and around 15 participating wineries.

01

[Victoria]

RUTHERGLEN

Deep in northern Victoria, there's something sweet and unique happening. Some of Australia's oldest wineries make its most unusual wines in this rural region.

Rain in Rutherglen. The farmers are rejoicing. The cockatoos, washing-powder white against the greenery, seem happy. And the winemakers have that look of bewilderment that comes with unexpected good fortune. For Rutherglen, deep in northern Victoria, four hours from Canberra, seven from Sydney, can suffer from 40°C (104°F) summers, with grapes having to be harvested in a mad rush – even in the middle of the night – before they cook into a jam. But the rain cools things down and prolongs the ripening time of the region's unique Muscat and Tokay vines. And the longer on the vine, the better for Rutherglen's remarkable fortified Muscats and Tokays – butterscotch-flavoured, raisin-rich dessert wines.

Aside from the heat, Rutherglen has its own challenges: newer wine regions such as King Valley, closer to Melbourne, have siphoned off visitors. Then there's the wine itself: in the age of the calorie-conscious diner, who orders a sweet wine (a 'sticky' in Aussie lingo) any more? Who even orders dessert? But Rutherglen's Muscats and Tokays, like Banyuls of southern France, deserve their place at the table, for being heady, idiosyncratic and wantonly indulgent. Wines aside, another reason to tour Rutherglen is the region's history. Several of its key wineries, such as All Saints and Morris, started in the mid-19th century and their stories are entwined with that of Australia, featuring colonial pioneers and gold miners, all set to a backdrop of the broad Murray River.

GET THERE

You'll need a car to drive from Melbourne (3hrs) or Canberra. Base yourself in Rutherglen.

01 MORRIS WINES

Starting a 'stickies' winery is a 20-year investment, which is why Rutherglen is dominated by fourth- and fifth-generation family wineries and has few new openings. This winery's family roots reach back to George Francis Morris, from Lancashire, England, who founded it in 1859. Like many of his peers, he'd moved to Australia in his teens in search of opportunity, specifically gold. The adage that the people who make money in gold rushes are those selling the picks was true in Morris' case. But eventually he sold his share in a gold-mining outfitters and started planting vines with the proceeds. By 1885 Morris had more than 80 hectares (198 acres) of vines and was the largest producer in the southern hemisphere. Five generations later, the Morris family is still making award-winning wines; the silverware in the trophy room dates back to the 19th century. They make a huge range of fortified wines, including tawny ports, and some full-bodied red wines, including a rustic Durif that has a cult following in Australia.

www.morriswines.com.au; tel 02-6026 7303 ; Mia Mia Rd, Browns Plains; 9am-5pm daily

02 ALL SAINTS

Don't be deceived by appearances: All Saints winery may look like a Scottish castle, complete with flag-topped turret (indeed, it's based on the Castle of Mey in Caithness, Scotland) but it's an all-Australian icon. Back in the 1860s, when it was founded, the winery had an earth floor and was built from red bricks fired on-site. The estate's history is tied to that of the Rutherglen region: its original owners, George Sutherland Smith and John Banks arrived from Scotland aged just 23 and 20 respectfully. Trained as engineers, they designed bridges and buildings throughout Victoria, including part of the jail in nearby Beechworth that accommodated the bushranger Ned Kelly. Then the friends started planting vines at the current site in 1869, winning the first gold medal for Australian wine in 1873 in London.

Today, under the guidance of (now former) winemaker Dan Crane, All Saints' wines have continued to win awards. 'A long autumn and cool nights, thanks to the cold air rolling off the Australian Alps, mean the grapes retain their acidity,' he explains. This gives the fruit's flavours a chance to catch up with

01 Rural Rutherglen

02 A tasting at Campbells Winery

03 All Saints winery

04 All Saints' distinctive facade

'There's no recipe – I look at the fruit as it comes in and how it is best going to express itself.'

–Anton Therkildsen, Valhalla Wines

its sugars. The Muscat and Tokay grapes are picked as late in the season as late May then pressed using their weight. But you'll have to wait at least eight years and up to 20 to taste the results in All Saints' fortified wines. ***www.allsaintswine.com.au; tel 02-6035 2222; All Saints Rd; 9am-5.30pm Mon-Sat, 10am-5.30pm Sun***

03 VALHALLA WINES

You can take a break from the history lessons when you reach Valhalla. Anton Therkildsen – half-Danish, half-Scottish – arrived in Rutherglen in 1997 when studying winemaking. Within two years he'd bought a plot of land and was married to a local GP, Antoinette. He planted Durif and Shiraz in the heavier soils, Grenache and Mourvedre in the loamy midweight soils and Marsanne and Viognier in the lightest soils. With the help of free cuttings from other vineyards, borrowed tractors, and the corner of a friend's winery, Anton's first vintage was on its way.

But he still needed a winery – and he wanted it to be sustainably built. They decided on a straw-bale design with 1m-thick walls. In 2007 the walls went up in three weeks, the double-insulated roof in another three weeks and the rendering in a final three week burst. In just over two months they had a passive solar-powered winery that didn't require air conditioning – quite an achievement when temperatures in Rutherglen range from -4°C to 40°C (25°F to 104°F). And all the rainwater is captured.

Anton's sustainable approach extends to the vines, with free-

05 Campbells winery

06 A good vintage

07 Enjoying the Campbells gardens

range geese providing fertiliser, and wild flowers to attract predators and deter pests. 'I wanted to bring different energies to the vineyard, working with natural rhythms, which is something we've lost as a society,' he explains. 'It was important to us to farm naturally and sustainably and to return to traditional winemaking principles. Our ethos is to do the best we can and make it available to the average consumer. Make it well and with integrity.'

Valhalla also aims to spread the word about winemaking. Not only does Anton get his children to help at harvest, but he also offers winemaker-for-a-day workshops. 'I love it,' he says. 'It's a big part of vintage, showcasing how it's made. Big wineries can be dangerous places but I encourage people to get stuck in and have a taste' Dip a finger into a foaming and fermenting vat of just-pressed Durif and it'll taste of deep, sweet blackcurrants. ***www.valhallawines.com.au; tel 02-6033 1438; 163 All Saints Rd; 10am-4pm Fri-Mon; tours & winemaking experiences by appointment***

04 CAMPBELLS WINES

Campbells is a family-owned winery that is part of Australia's winemaking heritage. In the mid-19th century, John Campbell, another Scottish immigrant, arrived in Rutherglen to seek his fortune in northeast Victoria's gold rush. But he realised there was no gold. Instead, as he was told by one of the region's first winemakers, there was more gold in the top six inches of soil. Following suit, Campbell planted the family's first vines 140 years ago. He named his first wine Bobbie Burns, after a gold mine opposite the cellar.

Campbells retains a lot of history. The storehouse, reinforced to keep people out, was used until the 1920s. Under the beams in the original part of the winery are 1000L, 100-year-old barrels of Muscat and Tokay. Every three months the winemaker tastes each barrel and between vintages a catflap-like door in the front lets (small) people crawl inside to clean them.

All the grapes used are grown on the site and include Durif, a variety developed by French botanist Dr Durif in the 1880s, which is resistant to heat. Having a dark colour and high alcohol content, it is used for port and robust table wines. Campbells also does its own bottling so whatever time of year it is, there will be something going on. ***www.campbellswines.com.au; tel 02-6033 6000; 4603 Murray Valley Hwy; 9am-5pm Mon-Sat, 10am-5pm Sun***

WHERE TO STAY

TUILERIES

This luxurious place stands next to Jolimont Cellars. There's a tennis court, pool and an outstanding restaurant. No prizes for guessing what the self-contained King Vineyard units overlook.
www.tuileriesrutherglen.com.au; tel 02-6032 9033; 13 Drummond St, Rutherglen

WHERE TO EAT

Most of the eating options in Rutherglen are strung along the handsome Main St, which gives a taste of rural Australian architecture.

TASTE

The top fine dining destination in Rutherglen is this multipurpose venue on the Main St. Cafe by day, swanky restaurant by night, serving a degustation menu with matching wines or à la carte. The bar has an interesting range of local Durif wines too. Open for breakfast, lunch and dinner (Wed-Sun).
www.taste-at-rutherglen.com; tel 02-6032 9765; 121b Main St, Rutherglen

WHAT TO DO

If you've made it up to northeast Victoria, it makes sense to explore as much as possible of this fantastic part of Australia. Half an hour by car southeast of Rutherglen is Beechworth, arguably Australia's most appealing country town. It's based around a crossroads, with plenty of well preserved buildings along each road, many with stories attached, such as the jail. There's also an excellent brewery and several good pubs and restaurants.
A couple of hours west of Rutherglen is Echuca, on the Murray, where riverboats ply their trade.
www.visitvictoria.com

CELEBRATIONS

Rutherglen's annual Winery Walkabout takes place in June on the Queen's Birthday long weekend holiday in Victoria. There are tastings at around 20 wineries and plenty of activities for families to take part in; the Country Fair on the Sunday features a grape stomp and a barrel-rolling competition.
www.winemakers.com.au

01

[Victoria]

YARRA VALLEY 1

Fabulous wineries, attractive towns, innovative art galleries, roaming 'roos: the Yarra Valley easily tempts as a perfect weekend retreat, moments from Melbourne.

It doesn't take long for the outer suburbs of Melbourne to give way to the rolling hills of the Yarra Valley as you approach from the Maroondah Highway. The transition from backyard to vineyard is sudden and by the time you reach Coldstream it's time to make some decisions. There's a large tourist sign that looms off to the left-hand side of the road listing dozens of wineries to visit. It doesn't really matter whether you veer off and follow the Melba Highway or stick to the Maroondah, both have wineries branching off either side and you're spoiled for choice. This, the first of our Yarra Valley trails, focuses on the classics – the more established and extravagant wineries offering much more than a cellar door tasting experience. The proximity to Melbourne makes this an easy day trip, with all of the cellar doors within easy reach of the town of Healesville, a convenient base for exploring.

This is Victoria's oldest wine grape-growing region, with the first vineyards planted back in 1838 at Yering Station. Things slowed down during the depression of the 1930s until a resurgence in the '60s and '70s which hasn't abated since. The legacy of early producers remains, with places like Yarra Yering still making the wines that first drew attention and critical acclaim to the region, while a new wave of winemakers build upon this intrepid spirit and experiment with alternative varieties.

Many grapes have been tried and tested over the years but it's the Burgundian varieties of Chardonnay and Pinot Noir that have consistently performed well, as have Cabernet and Shiraz. Most producers will have these as a staple but there are plenty of smaller plantings, of varieties such as Marsanne, Roussanne, Tempranillo and Nebbiolo, which are showing great promise.

GET THERE
Healesville is a 1hr drive from Melbourne, and a lot quicker by helicopter.

01 Clare Halloran of TarraWarra

02 Harvesting at TarraWarra

03 Domaine Chandon

04 Yarra Yering's team

05 Dining at TarraWarra

01 CHANDON

The meticulously manicured lawn and gardens that fringe the driveway approaching Chandon are an insight into what to expect here – a taste of the Champagne lifestyle. As the name suggests this is a venture by the French champagne house Moët & Chandon – their first in Australia having previously established outposts in Argentina, Brazil and California.

You can take a short, self-guided tour of the estate which takes you from the history of Moët & Chandon to the regions it sources grapes from in Victoria, and then on to the sparkling winemaking process including a look inside the riddling hall. If you're keen to learn more, sign up for the Sunday School lesson which explores 250 years of Champagne-making and the story of Aussie sparkling, complete with exquisite paired canapés.

There are sparkling wines to taste but you're better off enjoying the view, and wines, from the lounge bar and restaurant. If you have time and a designated driver, settle into one of the comfy chairs in the restaurant for the afternoon. Otherwise, the lounge bar is a great place to raise a glass of bubbly and propose a toast. On a sunny day with the Yarra Ranges as a backdrop, there's plenty to celebrate. *www.chandon.com.au; tel 03-9738 9200; 727 Maroondah Hwy, Coldstream; 10.30am–4.30pm daily*

02 OAKRIDGE

The big Burgundy glasses suggest that they take their tastings very seriously here, and so they should. Chief winemaker David Bicknell is a master of the craft, who is celebrated for his ability to coax the best out of the region's Chardonnay and was awarded Gourmet Traveller's winemaker of the year in 2017. Oakridge have not only got the wine experience covered, the restaurant which is run by Matt Stone and Jo Barrett is also top drawer, with panoramic views of the vineyard.

There's no charge to taste the wines and it's worth visiting for the Chardonnay alone, but this is not an experience you want to rush. The restaurant's weekend menu is a two- or three-course

From top let: courteesy of TarraWarra / Sally Goodall; Chandon; Yarra Yering; TarraWarra

celebration of locally sourced, foraged and sustainable produce and the matching wines are as good as you'll find anywhere in the Valley.
www.oakridgewines.com.au; tel 03-9738 9900; 864 Maroondah Hwy, Coldstream; 10am–5pm daily

03 YARRA YERING

The legacy of the revered founder and winemaker Dr Bailey Carrodus abides at Yarra Yering – one of the most iconic wineries in the region. The tasting experience here is an insight into the history of the Yarra Valley and a rare opportunity to taste wines that are not so readily available, coveted as they are by collectors and loyal customers.

Dr Carrodus' house was converted into the tasting room in 2011 and it retains the comfortable vibe of a lounge room, complete with a large window overlooking a magnificent view of vines and the valley. There are a few options for the guided tasting and each are priced based on the wines poured. It's only an extra $10 to try them all (including the Carrodus range and a few museum releases) and it's well worth it, if only to taste three vintages of the glorious Carrodus Shiraz ($250/bottle).
www.yarrayering.com; tel 03-5964 9267; 4 Briarty Rd, Gruyere; 10am–5pm daily

04 ROCHFORD

You could stop in for a quick tasting here but that would be missing the point – Rochford don't do anything by halves so why not set the afternoon aside and settle in to appreciate the huge scale of this venture. Whether it's lunch, dinner or a day on the green watching megastars like Elton John tinkle the ivories, this place draws the crowds.

The festival calendar is booked well in advance so chances are you'll stumble on some sort of event, and it's likely to involve at least great food and wine. The cellar door and winery are perched at the top of the amphitheatre providing sweeping views of the stage and the sprawling vineyards on either side. You can even take a tour of the vineyard on a Segway, helicopter or hot air balloon before coming back down to earth to

06 Out on the Rochford estate

07 The Chandon boutique

blend your own wine. Amid all the entertainment, there are great wines being produced, the sparkling Isabella's Vineyard Chardonnay a highlight.
www.rochfordwines.com.au; tel 03-5957 3333; 878-880 Maroondah Hwy, Coldstream; 9am-5pm Mon-Fri, 9am-6pm Sat-Sun

05 GIANT STEPS

Giant Steps is a relatively new winery in the Valley but has had a huge impact since launching in 2003, racking up an impressive list of awards. Founder Phil Sexton is a visionary who has created, among other things, a winery that's become regarded as one of the best Pinot producers in the country. This is due in no small part to the work of Steve Flamsteed – a winemaker with a deft touch when it comes to bringing out the best of the terroir. Here, as is the case throughout the Valley, it's Pinot Noir and Chardonnay that shine.

Giant Steps is not exactly the typical cellar door experience, with the tasting room at the back of their restaurant in the main street of Healseville. The restaurant offers wine flights at the table – $15 for three wines by the glass, with twilight tastings held at the bar on Friday or Saturday nights.

At other times, you're perched up at a long bar overlooking the working barrel room and winery, giving you a glimpse of the action – when we visited Steve Flamsteed was moving barrels around to make room for a function later that night. He'd also opened a few back vintages which were shared around. These and all the wines available for tasting are excellent – keep an eye out for the Gruyere Farm Ocarina Chardonnay which is fermented in a ceramic egg.
www.giantstepswine.com.au; tel 03-5962 6111; 336 Maroondah Hwy, Healesville; 11am-late Thu-Mon

06 TARRAWARRA

No other winery in the Yarra Valley has quite the same visual effect as Marc and Eva Besen's remarkable creation. Shadows cast by concrete columns sweep across a courtyard framed by rammed-earth walls and the arcing glass of the TarraWarra Museum of Art. The complex rests atop a ridge between Healesville and Yarra Glen and is the work of Melbourne architect Allan Powell, who seems to have been inspired by the Yarra's light and earth.

With a car park often filled with sports cars, an entrance that curls between high-sided walls before opening out to views over vines and landscaped grounds to the north, visiting this winery is a real event. Luckily Clare Halloran's wines stand up to the build-up: her Chardonnay, typically aged 10 months in oak, is a well-defined example of the grape. The other big draw here is the TarraWarra Museum of Art, which hosts exhibitions of modern (post-1950) Australian art from the Besens' own collection.
www.tarrawarra.com.au; tel 03-5957 3510; 311 Healesville-Yarra Glen Rd, Yarra Glen; 11am-5pm

ESSENTIAL INFORMATION

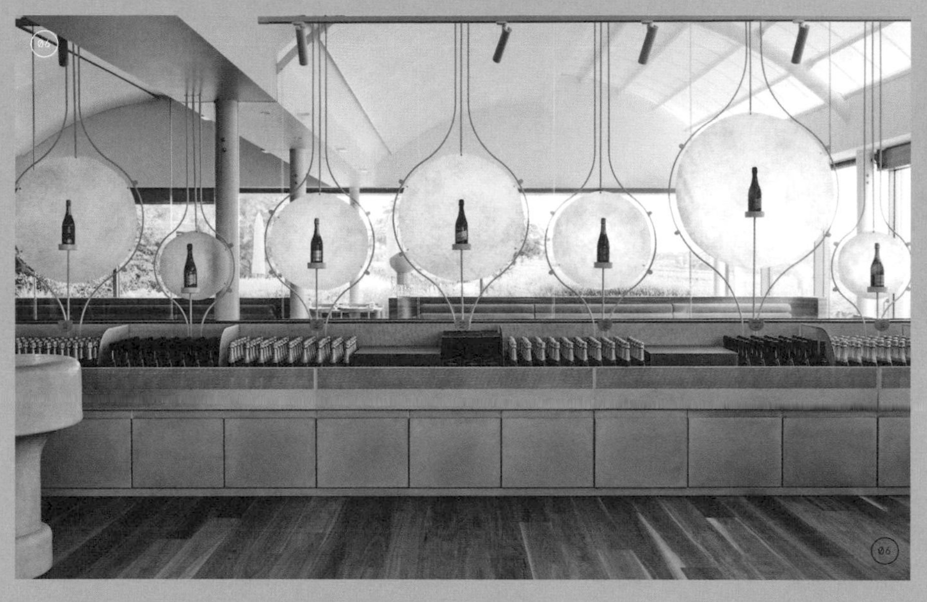

WHERE TO STAY

HEALESVILLE HOTEL

An iconic Healesville landmark, this restored 1910 hotel offers boutique rooms upstairs with crisp white linen, pressed-metal ceilings and spotless shared bathrooms plus chic apartments behind the hotel in Furmston House. Its renowned restaurant and bar is downstairs. *www.yarravalleyharvest.com.au; tel 03-5962 4002; 256 Maroondah Hwy, Healesville*

WHERE TO EAT

ELENORE'S RESTAURANT

Within the historic 1850s Yering chateau and winery is this contemporary fine dining restaurant with a reputation as one of the region's best. Featuring a chef who's worked at Michelin-star restaurants, here you can select multiple courses from its à la carte menu with items such as twice-cooked brisket with betel-leaf farci or smoked duck pie with crispy-skin salad. *chateauyering.com.au/dining/eleonores; tel 03-9237 3333; 42 Melba Hwy, Chateau Yering; 6pm–9pm daily*

ZONZO

This stylish Italian and traditional pizza restaurant at the Zonzo Estate Winery has superb views out over the valley. The thin-crust pizzas just fly off the table. They also offer tastings of their wines in their cellar door converted from old horse stables. *www.zonzo.com.au; tel 03-9730 2500; 957 Healesville-Yarra Glen Rd; noon–3pm Wed–Sun, 6pm–late Fri–Sun*

YARRA VALLEY DAIRY

Pay homage to the fromage at the Yarra Valley Dairy, the best place to buy cheese in the area. Hard or soft, most cheeses are made on-site. An eating area behind the counter is where you can enjoy a platter of cheeses, crackers and olives. *www.yvd.com.au; tel 03-9739 0023; McMeikan's Rd, Yering; 10.30am–5pm daily*

WHAT TO DO

Get up close to more than 200 species of Australian creatures, including Tasmanian devils, koalas and sleepy wombats at the Healesville Sanctuary. *www.zoo.org.au/healesville*

Lift off at sunrise for flight over the vineyards followed by breakfast at Yering Station. *www.gowildballooning.com.au*

CELEBRATIONS

YARRA VALLEY WINE AND FOOD FESTIVAL

The annual Yarra Valley Wine and Food Festival (Apr) is hosted by Rochford and features food, wine, ciders and local produce.

01

Courtesy of Soumah / Jessica Roberts

[Victoria]

YARRA VALLEY 2

Melbourne presents a pretty solid case for being crowned Australia's food and wine capital and the Yarra Valley's smaller wineries dazzle as jewels in that crown.

Many good things came out of the 1960s. One of the best was the idea by such pioneers as Guill de Pury of Yeringberg winery to plant vines in the Yarra Valley again. Grapes had been planted around the gentle slopes of the Yarra Ranges since the first settlers arrived in the 1830s but winemaking had petered out until Guill's group of hobbyist winemakers picked up the reins again. Starting with just two hectares at Yeringberg, Guill now farms more than 20 hectares. That expansion has been mirrored across the valley, with about 100 wineries and more than 50 cellar doors, large and small, now sprinkled around the country towns of Yarra Glen and Healesville.

Described by wine writer and resident James Halliday as 'a place of extreme beauty', the Yarra Valley is just an hour from Melbourne. But the large numbers of visitors from the big city – especially at weekends – seem to be effortlessly absorbed into this Arcadian retreat. There are more than enough wineries and beauty spots to find some space of your own. The Yarra river, marked by a line of River Red gum trees, runs straight through the middle of the valley, north of the Maroondah Highway. On a hot day the temptation to find a shady swimming spot and chill a bottle of Chardonnay in the river is irresistible.

With all the daytrippers, the valley can sustain a stellar supporting cast of swanky restaurants (often in the wineries), foodie shops, such as the Yarra Valley Dairy and numerous delicatessens in Healesville, plus boutique B&Bs. This makes the Yarra Valley Victoria's leading wine-touring destination, and perhaps Australia's. But remember that you're more likely to meet actual winemakers like Guill de Pury at the smaller cellar doors which are the focus of this trail – and that's the joy of wine touring.

GET THERE
The closest airport is Melbourne's, about an hour away by car.

01 YERINGBERG

It was the gold diggers who first followed the Yarra Track up to Victoria's goldfields in the 1850s, because the Yarra River couldn't be crossed in flood. The track became a road, and as people settled in the valley, vines started to flower and the first wine boom swept the Yarra in the 1880s.

The second wave of pioneers, among them Guill de Pury, arrived in the 1960s. His Yeringberg winery stands on the site of an original 150-year-old vineyard and many of its features date from that era. Another connection with the past is Yeringberg's Marsanne Roussane white wine, which uses the grape varieties originally planted in the Yarra and just happens to age beautifully.
www.yeringberg.com; tel 03-9739 0240; 810 Maroondah Hwy, Coldstream; visits by appt

02 MADDENS RISE

This is the antithesis of the large-scale, tour-group cellar door. There's no grand architecture, chef-hatted restaurant, art gallery or manicured sculpture gardens. But there is great wine, plenty of attention to detail and a passionate team who are keen to share it with you.

You'll be welcomed as soon as you step out of the car. The cellar door looks like a shed – a fancy shed, and it suits the philosophy of the winery beautifully. It was built to showcase the view over their 'front block' and retains a cosy, farmhouse vibe.

They have 17 varieties spread across 60 acres with plenty of northern Italian varieties. It's a minimal-intervention approach which applies biodynamic principles to let the purity of the fruit shine. The Nebbiolo is worth tasting, and if you're looking for a bottle to throw in the boot as a souvenir, the Arcobaleno (Italian for rainbow) is an interesting blend of Vermentino, Arneis, Garganega, Fiano and Chenin Blanc. Oh, and the 'Pink Fizz' (sparkling Chardonnay and Shiraz blend) will become your new festive sparkling staple – it pairs beautifully with christmas cake, and breakfast.
www.maddensrise.com; Cnr

From top left: courtesy of Soumah / Jessica Roberts; Payten & Jones / Phoebe Powell; Soumah / Jessica Roberts

01 Soumah of Yarra Valley

02 Soumah's HQ

03 The team at Payten & Jones

04 Italian-style servings at Soumah

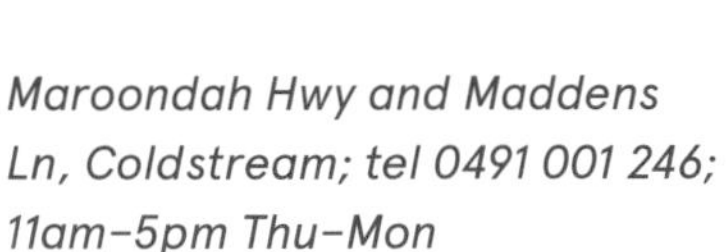

Maroondah Hwy and Maddens Ln, Coldstream; tel 0491 001 246; 11am–5pm Thu–Mon

03 SQUITCHY LANE

Tucked away at the top of the gravel driveway off Medhurst Road is Squitchy Lane. It's the passion project of former two-time premiership Captain and Rhodes Scholar, Mike Fitzpatrick, who met his wife in Squitchy Lane, Oxford, when he was studying there in the '70s. Cute name, great story and the wines are awesome.

With only a small cellar door – a converted tractor shed – the tasting experience is rather low-key, but there's a wonderful view of the vineyard from the deck. Of course the staples of Shiraz, Cabernet Sauvignon, Pinot and Chardonnay are on offer, but Squitchy Lane are keen to work outside the box and also produce an excellent Fumé Blanc and a spicy Cabernet Franc.

www.squitchylane.com.au; tel 03-5964 9114; 9 Medhurst Rd, Gruyere; 11am–5pm Sat–Sun or by appt

04 PIMPERNEL

Pimpernel began as a passion project for cardiologist Mark Horrigan but, as is often the case, the hobby took serious hold. Hard to resist when you have some of the region's great Pinot Noir being made by winemaker Damian Archibald, who knows his stuff having worked under the tutelage of Dr Bailey Carrodus of Yarra Yering.

Mark was obsessed by the vineyards of DRC (Domaine de la Romanée-Conti in Burgundy) and on a visit there with his mum, she leapt the fence and borrowed a few rocks from the vineyard. He bought them back to Australia to be tested and identified that the specific composition of these rocks was similar to those excavated at the nearby Lilydale quarry. He set aside a half acre of the Pinot block, dug two metres down then deposited 250 tonnes of the limestone. Pinot vines were then close planted – et voilà! DRC meets the Yarra Valley. A little extravagant, maybe, but the results are extraordinary and can be tasted in the Pinot Noir Three wine.

Pimpernel make five different

05 Cooling off at Payten & Jones

06 The Yarra River flows through Warburton

Pinots from the single vineyard, each varying in style. The vineyard is dry-grown and the winemaking style is French-inspired, resulting in complex and savoury wines. The cellar door is a small room with a barrel spittoon centre stage and a couch for when you need to take a moment to let the magnificence of Yarra Pinot sink in.
pimpernelvineyards.com.au; 6 Hill Rd, Coldstream; tel 0408 134 662; 11am–5pm Fri–Sun

05 SOUMAH OF YARRA VALLEY

It's a lovely approach to Soumah as you drive along narrow, undulating, winding back roads lined with vineyards. Owner and CEO Brett Butcher is obsessed with Italian wines and Soumah is his homage – pretty handy having a site similar in climate and soil composition to the revered vineyards of northern Italy.

Of course, Nebbiolo was always on the cards and the first vintage in 2015 receiving critical acclaim. The decision was then made to graft over the Sauvignon Blanc vines to Nebbiolo so we can expect more of this variety from Soumah in due course.

There are a couple of options for tasting – at the bar in the tasting room, or you can pay for the deluxe experience which features the premium range of wines, including a Savarro and a Brachetto, an ancient Italian variety dating back to Roman times, which is only planted in a few vineyards in Australia. The Italian theme continues with the food – think shared plates, pizzas and long tables laden with delicious salumi and antipasti.
soumah.com.au; 18 Hexham Rd, Gruyere; tel 03-5962 4716; 10am–5pm Mon–Fri, 10am–6pm Sat–Sun

06 PAYTEN & JONES

Payten & Jones is good mates Behn Payten and Troy Jones. Ben is the winemaker and his dad Peter is the viticulturist who sources the region's finest fruit. Family is a theme that runs through the entire experience here, with Behn's wife Emmanuelle running the cellar door.

It's a relatively new spot, opening in 2017 and located in the heart of Healesville. Payten & Jones have been making wines since 2007 but have broadened their reach with this engaging urban cellar door. Emmanuelle is an excellent host, taking time to pour wines in pairs to allow comparison – they produce 10 different varieties under three labels. Time is spent explaining the labels too, which feature artists and their stories, adding further layers of interest to these already fascinating wines.

Theirs is a minimal intervention approach to winemaking and it's a philosophy that invites you in, encouraging you to get involved, to share with friends, to eat and drink. When Behn talked about making a Sangiovese, Peter asked, 'why, and how will it sell?' Behn's response was, 'If we can't sell it at least we'll have 10 years of drinking with family and friends!'
www.paytenandjoneswine.com.au; 3 Lilydale Rd, Healesville; tel 0418 596 627; 10.30am–5.30pm Sun, Mon, Thu, 10.30am–7pm Fri–Sat

ESSENTIAL INFORMATION

WHERE TO STAY

If the creaky floorboards and antique plumbing at the Healesville Hotel (www.healesvillehotel.com.au) aren't your thing, opt for one of the many cottages, farmstays and B&Bs in the region for a tranquil escape.

WHERE TO EAT

HEALESVILLE HARVEST CAFE

Next to the Healesville Hotel, the Harvest is perfect for fresh coffee, snacks and light meals made with local produce. Head next door to its Kitchen & Butcher to pick up gourmet picnic goodies and hampers. *www.yarravalleyharvest.com.au; tel 03-5962 4002; 256 Maroondah Hwy, Healesville; 8am–4pm daily*

EZARD @ LEVANTINE HILL

This restaurant by acclaimed chef Teage Ezard is a collaboration with the Levantine Hill winery. Within its striking contemporary cellar door overlooking the vineyards, it has barrel-inspired booth seating to perch on during a long lunch of creative cuisine from a degustation menu designed specifically to match the wines. *www.levantinehill.com.au; tel 03-5962 1333; 882 Maroondah Hwy, Coldstream; 11am–5pm Mon & Wed–Fri, 10am–10pm Sat, 10am–5pm Sun*

WHAT TO DO

FOUR PILLARS GIN DISTILLERY

Directly opposite the Payten & Jones Cellar door, this is one of Victoria's best-run microdistillers. It's a class operator that specialises in inventive gins that you can watch being made while sampling the goods. Grab a paddle to taste their range, including an Australian gin, Spiced Negroni, Rare Dry and Navy Strength (58.8%). Staff are enthusiastic, friendly and knowledgeable. *www.fourpillarsgin.com.au; tel 03-5962 2791; 2a Lilydale Rd, Healesville; 10.30am–5.30pm Sun–Thu, to 9.30pm Fri–Sat*

WARBURTON

The town of Warburton is a short drive away, with Seville Estate a worthwhile stop en route. In Warburton, drive past outdoor artist Boinga Bob's house and if he's home you may get to chat to one of the region's most interesting characters.

CELEBRATIONS

SHEDFEST

On the second weekend of October each year, the smaller wineries along the Warburton Hwy open their doors for ShedFest. It's an opportunity to meet the winemakers, try wines you'd otherwise miss, and enjoy great food and some live music. *www.yarravalleysmallerwineries.com.au*

01

Courtesy of Forest Hill Wines

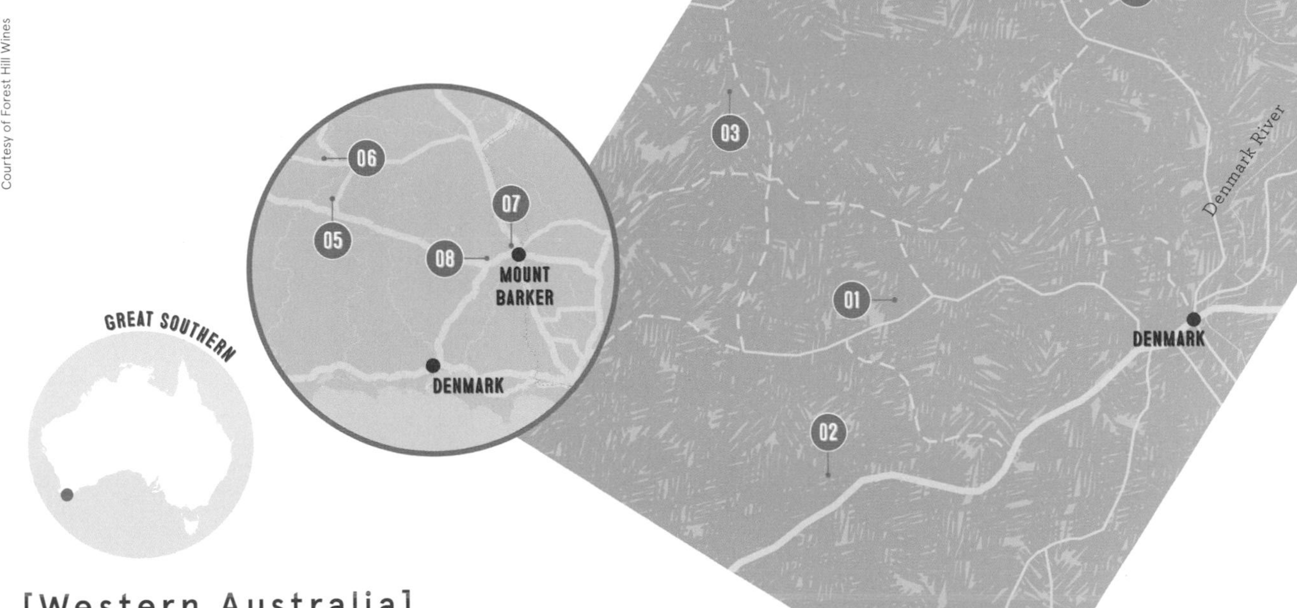

[Western Australia]

GREAT SOUTHERN

Explore coast and country in this epic region and be rewarded with white-sand beaches and brisk bush walks, as well as zesty Rieslings and spicy Shiraz.

Great in name and nature, this is the largest wine region in mainland Australia, encompassing wild coastline, rolling hills, open grazing land, eucalypt forests and granite outcrops. The western extremity is marked by coastal country town Denmark, the east, Porongurup, with its dramatic National Park. The first vineyard was planted in 1965 and Riesling is now, as it was then, the star variety, with Shiraz its red playmate. The Great Southern is also one of the most remote wine regions in the world: Perth to Albany is about five hours by car or a little over one hour's flight time.

Five sub-regions make up the Great Southern: Frankland River, Mount Barker and Albany, in addition to Porongurup and Denmark. With its high altitude, inland position, continental climate, cool air and granite soils, Porongurup produces some of the finest Riesling and spiciest Shiraz but is just beyond the limits of this trail. Mount Barker and Frankland River are warmer and make richer, fuller but no less charming Rieslings. There are also impressive Cabernet and other Bordeaux red varieties to seek out, and Denmark is well-regarded for Chardonnay while Albany has yielded some surprising Pinot Noirs.

Many vineyards are small and family-owned, often springing out of large grazing stations – you'll spot many a sheep between vineyards (if not between the vines). There are 70 producers in the area, but only about 15 wineries. Some of the state's bigger players, notably Houghton and Howard Park, truck some Great Southern grapes up to the Swan Valley or Margaret River for winemaking. Remote as it is, the region doesn't attract as many visitors as the Swan Valley or Margaret River, so you'll often have a relaxed reception at the cellar doors, several of which can be found in the towns of Denmark, Albany and Mount Barker.

GET THERE
Perth to Albany is about five hours by car or a little over one hour's flight time.

Courtesy of Castelli Estate; Forest Hill Wines

01 CASTELLI ESTATE

This relatively new winery, opened in 2007, is perched in a beautiful location on the slopes of Mt Shadforth, outside Denmark. The adjoining bistro serves wines chosen from Castelli's five-tiered offering, for which winemaker Mike Garland selects grapes from across the Great Southern as well as Pemberton and Geographe regions, for small batch processing back at Castelli's state-of-the art winery.

Look out for the 2016 Castelli Riesling, an outstanding example with a fragrant aroma of fresh herbs and lemon citrus, and a crisp, dry, lively palate – a wine that manages to perform a delicate and intense double act.

www.castelliestate.com.au; tel 08-9848 3174; 380 Mount Shadforth Rd, Denmark; 11am–3pm daily

02 FOREST HILL WINES

The Forest Hill vineyard was the first to be planted in the Great Southern, in 1965, at Mount Barker. The grapes for all the Estate and Single Block wines come from that substantial 65-hectare vineyard. To taste the end product, though, you need to head to the cellar door and winery at Denmark – the vineyard's current owners, the Lyons, opted to set up shop nearer town.

The old vines rely entirely on natural rainfall – eschewing irrigation is only possible because of the warm, dry summers and chilly, wet winters, combined with well-drained soil on a clay base. Wines created from these original plantings include the Block 1 Riesling, a drop of terrific fruit intensity and precision, while the Block 8 Chardonnay has impressively pungent lemon/citrus aromas.

www.foresthillwines.com.au; tel 08-9848 2399; 1564 South Coast Hwy; 10.30am–5pm Thurs–Sun

03 SINGLEFILE WINES

A background in geology certainly comes in handy when you're setting up a vineyard. Phil and Viv Snowden, both retired geologists, tapped into their experience when researching Australia's wine regions. They settled on this southwestern pocket in the Scotsdale Valley, buying an established vineyard 7km outside Denmark and enlisting the help of a

01 Forest Hill vineyard

02 Fun and games in the Castelli grounds

03 Serene scenes at Forest Hill

team of top consultant winemakers. Dedicated to producing wines that express the characteristics of such a carefully considered terroir – such as The Vivienne, a powerful but low-alcohol Chardonnay – their award winning cellar door has twice been named the Great Southern's best.

Have a wander through the grounds and you might just come across the resident flock of graylag geese, whose customary single file parade gives the estate its name.
www.singlefilewines.com; tel 1300 885 807; 90 Walter Rd, Denmark; 11am–5pm daily

04 ROCKCLIFFE

Close enough to the coast to benefit from sea breezes all summer long, Rockcliffe's name reflects its debt to the coastline in producing its superb cool-climate wines. The surf theme extends to the ranges Third Reef and Quarram Rocks and the port muscat, Forty Foot Drop.

The Scotsdale valley is a former fruit-growing area with fertile soils and tall karri forests. In fact, the site of this vineyard used to be given over to apple orchards. Nowadays, the harvest consists of Chardonnay, Riesling and some of the Great Southern's most serious, strongly structured Pinot Noir, among others.

First aid is at the ready if you've come on a scorching day – the Gelateria cafe scoops up artisan ices, including some made with the house wines. Rockcliffe is also active in entertainment, organising regular live music (the Summer Sunday Sessions), markets and film screenings.
www.rockcliffe.com.au; tel 08-9848 1951; 18 Hamilton Rd, Scotsdale; 11am–5pm daily

05 FRANKLAND ESTATE

The Frankland River sub-region comprises the most far-flung reaches of this wild part of Western Australia, but a trip to Frankland Estate is worth the effort – there's a grand emptiness to the landscape here, and the Smith family happen to make pretty outstanding wines, too.

The Smiths carved out a vineyard from their sheep and wheat farm in the 1980s and their son Hunter and daughter Elizabeth are now involved, operating the cellar door from a classic Aussie galvanised iron shed. The Isolation Ridge vineyard is certified organic, and Riesling is the speciality, with three single-vineyard Rieslings which aim to define separate terroirs. The flagship red is Olmo's Reward, a blend of Bordeaux varieties, unusual as Cabernet Franc is the lead grape.
www.franklandestate.com.au; tel 08-9855 1544; Frankland Rd, Frankland River; 10am–4pm Mon–Fri & weekends by appt

04 Welcome to Singlefile Wines

05 Work in progress at West Cape Howe

Plantagenet houses its welcoming cellar door and cafe in a building constructed from handmade mud-bricks in Mount Barker's main street. Tuck into a light lunch made from locally sourced ingredients, and paired with Plantagenet wines, al fresco in summer or by the open fire in winter.
www.plantagenetwines.com; tel 08-9851 3111; 45 Albany Hwy, Mount Barker; 10am–4.30pm daily

06 ALKOOMI

Like Frankland Estate, Alkoomi's vineyard was created as an extension of a sheep and wheat farm, and has now shifted on to the second generation, with the founders' daughter and son-in-law, Sandy and Rod Hallett, taking the reins. In the process, it's grown from a single hectare to over 100, becoming one of the largest family-run concerns in the state. All the more impressive, then, that Alkoomi is making strides to reduce its environmental impact, with the installation of solar panels, 'wall-to-wall grass' acting as weed-inhibitor and improving water retention, and sheep in charge of weed control in the colder months.

Alkoomi wines exemplify grape variety and region and have always delivered excellent value for money. The aromatic white wines, led by Riesling, are particularly stylish. The winery cellar door is located in an atmospheric stone building, and there's a second venue on the coast, at Albany.
www.alkoomiwines.com.au; tel 08-9855 2229; 1141 Wingebellup Rd, Frankland River; 10am–5pm daily. Also at 225 Stirling Terrace, Albany; 11am–5pm Mon–Sat

07 PLANTAGENET

Established by Tony Smith in 1974, Plantagenet is one of the earliest wine producers in the Great Southern. The wines are still sourced largely from the five vineyards Smith planted, all in the Mount Barker area. Shiraz and Cabernet Sauvignon were the initial grapes to be grown – the resulting Shiraz was one of the first in Australia to demonstrate how spicy this varietal could be when the grapes are grown in a cool climate. The fragrant Riesling, rich Chardonnay and elegant Cabernet Sauvignon are also recommended.

08 WEST CAPE HOWE

This is the region's leading winery, with a capacious cellar door showcasing its astonishingly good-value wines, as well as views of the Langton vineyard and glorious gardens. Every wine West Cape Howe produces punches well above its weight, but the Book Ends Cabernet Sauvignon and Two Steps Shiraz are the stand-outs.

Gavin Berry is the key figure behind the business, and a small upmarket range of wines which he makes with Margaret River winemaker Mike Kerrigan under the Kerrigan + Berry label is also available at the cellar door.

Along with the wines there's a gallery exhibiting work by local artists and a children's play area, and the knowledgeable staff also serve an excellent cup of coffee.
www.westcapehowewines.com.au; tel 08-9892 1444; 14923 Muir Hwy, Mount Barker; 10am–5pm daily

ESSENTIAL INFORMATION

WHERE TO STAY

CAPE HOWE COTTAGES

For a remote getaway, these five cottages in bushland southeast of Denmark really make the grade. They're all different, but the best is only 1.5km from dolphin-favoured Lowlands Beach and is properly plush – with a BBQ on the deck, a dishwasher and laundry facilities.
www.capehowe.com.au; tel 08-9845 1295; 322 Tennessee Rd S, Lowlands

31 ON THE TERRACE

Good-value, stylish en-suite rooms – some with balconies – fill this renovated corner pub in the centre of town. Compact apartments sleep up to five people.
www.denmarkaccommodation.com.au tel 08-9848 1700; 31 Strickland St, Denmark

WHERE TO EAT

PEPPER & SALT

With his Fijian-Indian heritage, chef Silas Masih's knowledge of spices and herbs is wonderfully showcased in his fresh and vibrant food. Highlights include king prawns with chilli popcorn and lime mayonnaise, or the excellent tapas platter, which effortlessly detours from Asia to the Middle East. Bookings essential.
www.pepperandsalt.com.au; tel 08-9848 3053; 1564 South Coast Hwy, Forest Hill Vineyard; noon–3pm Thu–Sun, from 6pm Fri

MRS JONES

Denmark's best coffee is at this spacious spot with high ceilings and exposed beams. Settle in with locals and tourists for interesting cafe fare, often with an Asian or Mediterranean spin. Try the hearty shakshuka baked eggs for breakfast or the robust harissa-spiced lamb burger for lunch. There's a good selection of vegan and gluten-free options too.
www.mrsjonescafe.com; tel 0467 481 878; 12 Mt Shadforth Rd; 7am–4pm daily

WHAT TO DO

WALKING AND SWIMMING

There are myriad options for stretching your legs, from some excellent bush walks in Porongurup National Park to the Wilson Inlet Heritage Trail (12km return, starting at the mouth of the Denmark River) which forms part of the longer Nornalup trail. William Bay National Park, about 20km west of Denmark, offers sheltered swimming in gorgeous Greens Pool and Elephant Rocks, and also has good walking tracks.

MARKET DAYS

Four times a year (mid-December, early and late January and Easter) Denmark hosts riverside markets days with craft stalls, music and food.
www.denmarkarts.com.au

05

ENTON BRAE
MARGARET RIVER
LLON SAUVIGNON BLANC
2017
LENTON BRAE
MARGARET RIVER
SOUTHSIDE CHARDONNAY
2015
01

Courtesy of Lenton Brae / David Dare Parker

[Western Australia]

MARGARET RIVER NORTH

Margaret River is an oasis of amazing food and wine in vast Western Australia. A weekend here combines wine with Indian Ocean beaches and magical landscapes.

Few wine regions anywhere in the world have rocketed to fame as quickly as Margaret River – 50th anniversary celebrations were in full swing in 2017 and into 2018. It's never been a secret to Australians that much of the country's finest wine is made here, and with vast surf beaches, deep forests of tall karri and robust jarrah trees, networks of limestone caves, and pristine air refreshed by its journey across the Indian Ocean from Africa, there's plenty beside the bottle to waylay visitors.

Extending about 90km north and south between Cape Naturaliste and Cape Leeuwin, Margaret River is the most geographically isolated wine region in the world. Its rich gravelly loams cultivate exceptionally high-quality fruit – 3% of Australia's wine, but 20% of its premium wine, is produced here. Wine critic Jancis Robinson has said: 'Margaret River is the closest thing to paradise of any wine region I have visited in my extensive search for knowledge.'

The area's lifeline is Caves Road, which runs parallel to the coastline, linking up the array of superbly appointed wineries, many with great restaurants, plus flourishing artisan food and craft beer scenes. In recent years, Margaret River has stolen the mantle of Australia's leading Cabernet region from Coonawarra, and added great Chardonnay to the menu. Its Semillon Sauvignon Blanc blends are affordable, everyday dry white wines and lately Shiraz has also been hitting the heights. The received wisdom designates the north as best for Cabernet Sauvignon, and the south for whites, particularly Chardonnay, but exceptions can always be found. We have divided Margaret River into two wine trails: approximately north and south. This northern section begins in Yallingup and Dunsborough and descends south to the halfway mark of Wilyabrup and Cowaramup.

GET THERE

The Western Australia capital of Perth has the closest airport. Margaret River is about 3hrs to the south by car.

01 FLAMETREE

Little more than a decade old, Flametree had a charmed beginning, winning the coveted Jimmy Watson Trophy with a 2007 Cabernet Merlot from its very first vintage. Soon afterwards, the owners, the Towner family, lured winemaker Cliff Royle away from Voyager Estate where he had made his name with ultra-refined Chardonnays that sat somewhat outside the Margaret River mainstream.

Rather than grow their own, Flametree select the best grapes from the region to craft in their state-of-the-art winery near Dunsborough, on the edge of Geographe Bay. Their top wines are labelled SRS, standing for sub-regional series. The SRS Chardonnay is from Wallcliffe in the cooler south and the SRS Cabernet from Wilyabrup, further north where the gravel soil and warmer climate especially suit this grape. The cellar door – all glossy wood and bright white walls – offers up make-your-own platters to accompany its wines, and a sun-trap lawn on which to enjoy them.

www.flametreewines.com; tel 08-9756 8577; 7 Chain Ave, cnr Caves Rd, Dunsborough; 10am–5pm daily

02 DEEP WOODS ESTATE

Up in the Yallingup Hills, with views extending across forests of jarrah and marri trees, Deep Woods occupies a prime position in Margaret River, and in the disparate wine empire of Perth businessman, Peter Fogarty. Admittedly, he'd strain to see the other vineyards in his portfolio, Lakes Folly in the Hunter Valley and Millbrook in the Perth Hills, from Deep Woods' lofty perch.

Grapes are sourced from far and wide with most ranges produced in small batches by talented winemaker Julian Langworthy. The Reserve Cabernet Sauvignon, in particular, is a tour de force. Stock up on the good-value, inexpensive red, white and award-winning rosé – Ebony, Ivory and Harmony – in the Margaret River range.

www.deepwoods.wine; tel 08-9756 6066; 889 Commonage Rd, Yallingup; 11am–5pm Wed–Sun, daily during hols

03 LENTON BRAE

Get a bird's eye view of the work behind each bottle at Lenton Brae from the viewing platform, a masterstroke of founder, town planner and architect Bruce

Courtesy of Woodlands / Jaden McLean; Flametree

01 Sampling the wines of Lenton Brae

02 The Margaret River coastline

03 Flametree's cellar door

Tomlinson. You can also admire sweeping views of Wilyabrup valley and listen out for the chiming of the two towers' brass bells.

Bruce's son, Ed Tomlinson, is the winemaker here. He crafts a fine selection of wines including one of the region's longest-running Semillon Sauvignon Blancs, with 32 consecutive releases and counting. A speciality is the region's first and only Pinot Blanc, a light-bodied, early-drinking fresh dry white that most Australian winemakers have inexplicably overlooked.
www.lentonbrae.com; tel 08-9755 6255; 3887 Caves Rd, Wilyabrup; 10am–6pm daily

04 WOODLANDS

Established in 1973, Woodlands is one of the region's earliest vineyards but flies somewhat under the radar. A hiatus in wine-producing meant it missed out on some early profile-building but when the sons of founders David and Heather Watson, Stuart and Andrew, completed their education and took over the business (Stuart as winemaker), Woodlands rapidly made up for lost ground.

Andrew swears by fermenting with naturally occurring yeasts and sorting the grapes on an expensive French sorting table to raise their wine quality. The Cabernet-based reds, of which there are several, are among the most elegant in the region. Taken from the oldest vines, dry-grown and producing low yields of concentrated grapes, the flagship is simply titled Woodlands Cabernet Sauvignon and bears the name of a different family member each year. The 2014 Matthew is a cracker.
www.woodlandswines.com.au; tel 08-9755 6226; 3948 Caves Rd, Margaret River; 10am–5pm daily

05 PIERRO

Peterkin, doctor turned winery owner, regards the Margaret River region as a 'viticultural paradise'. His vineyard is on a prime spot on Caves Road, Wilyabrup terroir, which yields one of the most complex and consistently brilliant Chardonnays in the region. The Reserve Cabernet Merlot, by contrast, is one of the finer-boned examples of these varieties, and is all about refinement, poise and subtle complexities rather than power or body. Fire Gully is Peterkin's second brand: these less expensive wines are lighter and more approachable younger. They are sourced from a separate vineyard on different soils, although the wines can be tasted and purchased at Pierro.
www.pierro.com.au; tel 08-9755 6220; 4051 Caves Rd, Wilyabrup; 10am–5pm daily

06 BROOKLAND VALLEY

Not far from Pierro along Caves Road, overlooking Wilyabrup Brook, Brookland Valley was established in 1984 and was acquired by Hardys (now part of Accolade Wines)

04 Glass half full at Deep Woods Estate

05 Watch for whales at Flinders Bay, Augusta

between 1997 and 2004. The wines are made by Courtney Treacher, off-site, at Accolade's other WA wineries: Houghton in the Swan Valley and the Nannup winery near Pemberton.

The soils are sandier than elsewhere in the prized Wilyabrup sub-region, giving the wines a distinctive style; concentrated yet fine-boned and aromatic. Whites are especially good on these soils and Brookland Valley Chardonnays are among the region's best. Of the three main ranges, Reserve, Estate and Verse 1, the latter can be blended from anywhere in the region, whereas the Estate and Reserve wines are predominantly Wilyabrup and mainly estate-grown. There's pleasant browsing to be had in the on-site cafe and gallery of food and wine-related art and accessories.
www.brooklandvalley.com.au; tel 08-9755 6042; 6284 Caves Rd, Wilyabrup; 11am–5pm daily

07 FRASER GALLOP ESTATE

A relative newcomer, the vineyard planted in 1999, Fraser Gallop has quickly secured its place among the elite producers of the region. Appointing former Vasse Felix chief winemaker Clive Otto was a masterstroke by owner Nigel Gallop – Otto is a Cabernet specialist who has worked in top Bordeaux estates.

The vineyards are unirrigated, unusual in Margaret River, and all the fruit is hand-picked. The wines are exemplary and reasonably priced. The Parterre label denotes the top echelon – the Semillon Sauvignon Blanc is a serious, complex, ageworthy style reminiscent of a top Bordeaux blanc.

The Gallop residence is a grand Georgian mansion overlooking a lake and surrounded on three sides by vineyards. Quite the period drama backdrop, and the estate does in fact market itself as a wedding venue, but cellar door guests are also welcomed daily.
frasergallopestate.com.au; tel 08-9755 7553; 493 Metricup Rd, Wilyabrup; 11am–4pm daily

08 LARRY CHERUBINO WINES

Following a distinguished career at Hardys and Houghton, Larry Cherubino has poured his considerable energies into his own brands, of which there are several, and produced a bewildering cornucopia of wines. The Cherubino range is at the apex, with The Yard, Wallflower and Ad Hoc staggered below it. These are slick, polished wines of great style. Riesling is a speciality and a favourite of Larry's: he makes a number, covering several sub-regions, all superbly refined.

Larry is a busy man, overseeing Western Australian wines for eastern state wineries, most notably Robert Oatley Vineyards, for whom he is overall director of winemaking. He also has vineyards in Margaret River, Pemberton, Frankland River and Porongurup. The latest development is the opening of this spacious cellar door on Caves Road, Wilyabrup.
www.larrycherubino.com.au; tel 08-9382 2379; 3462 Caves Rd, Wilyabrup; 10am–6pm daily Dec–Jan, Easter & long w'ends; check website for other times

ESSENTIAL INFORMATION

WHERE TO STAY

WILDWOOD VALLEY COTTAGES

These luxury cottages are set across 120 acres; look out for grazing kangaroos as you meander up the unsealed road to reception. *www.wildwoodvalley.com.au; tel 08-9755 2120; 1481 Wildwood Rd, Yallingup*

INJIDUP SPA RETREAT

The region's most stylish accommodation perches atop an isolated cliff south of Yallingup. A striking facade fronts the car park, while inside there are heated polished-concrete floors, 'eco' fires and sea views. Each of the 10 suites has its own plunge pool. *www.injidupsparetreat.com.au; tel 08-9750 1300; 31 Cape Clairault Rd, off Wyadup Rd, Yallingup*

WHERE TO EAT

RUSTICO AT HAY SHED HILL

Vineyard views from Rustico's deck are the background for a Spanish-influenced menu using the best of southwest Australian produce. Albany rock oysters are paired with Margaret River Riesling, and paella is crammed with chicken from Mt Barker and local seafood. Consider a six-course degustation with wine matches. *www.rusticotapas.com.au; tel 08-9755 6455; 511 Harmans Mill Rd, Wilyabrup; 11am–5pm daily*

05

FISHBONE WINES

Fishbone brings something special to their cellar door game: a superb Japanese restaurant serving fresh seafood sushi and sashimi, and dishes such as Margaret River wagyu beef tataki from an authentic Japanese menu. Beer and sake is available, although a dry white wine will pair well with sushi. *www.fishbonewines.com.au; 422 Harmans Mill Rd, Wilyabrup; tel 08-9755 6726; lunch only*

WHAT TO DO

NGILGI CAVE

Between Dunsborough and Yallingup, this 500,000-year-old cave is associated in Wardandi spirituality with the victory of the good spirit Ngilgi over the evil spirit Wolgine. To the Wardandi people it became a kind of honeymoon location. A European man first stumbled upon it in 1899 while looking for his horse. Formations include the white Mother of Pearl Shawl and the equally beautiful Arab's Tent and Oriental Shawl. *www.margaretriver.com; tel 08-9755 2152; Yallingup Caves Rd; 9am–5pm*

From June to September, humpback and southern right whales make a pitstop in Flinders Bay, off Augusta, south of Margaret River. And from September to December, whales, including the rare blue whale, frequent Geographe Bay to the north; whale-watching cruises are available. *www.westernaustralia.com*

CELEBRATIONS

The annual Margaret River Gourmet Escape showcases the region's world-class food and wine over a weekend in November. It draws international guest chefs and has open-air events. *www.gourmetescape.com.au*

01

Courtesy of Vasse Felix / Michelle Troop

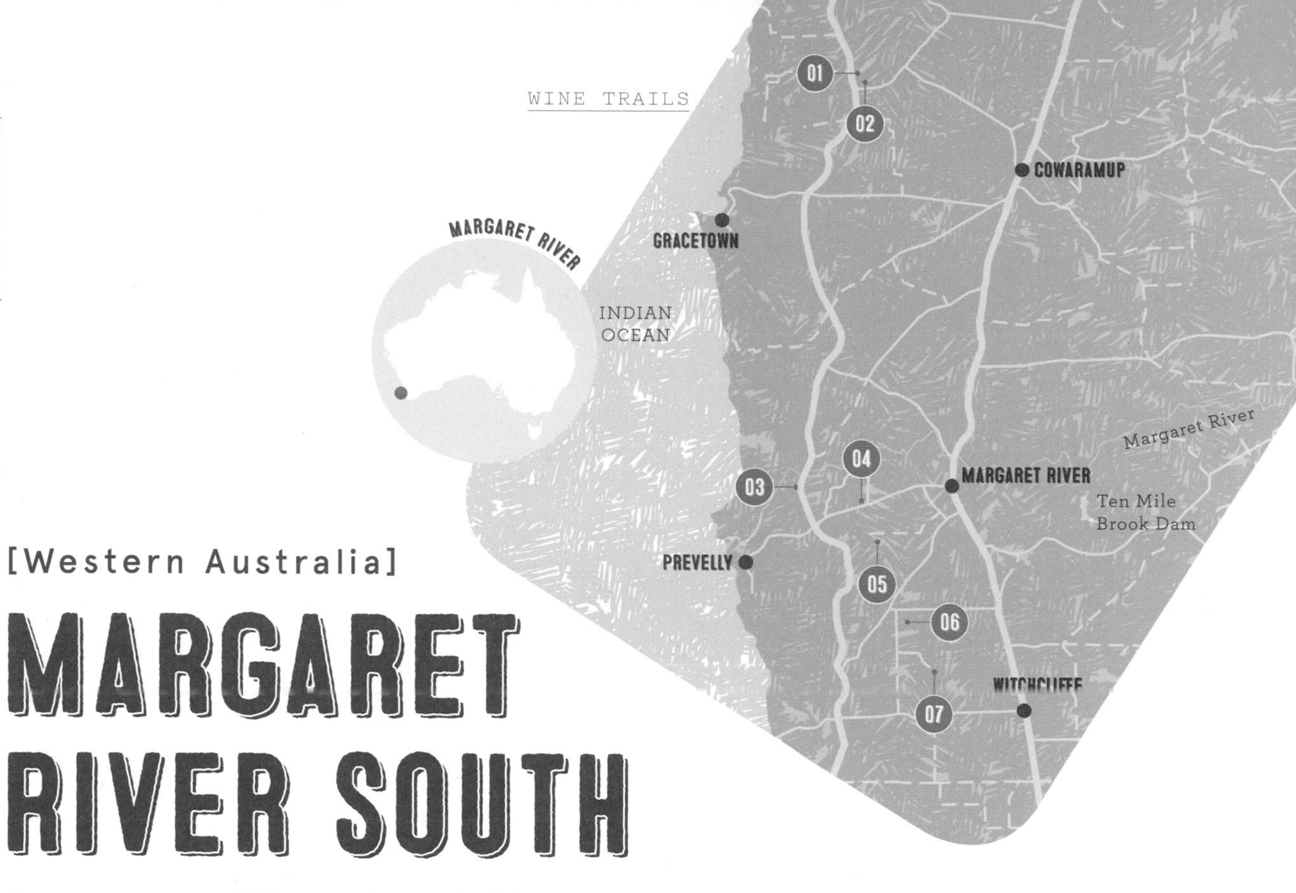

[Western Australia]

MARGARET RIVER SOUTH

Discover more of Margaret River's Edenic charms as you head south, towards the region's founding estate and beyond.

Our trail continues from just south of Wilyabrup down to the town of Margaret River itself. The dividing line could be said to be Wallcliffe Road, which connects Margaret River with the coast at the pretty beach village of Prevelly. The southern half of the region has a slightly cooler climate than the north, influenced by the colder currents of the Southern Ocean as well as the Indian Ocean. The vineyards start to thin out the further south you drive along Caves Road, but grapes are grown and fine wine made as far south as Hamelin Bay.

Dr Tom Cullity planted the region's first vines at Vasse Felix in 1967, on the basis of a report by viticultural research scientist Dr John Gladstones. Not the standard route for the inception of an Australian wine region, but even Gladstones couldn't have predicted how successful his 'baby' would prove to be.

Vasse Felix now includes four Margaret River vineyards and focuses its efforts on premium Cabernet Sauvignon and Chardonnay. The area to the southwest of Margaret River town is home to four of the region's other showpiece wineries: Leeuwin Estate, Cape Mentelle, Voyager Estate and Xanadu. Leeuwin is famous for its concerts and its Art Series Chardonnay, Voyager for its extraordinary Cape Dutch architecture, Mentelle for its statuesque Cabernets and Xanadu for exceptional success at wine shows in recent years.

With its stunning scenery and eye-opening clarity of light, Margaret River provides a feast for the eyes. Art lovers are particularly well catered for, with galleries at both Vasse Felix and Leeuwin Estate; the latter buys new paintings every year for each new vintage of its Art Series Cabernet, Chardonnay, Shiraz and Sauvignon Blanc. Vasse Felix is now owned by Paul Holmes à Court whose family have long held an outstanding collection of Australian art, including Aboriginal works.

GET THERE
The Western Australia capital of Perth has the closest airport. Margaret River is about 3hrs to the south by car.

01 CULLEN WINES

Cullen was founded in 1971, when Margaret River pioneers Kevin and Diana Cullen planted a plot of Cabernet Sauvignon and Riesling. The winery has a habit of being in the forefront of a movement: it was one of the earliest to become organic and it was the first vineyard in Australia to be carbon neutral.

Now led by daughter Vanya, who gained experience in Burgundy and California before becoming chief winemaker in 1989, Cullen Wines became a fully biodynamic winery in 2004. Biodynamic lore says that key processes such as planting and harvesting should be done in tandem with the cosmic rhythms of the planets; for example, planting should be done when the moon and Saturn are in opposition. There's much more to biodynamics than the moon's movement, such as cow horns filled with manure, but the core of the ethos is about working in harmony with nature so that chemicals are eschewed and nothing extra is added to the wines. A spiral garden has been planted at Cullen to explain biodynamics and it's a fascinating experience.

Vanya's wines are essentially natural wines, expressing the land on which they're grown, which is an old, granite and gravelly loam. Red or white, the results in the bottle are unerringly sublime wines that wow critics the world over.
www.cullenwines.com.au; tel 08-9755 5277; 4323 Caves Rd, Wilyabrup; 10am–4.30pm daily

02 VASSE FELIX

Luck is at the heart of Vasse Felix. The winery takes its name from French seaman, Thomas Vasse, who was swept overboard when his ship was surveying the Australian coast in 1801. Founder Dr Tom Cullity added Felix – lucky – to the lost sailor's name when he established Margaret River's first winery in 1967. But he didn't get any at the outset: the crop for the winery's first vintage in 1971 was mostly eaten by birds. A peregrine falcon was brought in to scare off the pests, but promptly disappeared into the distant trees; a falcon motif was added to the logo.

Things soon looked up, and under the present winemaker, Virginia Willcock, the wines, especially the Premier Chardonnay, have become

01 Alfresco servings at Vasse Felix

02 An outdoor concert at Leeuwin Estate

03 Crop thinning at Voyager Estate

04 Vasse Felix vineyards

classic examples of what Margaret River does best. To understand what that is, take the two-hour tutored tasting at the cellar door. The restaurant, reputed to be the best in the region, is open daily for lunch. *www.vassefelix.com.au; tel 08-9756 5000; cnr Tom Cullity Dr/ Caves Rd, Cowaramup; 10am-5pm daily, tutored tastings 10.30am Mon-Fri*

03 MCHENRY HOHNEN VINTNERS

When David Hohnen and his family company lost control of the winery they founded, Cape Mentelle, Hohnen launched a plan B with his brother-in-law Murray McHenry, a leading Perth wine retailer. Rather than re-invent the wheel and make the wines himself, Hohnen decided to delegate the winemaking to a talented employee, Julian Grounds. The grapes are sourced from several family-owned vineyards, including Calgardup Brook, Burnside, Hazel's and Rocky Road, all of which are biodynamically managed.

The cellar door shares premises with Hohnen's small butchery and smokehouse, The Farm House Margaret River. Or you can find the man himself selling his wares at the Saturday farmers market in town. *www.mchenryhohnen.com.au; tel 08-9757 9600; 5962 Caves Rd, Margaret River; 10.30am-4.30pm daily*

04 CAPE MENTELLE

One of Margaret River's original wineries, name after a nearby headland and first planted by the Hohnen family in 1970, Cape Mentelle is now owned by the French luxury goods giant Louis Vuitton Moët Hennessy. The place isn't all front row hauteur though – both the winery and outbuildings are constructed from stabilised rammed earth, a method pioneered by a member of the Hohnen family, and you can follow your visit to the cellar door with a relaxed a game of pétanque.

Cape Mentelle achieved significant early fame by winning the Melbourne Wine Show's famed Jimmy Watson Trophy twice in succession. The winning wine was its Cabernet Sauvignon, which has been the winery standard-bearer ever since.

05 Wining and dining at Vasse Felix

06 Bootleg Brewery

Reinforcing this, the winery has staged a biennial International Cabernet Tasting since 1982, most recently held as part of the Margaret River Gourmet Escape. *www.capementelle.com.au; tel 08-9757 0888; 331 Wallcliffe Rd, Margaret River; 10am–5pm daily*

05 XANADU WINES

What does the legend of Kubla Khan have to do with wine? Thankfully you don't have to be a Coleridge expert to appreciate the wonderful job Victoria's Rathbone family (owners of Yering Station in the Yarra Valley and Bayindeen's Mount Langi Ghiran) have done with this showpiece property. From its long, winding, tree-lined drive to its lawns and spacious buildings, which include a superb restaurant, it's a beautiful and visitor-friendly place. The wines, crafted by Glenn Goodall, are loaded with awards and outstanding across the board. Chardonnay and Cabernet Sauvignon are the specialities: don't miss comparing and contrasting the Reserve and single-vineyard Stevens Road bottlings of both. *www.xanaduwines.com; tel 08-9757 3389; Boodjidup Rd, Margaret River; 10am–5pm daily*

06 VOYAGER ESTATE

Continuing south, homing in on the town of Margaret River, you can choose between Voyager or Leeuwin, both among Margaret's grandest estates. If you want to check out elegantly understated Cape Dutch architecture, manicured gardens and Australia's second largest flagpole, Voyager's the one. The walled gardens, designed by South African landscape designer Deon Bronkhorst, are a beautiful place to wander when the rose bushes are flowering.

Voyager was established in 1978, but under winemaker Steve James it retains a spirit of adventure, using wild yeasts for the white wines, and experimenting with its project wines. There'll always be something interesting to sip. *www.voyagerestate.com.au; tel 08-9757 6354; 1 Stevens Rd, Margaret River; 10am–5pm daily*

07 LEEUWIN ESTATE

Superlative wines await at this family-owned winery, another of the estates in Margaret River dating from the 1970s. The Art Series Chardonnay is regarded as one of Australia's finest, alongside the Cabernet Sauvignon and Shiraz. The ethos at Leeuwin is to always reflect the land and the weather in the wine, as winemaker Tim Lovett says: 'Every vintage is different. It's about showcasing a sense of place.' All Margaret River's finest ingredients – the maritime climate, the ancient Australian soils, the skilled and thoughtful winemakers, such as Paul Atwood and Tim Lovett – come together at Leeuwin.

Add to that winning formula the annual outdoor concerts, which have attracted thousands since 1985 – the performers have ranged from the London Philharmonic Orchestra to Ray Charles, Tom Jones and Diana Ross. *www.leeuwinestate.com.au; tel 08-9759 0000; Stevens Rd, Margaret River; 10am–5pm daily*

ESSENTIAL INFORMATION

WHERE TO STAY

BURNSIDE ORGANIC FARM
These rammed-earth and limestone bungalows have spacious decks and designer kitchens, and the surrounding farm hosts a menagerie of animals and organic avocado and macadamia orchards. *www.burnside-organicfarm.com.au; tel 08-9757 2139; 287 Burnside Rd, Margaret River*

EDGE OF THE FOREST
Prepare to update your expectations of what a motel should be. This delightful spot is set in bird-filled gardens next to a State Forest, with walking trails from the front door. *www.edgeoftheforest.com.au; tel 08-9757 2351; 25 Bussell Hwy, Margaret River*

WHERE TO EAT

PROVIDORE
Voted one of Australia's Top 100 Gourmet Experiences by *Australian Traveller* magazine – given its amazing range of artisan produce, including organic olive oil, tapenades and preserved fruits, we can only agree. Look forward to loads of free samples and stock up your picnic basket. *www.providore.com.au; tel 08-9755 6355; 448 Tom Cullity Dr, Wilyabrup; 9am–5pm daily*

MIKI'S OPEN KITCHEN
Secure a spot around the open kitchen and enjoy the irresistible theatre of the Miki's team creating innovative Japanese spins on the best of WA seafood and produce. Combine a Margaret River wine with the $60 multi-course tasting menu for the most diverse experience, and settle in to watch the laidback Zen chefs work their tempura magic. Bookings recommended. *www.facebook.com/mikisopenkitchen; tel 08-9758 7673; 131 Bussell Hwy, Margaret River; 6pm–late Tue–Sat*

06

WHAT TO DO

While the Margaret River region's wine credentials are impeccable, the area is also a destination for craft-beer fans. Many breweries serve bar snacks and lunch – here are just a few:

BEER FARM
Located in a former milking shed down a sleepy side road, the Beer Farm is Margaret River's most rustic brewery. Try the hoppy Rye IPA. There's a food truck and plenty of room for kids (and pets) to run around. *www.beerfarm.com.au; tel 08-9755 7177; 8 Gale Rd, Metricup; noon–5pm Mon–Thu, to 7pm Fri–Sun*

CHEEKY MONKEY BREWERY
Set around a pretty lake, Cheeky Monkey has an expansive restaurant. Try the Hatseller Pilsner with bold New Zealand hops or the Belgian-style Hagenbeck Pale Ale. *www.cheekymonkeybrewery.com.au; tel 08-9755 5555; 4259 Caves Rd, Margaret River; 10am–6pm daily*

BOOTLEG BREWERY
More rustic than some of the area's flashier breweries, but lots of fun with a pint in the sun – especially with live bands on Saturday. Try the award-winning Raging Bull Porter – a West Australian classic. The food is good. *www.bootlegbrewery.com.au; tel 08-9755 6300; Puzey Rd, off Yelverton Rd, Wilyabrup; 11am–6pm daily*

01

Courtesy of Mandoon Estate

[Western Australia]

SWAN VALLEY

Head for the sunny Swan Valley if you're after bells and whistles, alongside fine wine and top-notch artisan food.

Just 30 minutes from the centre of cosmopolitan Perth, the Swan Valley is well placed to take advantage of the boom in wine tourism. It certainly has the credentials, with Western Australia's oldest vineyards and many multi-generational family-run wineries, but it's also going through something of a reinvention at present, with several newer wineries opening up and pulling out the stops for visitors.

The region has witnessed steady growth since botanist Thomas Water first identified the grape-growing potential offered by the Mediterranean climate and rich, fertile soils. Waves of southern European immigrants in the 20th century brought with them viticultural knowledge which helped the vineyards flourish – early Croatian settlers played a vital role and members of the founding families are still behind the scenes at John Kosovich and Talijancich.

The industry was founded on fortified wines and hearty full-bodied, high-alcohol reds that were popular in the 19th century, but it has re-oriented itself over the decades and today most of the wineries take at least some of their grapes from southern regions with cooler climates such as Margaret River, Pemberton and the Great Southern, where fruit for sparkling wines and delicate white table wines can be grown. Now it's common to find a Swan Valley winery selling robust local reds and fortifieds made from Shiraz, Cabernet and Malbec, fine dry Riesling from Mount Barker or Frankland grapes and Chardonnays from Margaret River grapes.

Common too are fine restaurants, micro-breweries, function centres, art galleries, coffee shops, children's playgrounds, helicopter rides and river cruises, all of them as much a part of the modern winery experience as the humble tasting room.

GET THERE
The Swan Valley is a 30min drive from Perth, or take a leisurely ferry ride up the Swan River.

01 MANDOON ESTATE

Mandoon is of the Swan's newest wine properties – established in 2008, with its first vintage in 2010 – and now something of a mini empire. The Erceg family are people in a hurry: they made an immediate impact on the wine shows, at the same time launching what is already the region's showpiece property, with a brewery, art gallery, tavern, fine-dining restaurant, cellar door, kids' playground, state-of-the-art winery and a function centre which seats 400. They've already enticed 5000 to 6000 weekly visitors. Newly added is The Colony, a 32-room accommodation complex overlooking vines and river. And next up, a distillery.

The wines, made by Ryan Sudarno, are very impressive. Margaret River reserve-level wines from Chardonnay and Cabernet Sauvignon are sensational, as is the Great Southern Riesling, while the Swan Valley is well represented with reds: Old Vine Shiraz, The Pact Shiraz and Surveyors Red Grenache Shiraz Mourvedre.

mandoonestate.com.au; tel 08-6279 0500; 10 Harris Rd, Caversham; 10am–5pm Mon–Thurs, 10am–10pm Fri, 7.30am–10pm Sat, 7.30am–5pm Sun

02 PINELLI

Pinelli was established in 1980 by Italian immigrants and is still owned and run by the family. Brothers Robert and Daniel are both trained winemakers – a rare luxury in a boutique winery. Their Aged Release Family Reserve Chenin Blanc is a smashing wine, released at 10 years. The Vermentino is also excellent but the winery is renowned for its Reserve Durif, a variety not common in the Swan. A key draw here is the excellent French (surprisingly) restaurant Fillaudeau's, with its attractive terrace shaded by twining vines.

www.pinelliwines.com.au; tel 08-9279 6818; 30 Bennett St, Caversham; 10am–5pm daily

03 HOUGHTON

This is the undisputed elder statesman of Swan Valley wineries, established in 1836, where the

From top left: courtesy of Mandoon Estate; Talijancich; © bellytubby / Shutterstock

01 An outdoor dinner at Mandoon Estate

02 Bush tucker tastings at Mandoon

03 Talijancich's vineyards

04 The Swan River

doyen of local winemakers Jack Mann plied his trade for 51 vintages. Today, Houghton's top Cabernet Sauvignon is named in his honour. The range of wines crafted by longstanding winemaker Ross Pamment is fantastic, although only one wine, a fortified, is from Swan Valley grapes.

The tasting room is bright and welcoming, set in lush grounds, and it's worth making time for tours of the winery and its historic underground cellars – where local bushranger Moondyne Joe was captured in 1869. Houghton wines are widely distributed throughout the country and often deeply discounted: they offer value for money at all levels. The modestly priced Red Stripe Shiraz, for example, is a bargain.
www.houghton-wines.com.au; tel 08-9274 9540; 148 Dale Rd, Middle Swan; 10am–5pm daily

04 SITTELLA

Perth doctor Simon Berns and his wife Maaike bought land in the Swan in 1998 and established a vineyard, boutique winery, charming cellar door and restaurant over the next few years. Their son Yuri is assistant winemaker to Colby Quirk, who previously worked at Domaine Chandon in Napa Valley. It's clearly no accident then that Sittella – named after a small local bird – specialises in sparkling wine. Grapes are sourced from cool Pemberton in the south as well as the Swan for the various cuvées, the best being an appropriately matured Pemberton vintage Pinot Noir Chardonnay. The Coffee Rock Shiraz is their standout local wine, while their Wildberry vineyard in Margaret River supplies grapes for an excellent Reserve Chardonnay.
www.sittella.com.au; tel 08-9296 2600; 100 Barrett St, Herne Hill; 11am–4pm Tues–Sun

05 JOHN KOSOVICH WINES

It seems appropriate that this traditional winery, the third oldest in the Swan Valley, is one of the few to operate a literal cellar door. Tastings taking place in the underground cellar dug by John's father – the axe hanging from the supporting beam serves as a reminder of his team's hard graft,

05 Fine dining at Sittella

06 Perth's superb coastal setting

and as quite a point of contrast with other wineries' slick facilities. This is a traditional winery where visitors will feel a close connection to the vignerons.

A boutique operation, John Kosovich Wines has always been famous for its outstanding fortified wines, including vintage and non-vintage dessert Muscats. Appropriate age is important here: you can also buy Reserve Chenin Blanc, aged for five or six years. *www.johnkosovichwines.com.au; tel 08-9296 4356; 180 Memorial Ave, Baskerville; 11am–4.30pm Wed–Mon*

06 FABER VINEYARD

Co-owner John Griffiths is one of the larger-than-life characters of the Swan, a former Houghton winemaker and wine science teacher, and a passionate ambassador for the region – a visit to Faber Vineyard is guaranteed to be an educational and entertaining experience. Many of the wines are sourced from the home vineyard, notably the Reserve Shiraz, Riche Shiraz and dry white Verdelho, and a luxurious old liqueur Muscat. Other wines are produced from vineyards in the Ferguson Valley, between Perth and Margaret River. *www.fabervineyeard.com.au; tel 08-9296 0209; 233 Haddrill Rd, Baskerville; 11am–4pm Fri–Sun*

07 LAMONT'S

The Lamont family are descendants of Swan Valley royalty, Jack Mann – daughter Corin Lamont runs the winery, with the help of a winemaker, and Jack's granddaughter, feted chef Kate Lamont, takes care of the restaurant (as well as another in Perth itself). The wines do a good job of respecting the Jack Mann traditions while introducing a little more polish and modern style. Most are sourced from southern areas Margaret River and Frankland, but there are also some Swan Valley wines. The dessert Muscat is a highlight. *www.lamonts.com.au; tel 08-9296 4485; 85 Bisdee Rd, Millendon; 10am–5pm Thu–Sun*

08 TALIJANCICH

Talijancich Wines doesn't offer much in the way of frills, but heaps of great atmosphere thanks to the present winemaker, affable James Talijancich. His predecessors were among the Yugoslav immigrants who did so much to establish winemaking in the Swan. Initially concentrating on fortified wine, the enterprise now follows a biodynamic approach, with most of the wines estate-grown.

Old and distinguished fortified wines remain the focal point – 30 Year Old Rare Tawny, 1974 Rare Pedro Solero and Julian James 1980 Solero Liqueur Shiraz are remarkable examples. James also makes Swan Valley table wines, though, none better than the Reserve Verdelho, which is released when mature at eight or nine years. *www.taliwine.com.au; tel 08-9296 4289; 26 Hyem Rd, Herne Hill; 10.30am–4.30pm Wed–Mon*

ESSENTIAL INFORMATION

WHERE TO STAY

DURACK HOUSE

A homely option if you're planning to make Perth your base. It's hard to avoid words like 'delightful' when describing this cottage, set on a peaceful suburban street behind a rose-adorned white picket fence. The three rooms have plenty of old-world charm, paired with thoroughly modern bathrooms.
www.durackhouse.com.au; tel 08-9370 4305; 7 Almondury Rd, Mt Lawley, Perth

SETTLERS REST FARMSTAY

Return to this idyllic, comfortable cottage, ideal for couples or young families, after a hard day's wine tasting and you'll feel like you're in bucolic heaven. There are farm animals to feed, including goats, sheep and llamas, plus eggs to collect for a wholesome breakfast ahead of the next trail.
www.settlersrest.com.au; tel 08-9250 4540; 90 George St, West Swan

06

WHERE TO EAT

PIZZA RUSTICA

A deliciously simple idea: tasty pizza, including a delicious-sounding range of veggie and vegan options, and a BYO policy, with no corkage charges, adding up to the perfect opportunity to try that Cabernet you picked up earlier.
www.pizzarustica.com.au; tel 08-6365 0477; The Courtyard, Ethel St, Guildford; 5pm–9pm Thu–Sun

TWILIGHT HAWKERS MARKET

Ethnic food stalls bring the flavours and aromas of the world to central Perth on Friday night in spring and summer. Look forward to combining your Turkish *gözleme* (savoury crepe) or Colombian *empanadas* (deep-fried pastries) with regular live music from local Perth bands.
www.twilighthawkersmarket.com; Forrest Chase, central Perth; 4.30pm–9pm Fri mid-Oct–late Apr

WHAT TO DO

CAVERSHAM WILDLIFE PARK

Get acquainted with over 2000 animals, birds and reptiles, including quokkas, kookaburras, wallabies and wombats (and even the valley's namesake swans) at this family-friendly attraction, located within Whiteman Park. Lots of daily special events should keep little ones happy for hours.
www.cavershamwildlife.com.au; tel 08-9248 1984; Unit B, Lot 99 Lord St, Whiteman Park; 9am–5.30pm daily

GUILDFORD

If you've chosen to stay in Perth, rather than in pretty Guildford, gateway to the Swan Valley, be sure to make time for an afternoon's visit. It's a well-preserved market town, dating back to 1829 – follow a walking trail to take in the colonial buildings, gaol, courthouse and antique shops, or simply follow your nose to Guildford's inviting pubs, cafes and restaurants.

CELEBRATIONS

ENTWINED IN THE VALLEY

An annual food, wine and cultural festival, held over a jam-packed October long weekend.
www.entwinedinthevalley.com.au

NEW ZEALAND

Courtesy of Mudbrick Vineyards

[Auckland]

AUCKLAND & WAIHEKE ISLAND

The country's most sophisticated wine trail will take you from the buzz of the city to the tranquillity of verdant vineyards in under an hour.

There are many reasons why around a third of New Zealand's population choose to live in Auckland – ruggedly beautiful beaches, a mild climate and all the benefits of a modern, thriving city. The region has produced wine for more than a hundred years and was once the beating heart of the country's wine industry, until the limited availability of good vineyard land took its toll and expansion spread elsewhere. Enough remains, though, to make up a vibrant trail catering to all tastes and budgets. Tantalisingly close to Auckland, blissful Waiheke Island is blessed with its own warm, dry microclimate.

Visitors to wineries in northwest Auckland or Waiheke are often surprised to find wine from other regions alongside local labels. Marlborough Sauvignon Blanc, for example, has become such an important calling card in export markets that it's a crucial addition to retailers' ranges. Auckland's temperate climate means that its own high-performers are Chardonnay, Syrah and the Bordeaux reds, Cabernet Sauvignon and Merlot. Heavy, mostly clay-based soils tend to produce rich, savoury red wines that are distinct from the more intensely fruit-focused reds of Hawke's Bay.

Arguably the most important factor shaping the style and quality of wines coming out of the Auckland region is also the most diverse: the winery founder/winemaker/viticulturist (often one and the same person), most of whom are fiercely individualistic with strong views to support their methods. What made them get into wine? Why did they choose this spot? If they had to do it all over again, what would they change? 'Visit us', enthuses Puriri Hills founder Judy Fowler, 'we love to share our experiences as much as we do our wines'. It's a sentiment shared by wine producers across the region.

GET THERE
Auckland wineries can easily be reached by car. The ferry operator to Waiheke Island, Fullers, offers a tour of three wineries.

Courtesy of Cable Bay / Jane Ussher

01 CABLE BAY VINEYARDS

Wind your way uphill from the ferry terminal on Waiheke Island, on a 15min walk through forest and a bird reserve, to reach Cable Bay. Here the focus is on the wines of two regions: Waiheke, where they planted their first vineyard 20 years ago, and Marlborough's Awatere Valley. Winemaker Chloe Somerset draws on her experience making wine in six countries to produce bright, fresh wines with purity and a sense of place. Cable Bay's Reserve wines certainly justify their flagship status.

The winery boasts two stylish restaurants with harbour views – a formal dining room and a more casual pizza spot.

www.cablebay.nz; tel 09-372 5889; 12 Nick Johnstone Dr, Oneroa, Waiheke Island; 11am–5pm daily

02 MUDBRICK VINEYARD & RESTAURANT

Mudbrick founders Robyn and Nick Jones were dazzled by the magnificent sea views when they bought their bare block of land in 1992. Nick kept his day job as an accountant while they planted a vineyard and eventually built a mud-brick house/winery/barn. A very successful restaurant was opened later with a more casual dining option, the Archive Wine Bar, added more recently.

While Mudbrick has a strong focus on producing Waiheke wines they also dabble with grapes from Hawke's Bay, Marlborough and Central Otago, selling 90% of their production through their cellar door and restaurants. Top drops to try are the red wines from Waiheke, such as the densely fruity Cabernet Sauvignon Merlot Reserve.

www.mudbrick.co.nz; tel 09-372 9050; 126 Church Bay Rd, Oneroa, Waiheke Island; 10am–5pm daily during summer, shorter hours in winter

03 KENNEDY POINT

Kennedy Point is a small-scale, certified organic vineyard, the only one to attain that status on the island. Best known for Syrah, Merlot, Cabernet Sauvignon and blended reds, they also make a robust rosé, full-

01 Winemaker Chloe Somerset of Cable bay

02 Mudbrick winery

03 Harbour views from Cable Bay

04 Alfresco offerings at Cable Bay

bodied Chardonnay as well as a Marlborough Sauvignon Blanc. Visitors get to taste three wines of the day, as well as estate-grown organic olive oil and avocado oil for the all-inclusive price of just $9. It's a great spot to kick back and enjoy sea views as you sip a Chardonnay paired with locally farmed oysters. *www.kennedypointvineyard.com; tel 09-372 5600; 44 Donald Bruce Rd, Surfdale, Waiheke Island; 11am–3pm daily or by appt*

04 STONYRIDGE

Waiheke's most famous vineyard is home to world-renowned reds, an atmospheric cafe and the occasional dance party (look it up if you're here around New Year). Owner Stephen White set up the vineyard with a determination to produce Bordeaux-style reds, and with the now world-famous Cabernt blend, Larose, he has outdone himself.

Red wines from Stonyridge's own Waiheke vineyards are supplemented by whites, rosés, sparklings and Pinot Noir under the Fallen Angel label, all made from grapes grown elsewhere.

Order a bottle of red and a gigantic deli platter and retreat to one of the cabanas in the garden. As one of Waiheke's most popular cellar doors, booking is essential, particularly during the busy summer months.
www.stonyridge.com; tel 09-372 8822; 80 Onetangi Rd, Waiheke Island; 11.30am–5pm daily

05 MAN O'WAR VINEYARDS

Waiheke's largest wine producer is still relatively modest in size when compared to wineries in Marlborough. They have just 59 hectares of vineyards in 76 individual hillside blocks – an incredibly labour-intensive site, devoted to making some of the island's best and most adventurous wines.

The beachfront tasting room is at beautiful Man O'War Bay on the relatively isolated eastern side of the island. It's worth taking the 30min drive along a twisty gravel road when your reward is tasting Man O'War's award-winning Gravestone Sauvignon Semillon, named after the basalt boulders which dot the nearby hilltops.
www.manowarvineyards.co.nz; tel

From top left: courtesy of Mudbrick / Amos Chapple: Cable Bay (2)

05 Stonyridge statuary

06 The tasting room at Man O'War

09-372 9678; 725 Man O'War Bay Rd, Waiheke Island; 11am–6pm Mon–Sun

06 VILLA MARIA

Anyone flying in or out of Auckland has the perfect excuse to visit Villa Maria – it's only a few minutes' drive from Auckland Airport. The winery and surrounding vineyards are nestled in the beautifully landscaped crater of a volcano, complete with an attractive lake and an arena used for big-name summer concerts.

Villa Maria is New Zealand's largest family-owned winery. It's also one of the best, if gold medals and trophies are anything to go by. There's a great range of wines at all price levels – from the complex Ihumatao Chardonnay to the aromatic Syrah. Look for limited-edition wines that are only sold through their cellar door. Short and informative daily tours at 11am and 2pm are worth the modest $5 charge.

www.villamaria.co.nz; tel 09-255 1777; 118 Montgomerie Rd, Mangere; 9am–6pm Mon–Fri, 9am–4pm Sat–Sun

07 KUMEU RIVER

If you're a Chardonnay fan, you owe yourself a pilgrimage to Kumeu River's cellar door to taste their world-beating vintages. What's the secret behind their soaring international reputation? Clay-rich soils with enough water-holding capacity to avoid the need for irrigation must be part of it. Meticulous attention to detail by winemaker Michael Brajkovich (Master of Wine) no doubt helps, too. Having made wine in the same spot for more than 70 years, the Brajkovich family clearly understand their vineyards and know how to get the very best out of them.

www.kumeuriver.co.nz; tel 09-412 8415; 550 State Highway 16, Kumeu; 9am–4.30pm Mon–Fri, 11am–4.30pm Sat

08 PURIRI HILLS

Puriri Hills is around 45 minutes by car from Auckland's CBD in the rolling rural hills of Clevedon. It may seem an unlikely spot to establish a vineyard but in fact it has a similar soil profile and climate to Waiheke Island, and is a must-visit for Bordeaux buffs.

Founder Judy Fowler has a little over two hectares planted with Merlot, Cabernet Franc, Carmenere, Cabernet Sauvignon and Malbec to produce wines in the style of 'right bank' Bordeaux. The wines are made in a small, purpose-built winery. Three quality levels are made: Estate, Harmonie du Soir and the flagship Pope. All are consistently good, with the best vintages, such as the yet-to-be-released 2014 Puriri Hills Pope, achieving greatness.

www.puririhills.com; tel 09-292 9264; Arcadia Farm, 398 North Rd, Clevedon; 1pm–4pm Sat–Sun or by appt

ESSENTIAL INFORMATION

WHERE TO STAY

HOTEL DEBRETT

This hip historic hotel has been zhooshed up with stripy carpets and clever designer touches in every nook of the 25 extremely comfortable rooms. Prices include a continental breakfast, free unlimited wi-fi and a pre-dinner drink. *www.hoteldebrett.com; tel 09-925 9000; 2 High St, Auckland*

Courtesy of Man O'War / Jim Janse

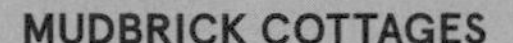

MUDBRICK COTTAGES

Mudbrick can put you up as well as quench your thirst – it has a variety of upscale accommodation including beachfront and vineyard cottages, both on- and off-site, perfect if you'd prefer to escape the city. *www.mudbrick.co.nz/accommodation; tel 09-372 9050; 126 Church Bay Rd, Oneroa, Waiheke Island*

WHERE TO EAT

THE FRENCH CAFÉ

Ask 100 Auckland foodies to name their favourite restaurant and The French Café is likely to come out on top. It's been around for a long time and has earned a thoroughly justified reputation for consistent, top quality food, great service and a cleverly curated wine list. Blow the budget on a tasting menu with paired wines or choose from a tempting a la carte menu. *www.thefrenchcafe.co.nz; tel 09-377 1911; 210 Symonds St, Auckland; open for dinner Tue–Sat, lunch Fri*

CABLE BAY

Impressive ubermodern architecture, interesting sculpture and beautiful views set the scene for this acclaimed restaurant. The food is sublime, but if the budget won't stretch to a meal, stick to a wine tasting or platters and shared plates at the Verandah bar. *www.cablebay.nz; tel 09-372 5889; 12 Nick Johnstone Dr, Oneroa, Waiheke Island; noon–3pm Tue–Sun, 6pm–late Tue–Sat*

WHAT TO DO

Auckland's War Memorial Museum has the world's largest collection of Polynesian exhibits as well as many other items of interest. Take a tour on an Auckland Explorer Bus – it costs just $45 for a 24hr pass with 18 'hop off, hop on' tourist stops across the city, including the museum. The price includes a ferry to Devonport and back. *www.aucklandmuseum.com; www.explorerbus.co.nz*

CELEBRATIONS

The Villa Maria Summer Concert Series takes place in January every year. Picnic at their vineyard near Auckland airport as you listen to top local bands doing what they do best. *www.villamaria.co.nz/news-and-events/concerts*

Man O'War Summer Lunch helps support the Auckland Rescue Helicopter Trust with its annual alfresco event, held in February each year (tickets available from October). *www.rescuehelicopter.org.nz/events/the-man-owar-summer-lunch*

01

Courtesy of Amisfield / Shantanu Starick

[Otago]

CENTRAL OTAGO

New Zealand's most beautiful wine region has the country's only continental climate with hot summer days and cool nights that ripen Pinot Noir to perfection.

Central Otago is the pin-up of New Zealand tourism, famed for sublime alpine scenery and the resort town of Queenstown. Vaunted for adrenalised pursuits such as skiing, hiking and biking. It's also the setting for some world-class winemaking.

The region's wild landscapes make up the world's southernmost wine region and New Zealand's highest, ranging between 200m and 450m (650ft and 1500ft) above sea level. Vineyards are spread throughout the deep valleys and basins of six sub-regions – Gibbston, Bannockburn, Cromwell Basin, Wanaka, Bendigo and Alexandra. In all, Central Otago boasts nearly 6% of the country's grape-growing area (although its wine output is less than 3%).

The few vines planted back in 1864 were an early forerunner of an industry that has only burgeoned since the mid-1990s. The scene remains largely in the hands of friendly boutique enterprises, and winemakers still experimenting with a terroir not yet fully understood.

Soils are predominantly glacial, with a high mineral content, while various microclimates share a common theme of hot days, cold nights, and low rainfall. These conditions have proven excellent for aromatics, particularly Riesling and Pinot Gris, but the hero is Pinot Noir, which accounts for more than 75% of the region's plantings. Indeed, Central Otago is lauded as one of the best places outside of Burgundy for cultivating this notoriously fickle grape.

With some 30 wineries regularly open to visitors, and more by appointment only, it would take a good two days' touring to get a comprehensive taste of the terroir. One focus could be on the Gibbston Valley (with cycle touring a possibility), but a much broader picture is revealed beyond the gates of the dramatic Kawarau Gorge at Cromwell Basin, where two-thirds of Central Otago's grapes are grow.

GET THERE
Auckland is the nearest major airport, with connecting flights to Queenstown airport, 9km out of town. Car hire is available.

01 AMISFIELD

Since it opened in 2005, Amisfield's cellar door restaurant has been an essential stop for gourmands and vinophiles visiting Central Otago. Indeed, its winning blend of fine wine, exciting cuisine, enviable architecture and stupendous views make it arguably the region's ultimate winery experience.

Capitalising on its proximity to the tourist hubs of Queenstown and Arrowtown, Amisfield Bistro lies within the mountain-lined Wakatipu Basin, overlooking Lake Hayes. The muscular building – fashioned from local schist and recycled timbers – is a fabulous setting for an alfresco lunch.

The 'Trust the Chef' shared menu is the way to go, where wines are matched to local ingredients. In season, Bluff oysters may arrive with a glass of bright, zesty Arcadia Brut NV, or Catlins *paua* (abalone) alongside a flinty, dry Riesling. Local venison is heavenly paired with Amisfield's plummy Pinot Noir.

The bistro and tasting room are the public face of the winery, located at Lowburn, north of Cromwell. On a former merino sheep station, it's one of Central Otago's largest single vineyard estates, though still relatively modest at 80 hectares (200 acres).

www.amisfield.co.nz; tel 03-442 0556; 10 Lake Hayes Rd, Queenstown; 10am–6pm daily

02 WILD EARTH WINES

Test your nerves as you cross the cascading Kawarau River and imagine stepping back 150 years to gold-mining days: crude huts, harsh winters and the slim chance of making a fortune. Nestled right at the river's edge, Wild Earth's cellar door and restaurant will return you to modern day comforts with wine that's gold standard and fantastic food. Owner Quintin Quider has come up with a novel way of reusing old French oak wine barrels, transforming them into outdoor 'stoakers', or cookers, to create tasty platters to accompany his excellent wines.

There is treasure here with old vintages of Wild Earth Pinot Noir

01 Amisfield Winery

02 Dining in the Amisfield Bistro

03 Wine and food at Wild Earth

04 Wild Earth restaurant

Central Otago is lauded as one of the best places outside Burgundy for cultivating the notoriously fickle Pinot Noir grape

dating back more than a decade – delicious, award-winning wines that demonstrate just how well good Pinot Noir can improve with bottle age.

www.wildearthwines.co.nz; tel 03-445 4841; 803 Kawarau Gorge Rd, State Hwy 6, Kawarau Gorge; 10am–5pm (subject to change in winter)

03 MT DIFFICULTY

The Gibbston Valley Hwy funnels through the rocky narrows of Kawarau Gorge before emerging into the Cromwell Basin where the undulating brow of the Carrick Range casts a rain-shadow across Bannockburn's famous vines. One of the forerunners here is Mt Difficulty, established in the early 1990s when five growers collaborated to produce wine from the promising but unproven Central Otago region.

Winemaker Matt Dicey joined in 1999 and, while still producing excellent Pinot Noir, he has developed a range of wines of enviable breadth and quality. We love their luscious lemon-and-lime Target Riesling, although some of the most captivating drops come from the Grower's Range, bursting with concentrated, nuanced flavours expressive of the local terroir.

But wait, there's more. Perched on a hill with vast views over Cromwell Basin, Mt Difficulty's alluring restaurant encourages lingering over lunch. Sharp and

From top left: courtesy of Amisfield / Benn Jae; Wild Earth Wines / Vaughan Brookfield (2)

05 Appetisers at Amisfield

06 Working in the Amisfield vineyards

modern with scrumptious fare and spectacular alfresco tables on the terrace, it will pay to book a table and sort out well in advance who's responsible for driving home.
www.mtdifficulty.co.nz; tel 03-445 3445; 73 Felton Rd, Bannockburn; 10:30am-4:30pm daily, to 5.30pm Christmas to Easter

04 AKARUA

Like most great Central Otago wineries, Akarua is the architect of delectable Pinot Noir, but it's the rosé and crisp bubbles that really pop our corks.

For this we have winemaker Matt Connell to thank. Joining this Bannockburn winery in 2008, he quickly focused on adding a bit of fizz to Akarua's range. Its first *méthode traditionelle* was launched in 2012, and within three years claimed four major trophies, including top New Zealand bubbles at the 2014 Sparkling Wine World Championships for its 2010 vintage brut.

A victory lap, however, should be reserved for Akarua's 100% Pinot Noir rosé: a bouquet of strawberries and cream and pretty hard to top on a classic Central Otago summer's day. An aperitif of champions!

The wines speak for themselves, so there's no need for bells and whistles at the cellar door. Accordingly, Akarua keeps it simple but smart, focusing on the warm welcomes and informative tastings that have been a hallmark of our repeated visits.
www.akarua.com; tel 03-445 0897; 210 Cairnmuir Rd, Bannockburn; 10.30am-4pm daily

05 CARRICK

The beauty of Central Otago's cellar doors is that they offer a classy wine experience low on snoot-factor, with Carrick a case in point. This slick outfit may host plenty of jetsetting types, but it treats visitors with equal fervour regardless of the taster's knowledge.

Like Mt Difficulty, Carrick is a spectacular spot for an indulgent lunch. The airy, art-filled atrium dining room opens on to a shady terrace and lush lawn. Framed by willows and vines is a view over Lake Dunstan's Bannockburn inlet to the Carrick Range, its foothills sculpted by old gold-mining sluices.

Starring its own olive oil and other local ingredients, Carrick's platters are a great complement to its wine range, which includes an intense, spicy Pinot Noir – its flagship drop – as well as a rich, toasty Chardonnay and citrusy aromatic varietals.

Between the wine, food and wonderful setting, Carrick rises to the occasion. To take things totally over the top, take a helicopter trip from the winery around the super-scenic Cromwell Basin with a landing atop the Pisa Range.
www.carrick.co.nz; tel 03-445 3480; 247 Cairnmuir Rd, Bannockburn; 11am-5pm daily

ESSENTIAL INFORMATION

WHERE TO STAY

VILLA DEL LAGO

With unobstructed lake views and a scenic 25-minute walk to downtown, these fully self-contained suites and villas make an ideal Queenstown base. *www.villadellago.co.nz; tel 03-442 5727; 249 Frankton Rd, Queenstown*

MILLBROOK RESORT

Set in 200 hectares (500 acres) of parkland with epic mountain views, this luxurious but unstuffy golf resort piles up the plaudits for its recreational facilities, day spa, 175 rooms and popular restaurants. *www.millbrook.co.nz; tel 03-441 7000; Malaghans Rd, Arrowtown*

WHERE TO EAT

CROMWELL FARMERS MARKET

Held in the Old Town heritage precinct on the lake edge, this sweet little summertime market (Sunday morning November–February) has everything from hot pies to produce with the bonus of live music and the chance to have a yarn with the locals. *Old Cromwell Town, cnr Melmore Tce & Mckinlay Lane, Cromwell*

PROVISIONS

Just one of many cafes housed in Central Otago's charming historic buildings, Provisions serves excellent espresso alongside irresistible home baking. Make a beeline for the sticky bun. *www.provisions.co.nz; tel 03-445 4048; 65 Buckingham St, Arrowtown*

WHAT TO DO

QUEENSTOWN TRAIL

This extensive, mostly easy, trail network is a memorable way to reach wine-tour highlights while soaking up the scenery and working up an appetite. Bike hire and regular shuttles make for enjoyable loops or tours around Lake Hayes and Gibbston Valley wineries, taking in AJ Hackett's bungy jump base at historic Kawarau Bridge. *www.queenstowntrail.co.nz*

CELEBRATIONS

With its endearing old schist stone buildings and interesting hydro-dam location, Clyde is an ambient setting for the annual Clyde Wine and Food Harvest Festival, held on Easter Sunday. Central Otago's largest culinary festival, it features 20-odd wine stalls and a raft of food producers, alongside live music and local art.

01

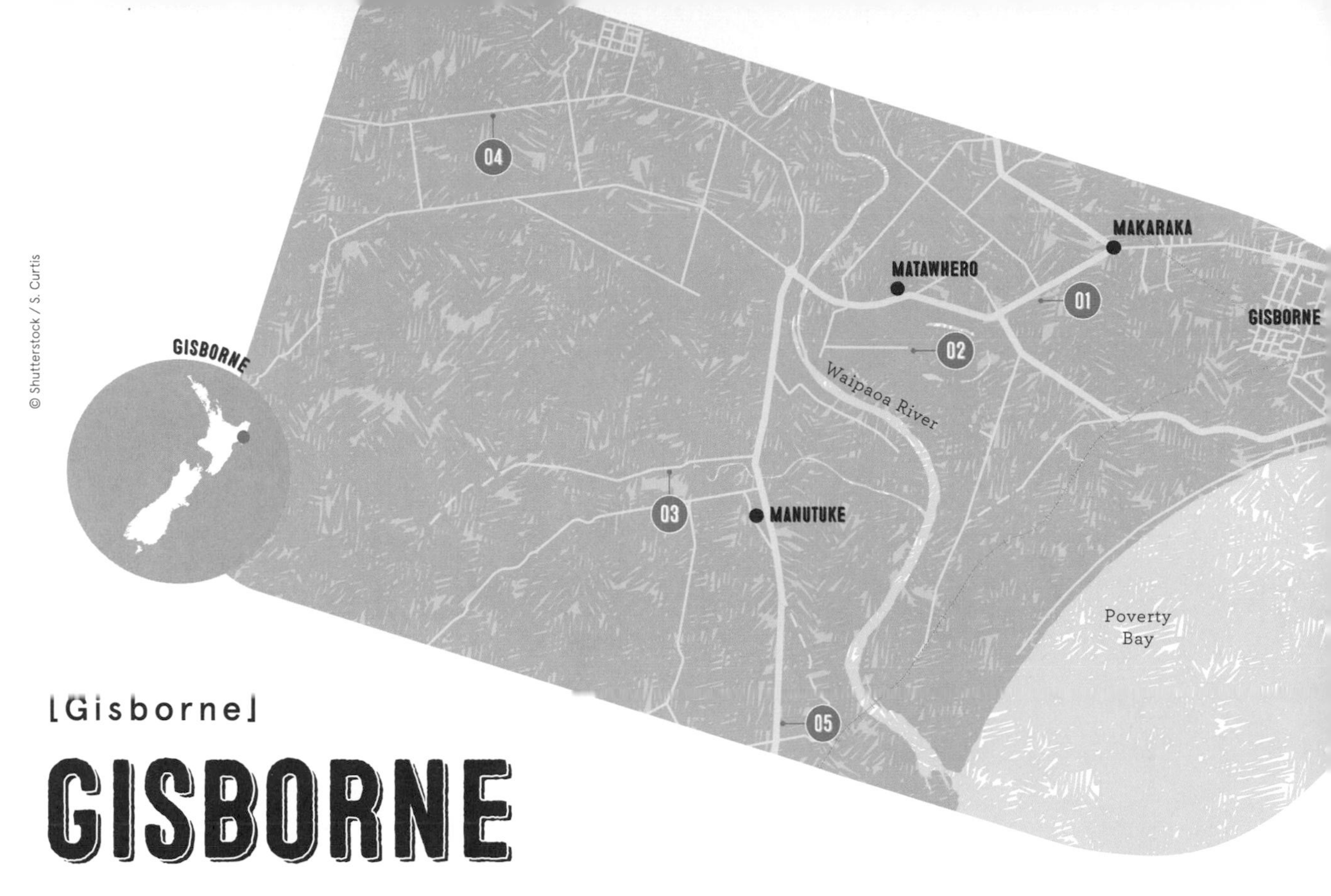

[Gisborne]

GISBORNE

Gisborne is a world apart where sun, sea and Chardonnay rule. The country's third largest wine region is a cool little surf town with a laid back approach to life.

On the easterly tip of the North Island, Gisborne proudly claims to be the first city in the world to see the sun. Indeed, it regularly records the highest sunshine hours and temperatures in New Zealand. So as you'd expect, sunshine is something the surrounding region has in abundance – along with fertile, free-draining river plains which are the perfect site for productive vineyards. The Waiapu River Valley, northwest of Gisborne, counts as one of New Zealand's foremost grape-growing areas.

This curve of the east coast is famous for its fresh-from-the-sea crayfish and mellow, creamy Chardonnay, a duo which also happens to make a devastating combination on the dinner table.

White wines are king here (and relaxed cafes and restaurants plentiful). Chardonnay takes the lead followed by a cluster of aromatic varieties: Pinot Gris, Gewürztraminer and Viognier; together with Sauvignon Blanc and the region's most significant red, Merlot.

But if you're looking for wines made from more obscure varieties Gisborne is still a good place to start your search. The local Riversun Nursery, the country's leading supplier of premium vines, introduced New Zealand to new grape varieties including Albariño, Arneis and Grüner Veltliner. Many new varieties were first trialled by local wine producers before being adopted elsewhere.

Gisborne's wines are unpretentious in both quality and price – its famous Chardonnay is typically smooth-textured and moreish, with ripe peach and other stone fruit flavours – and you'd do best to set aside at least a few days if you want to really unwind and get to grips with this wine region.

GET THERE
Fly to Gisborne from most major NZ airports. Take State Hwy 2 from Napier (three hours) or Opotiki (two hours).

01 BUSHMERE ESTATE

Bushmere owners David and Shona Egan have been growing grapes in Gisborne for more than 40 years. They've made the transition from grape-growers to winemakers with considerable flair, building up a smart winery complete with restaurant and function facilities. It's in the beating heart of Gisborne wine country where verdant vines stretch toward the horizon.

Bushmere Estate plays to Gisborne's strengths with a couple of stylish Chardonnays, a silken Pinot Gris and a delicately floral Gewürztraminer, all of which are worth shortlisting for a tasting flight of five wines. If you'd prefer to ration yourself to only one or two, smile sweetly and are lucky enough to be served by Shona, there's a chance you might not have to pay a fee...

For something more adventurous, veer away from whites to try a peppery, aromatic Montepulciano or sip an even more unconventional blend of Montepulciano and Sangiovese called The Italians – a pretty wine with delicious cherry and floral flavours. Rosé and two sparkling wines are also available together with an unusual and popular fortified sweet red wine called Diavolo Rosso.

www.bushmere.com; tel 06-868 9393; 166 Main Rd, Gisborne; 11am–3pm Wed–Sun Sept–May, with longer hours over the summer months; by appointment Apr–Aug

02 MATAWHERO WINES

Matawhero was one of the region's pioneering wineries, founded by Denis Irwin, an innovative winemaker building on the work of his father, Bill, who was the first to import many grape varieties to New Zealand from the late 1960s. You can still visit Irwin's original cellar and explore many long-forgotten labels. Present owners Richard and Kirsten Searle bought the property in 2008 and have revitalised it – with alfresco tastings and live jazz concerts – while preserving much of its history.

It's a family-friendly winery with plenty of space for children to run around, as well as a crowd-pleasing menu offering platters for youngsters, vegans and gourmets,

01 Gisborne's beautiful coast

02 Vineyards at Kirkpatrick Estate

03 Enjoying the wines at Matawhero

04 A Matawhero platter

This coast is famous for its crayfish and mellow, creamy Chardonnay, a duo which makes a devastating combination on the dinner table

and some tempting desserts.

Chardonnay is the hero here, with a choice of three labels including the flagship, Irwin Chardonnay. Chenin Blanc ranks highly too, with Gewürztraminer, Albariño and Pinot Gris close behind.

www.matawhero.co.nz; 06-867 6140; 189 Riverpoint Rd, Gisborne; noon–4pm Sat–Sun Oct–Nov; 11am–5pm Thurs–Mon Feb, Mar & Dec, 11am–5pm daily 27 Dec–end Jan

03 KIRKPATRICK ESTATE WINERY

Owner Simon has deep roots here – he grew up on the family farm opposite the winery and the Kirkpatricks have farmed on the Patutahi Plateau for 150 years. He bought the existing 8-hectare property with an established 5.5-hectare vineyard in 2003 and gained accreditation as a sustainable producer. All wines are made from the estate vineyard which surrounds the winery – grapes can be in the crusher, press and tank within minutes of being harvested.

The cellar door features an elevated terrace, with great views over the Malbec vineyard and the Patutahi Plateau beyond. You can taste a selection of wines, including the rich and spicy Malbec, as you enjoy an antipasto of estate-grown olives and other tasty morsels like freshly made onion marmalade, salami and aged cheddar.

Book ahead for a winery tour which includes a tasting of wines still

Ø5 Harvesting grapes at Matawhero

Ø6 The sun sets over Gisborne

in barrel. Kirkpatrick specialises in grape varieties with a proven record of success in the Gisborne region, including Merlot, Chardonnay, Gewürztraminer, Viognier, Malbec and Cabernet Sauvignon.
www.kew.co.nz; tel 06-862 7722; 575 Wharekopae Rd, Gisborne; opening hours vary – check the website

04 THE MILLTON VINEYARDS & WINERY

Certified organic since 1989, and biodynamic since 2009, and a true leading light in organic and biodynamic wine production in New Zealand, Millton Vineyards & Winery is a special place to visit, an impression that's only reinforced once you appreciate the dedication of owners James and Annie. Their aim is simply to produce the best possible wine, a true representation of its terroir – intuition and good sense led them to adopt the organic and biodynamic approach, over 30 years ago. Their vineyards flourish on rolling slopes, fed by biodynamic preparations, not chemicals. Lush flower gardens and grazing cattle enhance the idyllic tableau, but everything serves a purpose, too – cow horn manure, for example, plays an important part in improving the soil.

Millton's greatest wines come from their Clos de Ste Anne vineyard, a carefully tended 12-hectare hillside plot first planted in 1981 and now home to Chardonnay, Chenin Blanc, Pinot Noir, Syrah and Viognier vines. They consistently rank among the region's best with concentration and style reflecting vine age and winemaking experience. Cheese boards and antipasti provide a perfect match.
www.millton.co.nz; tel 06-862 8680; 119 Papatu Rd, Manutuke; Mon–Sat 10am–5pm summer, 2pm–5pm Mon–Fri winter, 10am–5pm daily Dec–Jan. By appt at other times

05 WRIGHTS VINEYARD AND WINERY

Juggling raising a young family and work in the legal profession, Geoff and Nicola Wright somehow managed to develop their own trio of organic/biodynamic vineyards which now cover over 18 hectares. The Terrace Vineyard is on a north-facing slope for maximum sun exposure; inland, the Valley Vineyard enjoys hotter summer and lower winter temperatures, while the Coastal Vineyard in Manutuke is cooled by coastal breezes. They've established native gardens and ponds, and have planted 500 olive trees, whose crop provides them with olive oil.

Kick back with gourmet pizza alongside a quartet of wines at the family-friendly cellar door, which boasts live music most Saturday afternoons. Both ranges on offer, The Natural Wine Co and Wrights, are certified organic and include a rich, smooth-textured Viognier and a gentle Gewürztraminer with subtle rose petal flavours.
www.wrightswines.co.nz; tel 06-862 5335; 1093 Wharerata Rd, Manutuke; open daily in summer – see website for opening hours

ESSENTIAL INFORMATION

WHERE TO STAY

AHI KAA MOTEL
This uptown motel is in a quiet backstreet, a short sandy-footed stroll across the road from Waikanae Beach in the heart of Gisborne.
www.ahikaa.co.nz; tel 06-867 7107; 61 Salisbury Rd, Gisborne

PACIFIC HARBOUR MOTOR INN
Overlooking the inner harbour marina and a short walk from Gisborne's main street, the Pacific Harbour Motor Inn is a popular choice.
www.pacific-harbour.co.nz; tel 06-867 8847; 24 Reads Quay, Gisborne

WHERE TO EAT

MARINA RESTAURANT
Often touted as Gisborne's best restaurant, the Marina offers casual bistro-style lunches and formal fine dining in the evenings – all with very Gallic vibes – served up in a grand old white weatherboard boathouse.
www.marinarestaurant.co.nz; tel 06-868 5919; 2 Vogel St, Gisborne

USSCO BAR & BISTRO
Housed in the Union Steam Ship Company building, this place is all class. The highly seasonal menu is offset by a wine list of impressive depth, with a good range of carefully selected Gisborne labels.
www.ussco.co.nz; tel 06-868 3246; 16 Childers Rd, Gisborne

WHAT TO DO

GISBORNE WINE CENTRE
Gisborne Wine Centre is a great place to get acquainted with a selection of stylish Gisborne wines in a waterside setting. An expert is on hand to help you choose from the wine list and menu.
www.gisbornewinecentre.co.nz; tel 06-867 4085; Shed 3, Inner Harbour, Gisborne

DIVE TATAPOURI
Join a reef ecology tour to feed stingrays and have an encounter with kingfish, kahawai, crayfish, octopus and conger eel.
www.divetatapouri.com; tel 06-868 5153; 532 Whangara Rd, State Highway 35, Tatapouri

GISBORNE BOTANIC GARDENS
The town gardens sit pretty beside the Taruheru River – a perfect spot for a picnic and a run around the big playground.
www.gdc.govt.nz/our-parks-and-reserves/showPark/botanical-gardens; tel 06-867 2049; Aberdeen Rd, Gisborne

CELEBRATIONS

Rhythm & Vines is a huge event on Gisborne's calendar, a three-day music festival culminating on New Year's day, when some 20,000 people flock to the Waiohika Estate to see in the first sunrise of the New Year and enjoy more than a hundred local and global bands and DJs – from Calvin Harris and Bastille to Kimbra and Moby.
www.rhythmandvines.co.nz; Waiohika Estate, Gisborne

Courtesy of Church Road

[Hawke's Bay]

HAWKE'S BAY

In-the-know wine-lovers head to this North Island bay not only for wines of enviable quality but also breathtaking scenery and a town full of art deco gems.

Known as the 'fruit bowl of New Zealand', Hawke's Bay is a patchwork of orchards, vegetable gardens and vineyards, with pasture in between. Alongside such delectable largesse is a raft of attractions ranging from art-deco architecture, farmers' markets and a sophisticated dining scene, to surf beaches and cycle trails. And as well as being the country's second largest wine region it's also the oldest, dating back to 1851 when Marist missionaries planted the first vines between Napier and Hastings.

While Hawke's Bay lacks a signature varietal such as Marlborough's Sauvignon Blanc or Central Otago's Pinot Noir, it grows a whole bunch of grapes very well. Warm, sunny conditions swiftly ripen fruit from highly varied soils throughout diverse sub-regions such as the Bridge Pa Triangle on the Heretaunga Plains, to the cooler Esk Valley and coastal Te Awanga.

The most famous sub-region is the Gimblett Gravels, laid down by Ngaruroro River as it changed course over the ages. Once considered a barren wasteland, the first vines were planted here in 1981, but it wasn't until the early 90s – when plans for a quarry were quashed – that winemaking in the gravels really gathered momentum.

Full-bodied reds rule the roost across the Bay, particularly the vast plantings of Merlot and Cabernet Sauvignon that lend the region its moniker 'Bordeaux of New Zealand'. Syrah is also produced in significant volume. The dense, peppery profile of this cooler-climate, Rhône-style red accounts for the locals' tactical move to eschew the name 'Shiraz', thus distinguishing it from the vibrant, jammy Aussie versions. Chardonnay is another leader, nosing its way through a respectable field of contenders – Pinot Gris, Gewürztraminer and Pinot Noir to name but a few. Like most other New Zealand wine-growing areas, however, experimentation is rife.

The abundance, quality and diversity of the Bay's wines make for enjoyable touring, amplified by the volume of restaurants, cafes and artisan food producers all sandwiched together, with splendid scenery and the option of cruising around by bike.

GET THERE
Hawke's Bay has flights from Auckland, Wellington and Christchurch. By car it's about 3.5hr from Wellington; 1.5hr from Taupo and 2hr from Gisborne.

01 Chris Scott of Church Road

02 Tasting at Craggy Range

03 Craggy Range vineyards

04 Elephant Hill platter

05 Te Mata

01 MISSION ESTATE

At the end of a tree-lined avenue, Mission Estate's centrepiece is the beautifully preserved seminary – La Grande Maison – built in 1880. Daily tours illuminate Mission's story and key chapters in the region's history (including a devastating 1931 earthquake), and foreground the wines available for tasting. Visitors can also sit down to a refined luncheon in the seminary's formal front rooms, or out on the sun-drenched terrace.

Made to 'gladden the human heart', originally by French Marist missionaries, Mission's wines have been tended by Paul Mooney for the last 30 years. The range features six tiers from the great-value Mission Estate wines through to the classy Jewelstone and Huchet drops made from Mission's most blessed grapes.

Hallmark Hawke's Bay exemplars include toasty Chardonnays from vines grown on-site, and Bordeaux-style reds and Syrah borne from the coveted Gimblett Gravels. A tasting at Mission, however, may also include aromatic Riesling, Pinot Gris and Gewürztraminer, an intense Marlborough Sauvignon Blanc or savoury Martinborough Pinot Noir.

www.missionestate.co.nz; tel 06-845 9353; 198 Church Rd, Taradale; 9am–5pm Mon–Sat, 10am–4.30pm Sun

02 CHURCH ROAD

Red wines flowed from this site on Church Road for most of the 20th century, but it took a new winemaking team to revive the winery in the '90s, setting its sights on creating reds in the Bordeaux style using fruit from across Hawke's Bay.

Today, Chardonnay is the signature wine of talented winemaker Chris Scott, who has also won many awards for his Syrah and blended reds. The cellar door features a trio of tutored tastings and a range of 22 wines for sale including old vintages and experimental labels only available from the winery. Hot tip: try Church Road's big, juicy red made from the Italian grape Marzemino.

www.church-road.co.nz; tel 06-833 8234; 150 Church Rd, Taradale, Napier; 11.30am–3pm daily, to 2.30pm in winter

03 TRINITY HILL

John Hancock, winemaker and co-owner of Trinity Hill, was an early pioneer and co-founder of the Gimblett Gravels Winegrowers Association. His impressive output has helped elevate the Gravels' reputation as the Bay's premier winegrowing district, particularly well-suited to full-bodied reds.

Indeed, Trinity Hill produces a Rhône-rivalling Syrah, the Homage, made only in superlative years and ranked among New Zealand's greatest reds. Other varietals include exemplary Chardonnay and Merlot, as well as unusual and experimental varieties including a delicate Arneis and richly textured Marsanne/Viognier blend, both excellent with food. Iberian influences surface in a sturdy fruit-driven Tempranillo, and Touriga Nacional port-style wine.

Located in the thick of cellar door territory in the countryside west of Hastings, Trinity Hill is not to be missed. Their high-ceilinged, concrete-slab tasting room is spacious, with platters in the garden in summertime.

www.trinityhill.com; tel 06-879 7778; 2396 State Hwy 50, Hastings; 10am–5pm summer, 11am–4pm Wed–Sat winter

04 TE AWA

Literally a stone's throw from Trinity Hill and making wines from the same Gimblett Gravels terroir, Te Awa is also home to a restaurant boasting some of Hawke's Bay's best food.

But let's not get ahead of ourselves, for this place is serious about its wines, produced under three labels. The flagship is Te Awa, a suite of single-estate wines – Bordeaux blends, Syrah and Chardonnay – that highlight the unique characteristics of the Gravels' terroir. The best drops work their way up to the Kidnapper Cliffs premium range, accordingly priced and suited to cellaring, while the Left Field label is appended to Te Awa's 'weird and wonderful', more affordable wines.

The timber-built tasting room and restaurant blends rural charm with a debonair panache, the menu presenting shared plates of exciting fare – lamb and green olive cigars with cumin salsa, fish crudo with ouzo mayo. With wine list in hand and warm sunrays playing through the trees, you could count yourself in for a very long lunch.

www.teawacollection.com; tel 06-879 7602; 2375 State Hwy 50, Hastings; 10am–4pm daily

05 BLACK BARN

Black Barn has all sorts of ways to lure in the passing visitor: a stylish cellar door, a growers' market held beneath the trees on summertime Saturday mornings, a kitchen store crammed full of only local produce, an outdoor concert venue and – for those who really want to make the most of all this bounty – luxurious cottages and retreats to rent.

The vineyard accompanying this mini-empire is decidedly boutique, with all wines estate-grown and many sold only through the cellar door. There's a good cross section of well-made varietal wines available to taste. Barrel-fermented Chardonnay and Viognier 'sur lie' (kept in contact with the residual

From top left: courtesy of Craggy Range (2); Elephant Hill / Brian Culy; Te Mata

06 The oceanside Elephant Hill

07 The cellar door at Trinity Hill

yeast) are two favourites. Pick a nice day and enjoy a heavenly lunch under the vines at the Black Barn Bistro.
www.blackbarn.com; tel 06-877 7985 Black Barn Rd, Havelock North; 9am–5pm Mon–Fri, 10am–5pm Sat–Sun

06 TE MATA

Te Mata is the country's oldest winery, with wines still being made in the original 1896 buildings and the vineyards recognised as important national heritage sites.

Best known for Coleraine, the country's most iconic and internationally respected red wine, Te Mata also makes a string of other stylish wines. No visit is complete without trying peppery, Rhône-like Bullnose Syrah, rich, complex Zara Viognier, suave and sophisticated Elston Chardonnay or deliciously fruity Gamay Noir.
www.temata.co.nz; tel 06-877 4399; 349 Te Mata Rd, Havelock North; 10am–5pm Mon–Sat, 11am–4pm Sun in summer; 10am–5pm Wed–Sat in winter (Mon & Tues by appt)

07 CRAGGY RANGE

In a sublime setting alongside the Tukituki River, at the foot of Te Mata Peak – the Bay's chief landmark – Craggy Range is worth visiting for the journey alone. Add in a modernistic collection of buildings housing the cellar door, restaurant and upscale accommodation, and pour in some of New Zealand's finest drops, and you've got yourself a wine-tour stop that's hard to beat.

After a serendipitous meeting between Craggy Range founder Terry Peabody and Master of Wine Steve Smith in 1997, the pair set out to create 'single-vineyard New World classics' from various New Zealand wine regions including Martinborough, Marlborough and Central Otago, where they own their own vines.

Quality is certainly high across the board, but it's Craggy's top-flight range where memories are made. Well-heeled wine-lovers may wish to indulge in a bottle of Le Sol Syrah, a dense and luscious drop from the Gimblett Gravels best savoured with something gamey in the excellent Terrôir restaurant. A treasure trove of other hen's teeth Craggy Range vintages can be found in its formidable wine list.
www.craggyrange.com; tel 06-873 0141; 253 Waimarama Rd, Havelock North; 10am–6pm daily Nov–Mar, Wed–Sun Apr–Oct

08 ELEPHANT HILL

Contrasting starkly with the rustic charm of other wineries, Elephant Hill is a striking, monolithic form clad in patinated copper and fronted with epic windows offering unobstructed views of Cape Kidnappers and the Pacific Ocean.

Elephant Hill's German owners fell for Te Awanga while on holiday. With the goal of creating a state-of-the-art winery marrying traditional and contemporary styles and techniques, they planted their first grapes in 2003 and set to it. The results are impressive; their Reserve Chardonnay displays a lovely fruit purity and depth typical of Te Awanga terroir, and their reds blend local and Gimblett Gravels' characters.

The circular tasting bar is an enticing introduction to the restaurant, a classy affair complete with a white leather sunken lounge, sundeck and an infinity pool.
www.elephanthill.co.nz; tel 06-872 6073; 86 Clifton Rd, Te Awanga; 11am–5pm Dec–Mar, to 4pm Apr–Nov

Courtesy of Elephant Hill / Brian Culy; Trinity Hill

ESSENTIAL INFORMATION

WHERE TO STAY

CLIVE COLONIAL COTTAGES

These courtyard cottages sit prettily amid gardens in a serene spot near the beach. Pick up the cycle trail alongside to ride around the vines. *www.clivecolonial cottages.co.nz; tel 06-870 1018; 198 School Rd, Clive*

MILLAR ROAD

Set in the Tuki Tuki Hills with vineyards and bay views, Millar Road is architecturally heaven-sent. Two plush villas (each sleep four) and a super-stylish house (sleeps eight) are filled with NZ-made furniture and local art. Explore the 20-hectare grounds or look cool by the pool. *www.millarroad.co.nz; tel 06-875 1977; 83 Millar Rd, Hastings*

WHERE TO EAT

HAWKE'S BAY FARMERS MARKET

If you're around on a Sunday morning, don't miss one of New Zealand's best markets, a lively affair set in bucolic showgrounds and bursting with produce, coffee and gourmet picnic supplies. *www.hawkesbay farmersmarket.co.nz; A&P Showgrounds, Kenilworth Rd, Hastings*

MISTER D

With something for everyone, morning, noon and night, Napier's hottest dining ticket sets a hip and stylish standard with food from cinnamon doughnuts to bone-marrow ravioli. *www.misterd.co.nz; tel 06-835 5022; 47 Tennyson St, Napier*

WHAT TO DO

Don your walking shoes or hop on a bike to admire Napier's internationally acclaimed collection of art deco buildings, which emerged in the aftermath of the devastating 1931 Hawke's Bay earthquake. This fascinating chapter in the Bay's history is well told at the Art Deco Trust visitor centre, a good place to start your tour. *www.artdeconapier. com; tel 06-835 0022; 7 Tennyson St, Napier*

Te Mata Peak (399m), part of the Te Mata Trust Park, rises dramatically from the Heretaunga Plains 16km south of Havelock North. The summit road passes sheep trails, rickety fences and vertigo-inducing stone escarpments, veiled in a bleak, lunar-meets-Scottish-Highlands atmosphere. On a clear day, views from the lookout fall away to Hawke Bay, Mahia Peninsula and distant Mt Ruapehu. The park's 30km of trails offer walks ranging from 30 minutes to two hours: pick up the Te Mata Park's Top 5 Walking Tracks brochure from local i-SITEs. *www.tematapark.co.nz; tel 06-873 0080; off Te Mata Rd, Havelock North*

CELEBRATIONS

The bay's major festival is the annual Art Deco Weekend in February, a 200-event extravaganza of art deco architecture, art, music and Gatsby-esque costumes. Epicures might like to coincide their visit with the Hawke's Bay's Food and Wine Classic (FAWC), a series of appetising events held twice yearly in June and November. *www.artdeconapier. com; www.fawc.co.nz*

01

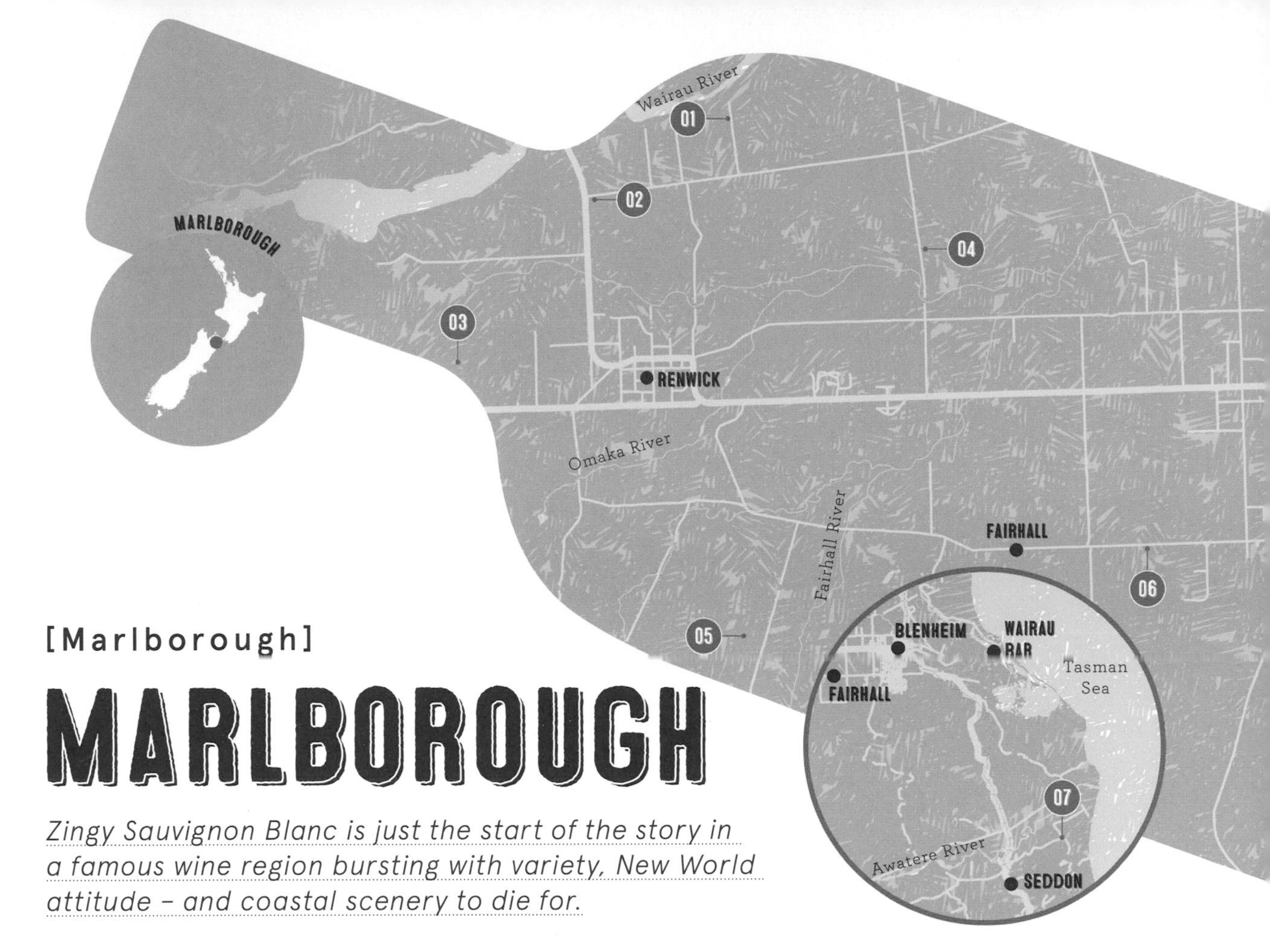

[Marlborough]

MARLBOROUGH

Zingy Sauvignon Blanc is just the start of the story in a famous wine region bursting with variety, New World attitude – and coastal scenery to die for.

Marlborough is a vinous colossus, accounting for around three-quarters of New Zealand's wine. At last count there were nearly 600 growers tending 23,000 hectares of grapes, working their way into the wines of 151 producers. Remarkably, it has taken just 40-odd years for the Marlborough region to grow from first vines into the billion-dollar industry it is today.

So that's why you've probably heard of Marlborough Sauvignon Blanc; this New World classic is pungently aromatic, fruity and herbaceous, a dominant varietal that has stormed the global wine scene. Indeed, the ubiquity of big brands flooding supermarkets worldwide has led to accusations that Marlborough 'sav' has become predictable – even one-dimensional – but the region produces plenty that is exciting and distinct.

The majority of vineyards line up around Renwick in the Wairau Valley, although side valleys and coastal fringes have been colonised in response to the demand for land. While growing conditions throughout are generally sunny and dry, the soil is a veritable kaleidoscope of glacial stone, shingle, sand and silt, shifted and settled by river flows. The result is a highly varied terroir.

To home in on memorable Sauvignon Blanc, set your sights on smaller, independent wineries. They are more likely to offer tastings of single-estate wines, not just of Sauvignon Blanc but also of Marlborough's other notable varietals such as Pinot Noir and Riesling.

With lots of accommodation in its rural surrounds, just 10km from Blenheim, Renwick makes a good base for wine touring. More than 20 of the region's 35 cellar doors can be found around here, along with bicycle hire, guided tours and shuttle services.

GET THERE
Auckland is the nearest major airport, with connecting flights to Marlborough, 7km from Rapaura. Or cruise up the Marlborough Sounds.

Courtesy of Yealands Family Wines / Jim Tannock

01 HANS HERZOG ESTATE

Hans and Therese Herzog left behind their winery in Switzerland and Michelin-starred restaurant respectively to start anew in Marlborough. The result? Seriously good Kiwi wines with a distinctly European flavour from 29 different grape varieties, some in achingly small quantities, all estate-grown and made. The limited edition Nebbiolo and seriously concentrated Montepulciano wouldn't look out of place alongside the best Italian examples of both varieties. And while the cuvée Therese rosé sparkling might not fool you into thinking it's champagne, it is still delicious.

They offer a choice of wine tastings and a 30-minute winery tour at 12pm or 6pm each day. Choose between fine dining in their lavish restaurant or a more casual meal in Herzog's Bistro, where the menu changes daily.

www.herzog.co.nz; 03-572 8770; 81 Jeffries Rd, Marlborough; 9am–5pm Mon–Fri, 11am–4.30pm Sat–Sun

02 NAUTILUS ESTATE

Nautilus wines are typically pure and ethereal, showing a clear expression of place but also packing a punch. So determined was the team to make great Pinot Noir that they built a separate, dedicated gravity-flow winery – the results speak for themselves. Elegant Chardonnay, seductively fruity Pinot Noir, taut, restrained Sauvignon Blanc and a complex, yeasty bottle-fermented sparkling wine which has won many well-deserved accolades – Nautilus sweeps the board.

Book in advance to tour the winery with a Nautilus winemaker.

www.nautilusestate.com; tel 03-572 6008; 12 Rapaura Rd, Renwick; Oct–Apr 10am–4.30pm daily

03 SERESIN ESTATE

Founded in 1992 by successful cinematographer Michael Seresin, who describes the estate as 'a new world winery with an old world philosophy', Seresin is farmed biodynamically and organically and encompasses olive groves, orchards and vegetable plots as well as vineyards.

01 Livestock among the Yealands vines

02 Brancott Estate

03 Summer at Cloudy Bay

04 The Cloudy Bay cellar door

To home in on memorable Sauvignon Blanc, set your sights on smaller, independent wineries more likely to offer tastings of single-estate wines

The flagship Sun & Moon heads a list of seven Pinot Noir labels, including the entry-level Osip Pinot Noir. A highlight of the three Sauvignon Blanc labels is the additive-free Osip; a sleek Chardonnay, spicy Pinot Gris and medium Riesling are also excellent. *www.seresin.co.nz; tel 03-572 9408; 85 Bedford Rd, Blenheim; 10am-4.30pm daily*

04 CLOUDY BAY

Visiting Marlborough without stopping at Cloudy Bay is like going to Agra without taking in the Taj Mahal. One of the region's pioneering winemakers, Cloudy Bay helped put New Zealand wine on the world map, particularly with its Sauvignon Blanc, which remains something of an international icon. Less well-known but even more delicious is its elegant and complex Chardonnay and plump, fruity Te Wahi Pinot Noir, the latter from Central Otago where Cloudy Bay has now purchased vineyards and a winery.

In summer, Jack's Raw Bar offers an exciting menu of fresh, local (mostly raw) produce that demands to be enjoyed alfresco. *www.cloudybay.co.nz; tel 03-520 9140; 230 Jacksons Rd, Blenheim; 10am-4pm daily*

05 BRANCOTT ESTATE CELLAR DOOR & RESTAURANT

Trailblazers Brancott Estate (then known as Montana Wines) planted the first Sauvignon Blanc

From top left: courtesy of Brancott Estate / Jessica Jones; Cloudy Bay / Jim Tannock; Cloudy Bay / Oliver Weber

05 Brancott's cellar door patio

06 Wither Hills winery

vines in Marlborough in 1973 and today remain a dominant force in the region and indeed the New Zealand wine industry. It's worth booking ahead for their 'Mastery of Marlborough Sauvignon Blanc' tutored tasting to hear the full story of the star varietal.

It's hard to beat lunch at the on-site restaurant which sits high above the vineyard, stretching across the Wairau valley floor below. The best local, seasonal produce goes into each dish, each of which is paired with Brancott Estate wines.
www.brancottestate.com; tel 03-520 6975; 180 Brancott Rd, Fairhall; 10am–4.30pm daily

06 WITHER HILLS

This modern, midsized winery, nestled in among vineyards bordering the Wither Hills, incorporates a stylish restaurant and a comprehensive menu of wine-tasting experiences, from a straightforward guided session to the chance to experiment with your own blends.

Wither Hills own vineyards throughout Marlborough and produce benchmark examples of the region's high-performing grape varieties. The single-estate Sauvignon Blanc from the coastal Rarangi vineyard is one of Marlborough's more concentrated examples, while the sophisticated Pinot Noir from the Taylor River vineyard offers outstanding value for money.

Wither Hills takes sustainability seriously, having established the Rarangi Wetlands Conservation Project in their Rarangi vineyard to create biological diversity and help protect rare flora.
www.witherhills.co.nz; tel 03-520 8284; 211 New Renwick Rd, Blenheim; 10am–4.30pm daily

06 YEALANDS FAMILY WINES

Yealands lies on the edge of the wine region, 31km southeast of Blenheim, but it's an easy trip for those driving to or from Kaikoura. Blanketing 1000 hilly hectares (2471 acres) in the Awatere Valley, it's the country's largest privately owned vineyard.

Yet despite its size, Yealands keeps its eyes on the prize – environmentally sustainable winemaking, a carbon-zero footprint, and total self-sufficiency. These efforts are evident on the enjoyable self-drive tour that loops through Seaview vineyard, passing picnic spots, windmills, wetlands and compost piles along the way. There's also the odd peacock, sheep, chicken or duck. (The pigs were banished after they piggybacked one another to chomp the grapes.)

The corporate but casual cellar door experience is best started with the short film relaying the colourful Yealands backstory. As for tasting, while the winery is known for an abundance of super-value drops, there are plenty of delightful single-vineyard wines and Reserves. Its S1 Block Sauvignon Blanc is a winner, while relative newcomers Grüner Veltliner and aromatic blend PGR are making waves.
www.yealands.co.nz; tel 03-575 7618; cnr Seaview and Reserve Rds, Seddon, Blenheim; 10am–4.30pm daily

ESSENTIAL INFORMATION

WHERE TO STAY

OLDE MILLE HOUSE

On an elevated section in otherwise flat Renwick, this charming old house is a treat. Dyed-in-the-wool local hosts run a welcoming B&B, with stately decor, and home-grown fruit and homemade goodies for breakfast. Lovely gardens, spa and free bikes make this a tip-top base for exploring wine country.
www.oldemillhouse.co.nz; tel 03-572 8458; 9 Wilson St, Renwick

MARLBOROUGH VINTNERS HOTEL

These smart suites make the most of panoramic, vine-lined Wairau Valley views. Opt for the Outdoor Bath suite to survey Marlborough's night skies while having a soak. The stylish reception building has a bar and restaurant opening out to a cherry orchard and organic veggie garden.
www.mvh.co.nz; tel 03-572 5094; 190 Rapaura Rd, Renwick

WHERE TO EAT

ROCK FERRY

This stylish cafe is a popular lunchtime spot for seasonal fare and stupendous sweet treats matched with Rock Ferry's own organic wines.
www.rockferry.co.nz; tel 03-579 6431; 130 Hammerichs Rd, Blenheim; 11.30am–3pm daily

GRAMADO'S

Injecting a little Latin American flair into the Blenheim dining scene, Gramado's is a fun place to tuck into unashamedly hearty meals such as lamb assado, feijoada (smoky pork and bean stew) and Brazilian-spiced fish. Kick things off with a caipirinha, of course.
www.gramadosrestaurant.com; tel 03-579 1192; 74 Main St, Blenheim; 4pm–late Tue–Sat

06

WHAT TO DO

OMAKA AVIATION HERITAGE CENTRE

Original and replica WWI aircraft are brought to life at this brilliant museum abetted by Peter Jackson's Wingnut Films and Weta Workshop. A new wing houses Dangerous Skies, a WW2 collection. Vintage biplane flights are a great way to survey the Wairau Valley. A cafe and shop are on site and next door is Omaka Classic Cars, with more than 100 vehicles from the '50s to the '80s.
www.omaka.org.nz; 79 Aerodrome Rd, Blenheim; 9am–5pm Dec–Mar, 10am–4pm Apr–Nov

MARLBOROUGH FARMERS MARKET

Come rain, hail or shine, this atmospheric market is open every Sunday 9am to 12pm, and Thursday 2pm to 5pm at the A&P Park on Blenheim's Alabama Road.

CELEBRATIONS

New Zealand's largest and longest-running wine and food festival is held at Brancott Estate in February. Watch a band, take in a cooking demo or just chill out on the grass enjoying the sun.
www.marlboroughwinefestival.co.nz

[Auckland]

MATAKANA

Escape from Auckland and discover the rolling, rural landscape of Matakana and the cellar door stories of its pioneering winemakers.

When brothers Petar and James Vuletic planted Cabernet Sauvignon, Merlot and Malbec in Matakana in 1979, they were convinced they could make world-class red wine. Their Antipodean label subsequently fetched record prices, inspiring others to follow their lead. Although grapevines had been planted in Matakana in the 1950s it was The Antipodean that launched winemaking in the region.

Winemaking has transformed unassuming Matakana from a nondescript rural village into a destination for Auckland's chattering classes. Locals watch bemused as urbanites idle away the hours in stylish wine bars and cafes. It's the area's boutique wineries that are proving such a lure – steadily gaining a name for themselves for Pinot Gris, Merlot, Syrah and a host of obscure varietals. Today 21 grape-growers and wine producers have a collective (and minuscule) vineyard area of 65 hectares (160 acres).

The biggest challenge to grape-growing here is rain and humidity during the ripening period. Tropical cyclones carry moisture-laden air from the Pacific; rain can cause dilution and rot. It can be avoided, or at least mitigated, by trellising systems that open up the vine canopy, or by choosing grape varieties that ripen early or are resistant to disease. Vineyards tend to be sited on hillsides for better sun exposure and drainage, and hand-picking ensures any sub-standard grapes are rejected during harvest. Soils often have a high clay content with enough water retention to avoid the need to irrigate. All in all, the conditions point most winemakers towards a minimal-intervention approach.

And minimal planning is all it takes to make a stimulating visit to the region – with a weekly farmers market, artisan shops and sculpture trails, plus breathtaking nearby beaches and snorkelling opportunities, it's simply a case of joining the dots.

GET THERE

Matakana is a 1hr drive north of Auckland, via the toll motorway, or take the slightly longer but more scenic route.

Courtesy of Brick Bay / Sam Hartnett

01 RANSOM WINES

Heading north from Auckland, Ransom Wines should be your first stop – a small, stylish winery making decent, often adventurous wines exclusively from their own vineyard, and hosting a welcoming cellar door. Its flagship wine is a spicy, complex blend of Bordeaux varieties called Dark Summit.

Ransom is also behind one of the few Kiwi wines made from the rustic red grape Carmenere, a gutsy rosé and tangy Albariño. Another less mainstream offering is the orange wine, made from Pinot Gris with plenty of skin contact. Try to taste them all, alongside platters heaving with local delicacies.

www.ransomwines.co.nz; tel 09-425 8862; 46 Valerie Close, Warkworth; 10am–4pm Tue–Sun

02 BRICK BAY

The undulating grounds at Brick Bay have seen all sorts of crops, livestock and activity over the last 30 years, from macadamias to angora goats, plums and pears to lake-building. While not everything has stuck, experimentation and perseverance have paid off and today the site is home to a sustainably accredited vineyard, olive groves and bee hives, a striking lakeside restaurant and a 2km sculpture trail. Featuring more than 50 works – ranging from large-scale pieces tucked into the landscape of palms, kauri forest and native bush, to smaller scupltures in the more intimate gallery and courtyard setting – the trail is full of surprises and also plays an important role in supporting local artists.

After a sculpture fix, the obvious next step is to while away an afternoon over a lunch of fresh, seasonal produce (much of it grown in the site's garden) at The Glass House Kitchen. You can also drop in for wine tasting, coffee or sweet treats. Recommended wines include a delicately scented, off/dry Pinot Gris, a soft and subtle rosé made from a blend of Bordeaux varieties and two blended reds, the elegant Martello Rock and

Winemaking has transformed unassuming Matakana from a nondescript rural village into a stylish destination for Auckland's urbanites

01 Wine tastings at Brick Bay

02 Ascension Wine Estate

03 Picking grapes at Brick Bay

04 Ascension's gently sloping vineyards

fuller-bodied Pharos.
www.brickbay.co.nz; tel 09-425 4690; 17 Arabella Ln, Snells Beach, Warkworth; 10am–5pm daily

03 RUNNER DUCK ESTATE

Clyde and Farida Cooper run this boutique estate dedicated to premium red wine. It's quite a change from their previous life in Mumbai, India, but they're putting their passion for the finer things in life to good use here. Their two small vineyards, the second adjacent to their restaurant, Plume, are planted in Syrah, Cabernet Franc and Merlot, among others, although they supplement their reds with a Marlborough Sauvignon Blanc and Auckland Chardonnay.

The rest of the plot comprises olive groves, bush and gardens, including ponds which attract ducks and other wildlife – it's the Indian runner duck, in fact, whose distinctive long neck recalls the shape of a wine bottle, that lends the Estate its name.

The cellar door is near the entrance to Runner Duck Estate's comfortable Plume restaurant, offering the chance to taste the wines on offer before you sit down to enjoy lunch. Look out for the fresh and flavoursome Matakana Pinot Gris and crowd-pleasing Passion Syrah.
www.runnerduck.co.nz; tel 09-575 4246, 49a Sharp Rd, Matakana; 11am–4pm Wed–Fri, 11am–3.30pm Sat–Sun

05 The cellar door at Runner Duck

06 Tawharanui Regional Park

04 HERON'S FLIGHT

When owners David Hoskins and Mary Evans first planted their vineyard in 1987 they chose the perenially popular French grape varieties. Then David tasted an Italian wine – 'It was an epiphany', he recalls. It was au revoir to the French varieties and benvenuto to red Italian varieties Sangiovese and Dolcetto, a decision partly based on the need to select varieties that could perform in a challenging vintage, which in Matakana usually means late summer rain.

Visitors to the cellar door are likely to be served by David or Mary. Both have been growing grapes and making wine for longer than most in their region and have plenty to say about their craft. Their wines are equally full of character – the 2013 Sangiovese Reserve, for example, is a ripe and complex red.

www.heronsflight.co.nz; tel 09-950 6643; 49 Sharps Rd, Matakana (down the drive); 10am–5pm daily

05 ASCENSION WINE ESTATE

This is a winery with kerb appeal, its Mediterranean-style buildings flanked by vineyards gently sloping down towards Matakana Road. Not that it depends on passing trade – this is a big, popular operation, able to cater for groups of up to 300 in its restaurant, function room and barrel hall.

All of Ascension's wines are made from grapes grown in the small 4-hectare vineyard next to the winery, although high demand by restaurant customers does limit availability. Eleven grape varieties produce a surprisingly diverse wine list. Try the rich and weighty The Accent Chardonnay or the peppery, herbal The Countryman's Hat Tannat, from a southern French grape variety that is reputed to reduce blood pressure when drunk in moderation.

www.ascensionwine.co.nz; tel 09-422 9601; 480 Matakana Rd, Laly Haddon Place, Matakana; 11am–4pm daily

06 HYPERION WINES

Heading east through Matakana village take the first road on the right and travel for 1.8km until you can go no further. You'll come upon a rustic setting created by Hyperion's two enthusiastic owners, John and Jill Crone, who planted the vineyard in 1994 and later converted a cowshed into their winery.

Pinot Gris and Syrah grapes are obtained from other Matakana growers but otherwise all Hyperion's predominantly red wines are sourced from their own two small vineyards. Of particular note is a delicately succulent Eos Pinot Noir and a fairly new wine made from the hardy French-American hybrid grape, Chambourcin, with an impressively dense colour and plum/berry flavours.

www.hyperionwines.co.nz; tel 09-422 9375; 188 Tongue Farm Rd, Matakana; 10am–5pm weekends, public holidays and every day in January

ESSENTIAL INFORMATION

WHERE TO STAY

TAKATU LODGE AND VINEYARD
Make your stay all the more wine-soaked by opting for a few nights at one of the four plush suites on this working vineyard in Matakana village.
www.takatulodge.co.nz; tel 09-423 0299; 518 Whitemore Rd, Matakana

BLACK FERN MATAKANA
Bordering Ascension vineyard, this luxurious lodge can accommodate large groups and boasts a heated swimming pool and small gym. Perfect for working off the excesses of a day's winery touring.
www.blackfernmatakana.com; tel 021 912 805; 454 Matakana Rd, Warkworth

HYPERION HEIGHTS
A good compromise between rural retreat and village convenience, with many cafes within walking distance and a stunning location overlooking Hyperion vineyard and rolling farmland. You'll find a complimentary bottle of Hyperion wine on arrival and no doubt get a chance to chat with the winery's friendly owners.
www.hyperionwines.co.nz; tel 09-422 9375; 569 Whitmore Rd, Matakana

06

WHERE TO EAT

THE MATAKANA
Following a trendy makeover, Matakana's heritage pub now features quirky decor, Matakana wines and craft beers, and decent bistro food including Mahurangi oysters. Occasional DJs and live acts enliven the cool outdoor space.
www.matakana.co.nz; tel 09-422 7518; 11 Matakana Valley Rd, Matakana; 11.30am–1am daily

WHARF STREET BISTRO
Settle in with the Warkworth locals at this popular riverside spot, open for inventive evening meals featuring fish of the day, fresh seafood and tasty slow-cooked organic meat.
www.wharfstreetbistro.com; tel 09-422 2511; 6 Wharf St, Warkworth; 5pm–9pm Tue–Sat

VINTRY
Located in the Matakana Cinemas Complex, this wine bar serves as a one-stop cellar door for all the local producers.
www.thevintry.co.nz; tel 09-423 0251; 2 Matakana Valley Rd, Matakana; 3pm–late daily

WHAT TO DO

MATAKANA VILLAGE
The striking Matakana Cinemas complex has a domed roof reminiscent of an Ottoman bathhouse, and an excellent farmers market (8am–1pm Sat) is held in its shadow. Stock up and picnic by the river.
www.matakanacinemas.co.nz; www.matakanavillage.co.nz

TAWHARANUI REGIONAL PARK
A partly unsealed road leads to this 588-hectare reserve at the end of a peninsula. This special place is an open sanctuary for native birds, protected by a pest-proof fence, while the northern coast is a marine park (bring a snorkel). There are plenty of walking tracks (1.5 to 4 hours) but the main attraction is Anchor Bay, one of the region's finest white-sand beaches.

[Nelson]

NELSON

Nelson has no problem satisfying a holidaymaker's every whim, from food, wine and beer, art, craft and festivals, to that most precious of pastimes, lazing in the sunshine.

At the tip of the South Island, with mountain ranges either side, the sunny, clear-skied Nelson region draws in the crowds. Many of its best wines are never sold outside the region, so those crowds must be pretty discerning – a collection of boutique wineries make mostly very small-production wines, so you have to get yourself there to be in with a chance of appreciating them. They are mostly family affairs with mum and dad looking after the vineyard, making the wine and serving customers with or without help from the kids. Visiting these cellar doors can be an intimate experience with stories shared by hard-working owners who persevere because every vintage gets a little better, if not a little easier.

Nelson has two distinct sub-regions, each of which can be toured in a day. The Waimea Plains near Richmond, southwest of Nelson, is our starting point. Waimea is Maori for 'river garden' and was traditionally a top spot for arable crops, orchards and hops before grapevines made an appearance. Stony, free-draining river gravels produce both white and red wines that are typically bright and perfumed. In the Moutere Hills region northwest of Nelson, many vineyards use the folding hills to increase sun exposure and ripening ability. Richer, clay-laced soils tend to produce more concentrated and often longer-lived wines.

Sauvignon Blanc is the most popular grape variety with a regional style that's perky and vibrant, often with a taut, mineral-like backbone of fresh acidity. Pinot Noir ranks second in terms of vine area although some would argue that it's the region's most prestigious wine. Nelson's cool nights and warm days through the ripening season produce top results from aromatic grape varieties Pinot Gris, Riesling and Gewürztraminer. Chardonnay is a local hero too, with the best examples absolute world-beaters.

GET THERE
Nelson is a 1.5hr drive from Blenheim or 1.75hr from Picton. Nelson's busy airport is a short drive from the city.

01 WAIMEA ESTATES

Waimea Estates is the closest winery to Richmond, a short 5min drive away, and relatively large by Nelson standards. Mainstream grape varieties such as Chardonnay Sauvignon Blanc, Pinot Gris, Riesling, Gewürztraminer and Pinot Noir are consistently good and often offer excellent value. More unusual varieties including Albarino, Grüner Veltliner and Sauvignon Gris add extra spice to their wine range.

The cellar door and cafe were once located at the winery but a fire forced both to move to new premises down the road.

www.waimeaestates.co.nz; tel 03-544 4963; 107 Appelby Hwy, Hope; 11am–5pm daily; winery tours possible with advance notice

02 BRIGHTWATER VINEYARDS

This small family-owned wine producer has always set its sights high, passionate about fine wine and focused on premium ranges while other wineries dabble with lower-cost labels. Awards and praise have come thick and fast, year in year out, despite the vagaries of vintage. One to try while gazing out towards the Western Ranges is Lord Rutherford Barrique Sauvignon Blanc – a rich and textural oak-aged wine, more interesting than the often simple, fruity examples from many producers.

www.brightwaterwine.co.nz; tel 03-544 1066; 546 Main Rd, Hope, Brightwater; 11am–4.30pm Mon–Fri (hours vary, check website)

03 SEIFRIED ESTATE

In 1973 Hermann and Agnes Seifried earned pioneer status by planting the first vines in the Upper Moutere, and subsequently building a winery. They moved to their present site in 1993, opening a restaurant and later a winery alongside. In the years since, Seifried Estate has grown to be Nelson's largest wine producer with over 300 hectares of vineyards in nine different Nelson sites.

The cellar door is a family-friendly place with a popular children's playground (grape juice is available, too!). There's usually a broad selection of wines to taste – it's worth asking to sample the award-winning Sweet Agnes Riesling, a luscious yet

wonderfully pure dessert wine which is remarkably consistent from year to year.
www.seifried.co.nz; tel 03-544 1600; 184 Redwood Rd, Appelby; 10am–5pm Mon–Fri Nov–Easter, closes 4pm in winter

04 MOUTERE HILLS

Moutere Hills' two adjacent vineyards are planted on clay-gravel soils that retain sufficient moisture to avoid the use of irrigation. Both are sheltered, sloping sites that enjoy the moderating effect of coastal breezes. A modern winery, built in 2006, is large enough to provide contract winemaking services to other local producers. Choose a spot indoors or out for lunch at the café/cellar door and enjoy seasonal food during the summer months. Dinner is served all year round at the rustic Fox n Grapes wine bar, converted from a nearby hop kiln. The weighty, smooth-textured Sarau Reserve Chardonnay and intense, limited-edition Sarau Reserve Pinot Noir, which thoroughly justify their Reserve status and elevated prices, are available by the glass or bottle.
www.mouterehills.co.nz; tel 03-543 2288; 42 Eggers Rd, Upper Moutere; 11am–5pm daily Jan–Easter, 11am–5pm Thu–Sun winter

05 KAHURANGI ESTATE

Kahurangi is the oldest cellar door in Nelson (built by Seifried in the early '70s) and boasts the oldest commercial Riesling vines in the South Island, planted in 1973. It's an elevated historic site with views across their vineyard to distant hills.

The International Wine Room is an unusual addition – although perhaps less surprising given founder Greg Day's background as a wine merchant – offering port, sherry, cognac and a selection of interesting wines from Australia, Italy, the Americas, Portugal, Spain and France. The winery is also an outlet for three local wine brands.

Kahurangi Estate offers a broad spectrum of grape varieties with an emphasis on aromatic Riesling, Gewürztraminer and Pinot Gris but including a tangy, fruity Italian-style Montepulciano. Entry label Trout Valley offers wines made from grapes supplied by seven contract

01 Autumn in Nelson

02 Helping with the harvest at Seifried

03 The nearby coastline

04 Night falls on Waimea Estates

05 Central Nelson

growers and is a rich hunting ground for bargain-seekers. *www.kahurangiwine.com; tel 03-543 2980; Sunrise Rd, Upper Moutere; 11am–5pm Wed–Sun (hours vary, check website)*

06 MAHANA ESTATES

This truly magnificent, elevated site in the heart of the Moutere Hills is home to a beautiful villa, state-of-the-art winery, art gallery, cellar door and restaurant, all the brainchild of art-lover and philanthropist Glenn Schaeffer. The site is organically farmed and wines are produced in a custom-built four-level gravity-flow winery – where the grapes gently flow from one level down to the next, without the need for pumps or unnecessary handling – which is built into this hillside and camouflaged by a living green roof of shrubs and grasses.

Mahana underwent a revolution recently with a new brand name (formerly Woollaston) and new winemaker, Michel Glover, who has a reputation for adventure in his craft. Try Davey's Lease Sauvignon Blanc, fermented on the grape skins and aged in acacia barrels, to experience an unusual but curiously appealing wine. Another unfamiliar example is the orange-hued Blood Moon Pinot Gris which was fermented on skins for four weeks then aged on its lees for a further 12 months.
www.mahana.nz; tel 03-543 2817; 243 Old Coach Rd, Upper Moutere; 11.30am–4.30pm Fri–Sun

07 NEUDORF VINEYARDS

Neudorf is an exciting cellar door offering equally thrilling wines. Concerted efforts in sustainable, organic and dry farming are paying dividends. Chardonnay is their signature wine, the best tasting similar to serious Burgundy, and the 2014 Moutere Chardonnay a rare recipient of a maximum 100 point critic's score. There's also a cracking, long-lived Pinot Noir, spicy Pinot Gris and new kid on the block, mineral Albariño, which is off to a flying start.

The cellar door is housed in restored buildings, with a mini-deli where you can put together your own platter to enjoy in the garden.
www.neudorf.co.nz; tel 03-543 2643; 138 Neudorf Rd, Upper Moutere; 11am–5pm daily

ESSENTIAL INFORMATION

WHERE TO STAY

SUSSEX HOUSE
In a quiet riverside spot, only a 5min walk to town, this creaky old villa dates back to around 1880. The five rooms feature upmarket bedding, period-piece furniture and bathrooms. Enjoy local fruit at breakfast in the grand dining room. *www.sussex.co.nz; tel 03-548 9972; 238 Bridge St, Nelson*

MOUTERE INN
Reputedly NZ's oldest pub, complete with retro interior, the Moutere Inn is a welcoming establishment serving meals and predominantly local craft beer, and hosting music nights with a folksy bent. There are also a couple of bedrooms available. *www.moutereinn.co.nz; tel 03-543 2759; 1406 Moutere Hwy, Upper Moutere*

WHERE TO EAT

DEVILLE
Most of DeVille's tables lie in its sweet walled courtyard, a hidden boho oasis and a perfect place for a meal or morning tea. The food's good and local – from fresh baking to a chorizo-burrito brunch, Caesar salad and proper burgers, with regional wines and beers. Open late for live music on Fridays in summer. *www.devillecafe.co.nz; tel 03-545 6911; 22 New St, Nelson; 8am–4pm Mon–Sat, 8.30am–2.30pm Sun*

SMOKEHOUSE
Eat fish and chips from this Mapua institution on the wharf while the gulls eye up your crispy bits. Get some delicious wood-smoked fish and pâté to go. *www.smokehouse.co.nz; Mapua Wharf, Mapua; 11am–8pm daily*

JESTER HOUSE
Long-standing Jester House is reason to take this coastal detour, as much for its tame eels as for the peaceful sculpture gardens that encourage you to linger over lunch. A simple menu puts a few twists into staples (venison burger, lavender shortbread), and there are local beers and wines. It's 8km to Mapua or Motueka. *www.jesterhouse.co.nz; tel 03-526 6742; 320 Aporo Rd, Tasman; 9am–5pm daily*

WHAT TO DO

WORLD OF WEARABLEART & CLASSIC CARS MUSEUM
Nelson is the birthplace of New Zealand's most inspiring fashion show, the annual World of WearableArts Awards Show. You can see 70 or so current and past entries in the sensory-overloading galleries of the World of WearableArt & Classic Cars Museum (WOW) which include a glow-in-the-dark room. *www.wowcars.co.nz; tel 03-547 4573; 1 Cadillac Way, Nelson; 10am–5pm daily*

TAHUNA BEACH
Nelson's playground takes the form of an epic sandy beach (with lifeguards in summer) backed by dunes, and a large park with a kids' play area, an espresso cart, hydroslide, bumper boats, roller-skating rink, model railway and an adjacent restaurant strip. Weekends will be busy.

CELEBRATIONS

Nelson Wine + Food Festival is held annually in mid-February at Middle Earth Vineyards. Proceeds from the family-friendly event are donated to local causes. *www.richmondrotary.org.nz/bwff*

[Northland]

NORTHLAND

Birthplace of New Zealand wine, the 'winterless north' is home to small family wineries that hug the coast to benefit from cooling sea breezes and breathtaking views.

For many Kiwis, the phrase 'up north' conjures up sepia-toned images of family fun in the sun, pohutukawa in bloom and dolphins frolicking in pretty bays. Beaches – often deserted and undeveloped – are the main drawcard, with surfing, sailing and diving opportunities galore, but there are also awe-inspiring sights on land, including remnants of the ancient kauri forest that once blanketed the top of the country. It's not just natural attractions that are on offer, though: there's history too. The site of the earliest settlements of both Maori and Europeans, Northland is the nation's birthplace.

It's also where the wine industry has its roots – the first recorded grapevines in New Zealand were planted in the Bay of Islands by the Reverend Samuel Marsden in 1819. James Busby, who took the title of first winemaker, recorded his content impression of vineyard life: 'A man who could sit under the shade of his own vines with his wife and children about him, the ripe clusters hanging within their reach, in such a climate as this, and not feel the highest enjoyment is incapable of happiness...' While his first forays inspired others to establish vineyards, Northland remains one of the country's smallest wine-producing regions.

Clay-based soils allow most vineyards to avoid using irrigation and hillside locations, providing exposure to the sun and drainage, are common. Chardonnay is the most popular grape variety, partly because it ripens early and can escape the damaging effect of warm, tropical cyclones that may sweep through Northland during the ripening period. Syrah, a late-ripening and reasonably hardy grape, is the next favourite.

There's a relaxed feeling in the north and it's not unusual to see a boat parked near the winery, ready for some fishing when the job allows. The climate presents challenges but it's clear there are some compensations.

GET THERE
Northland is a few hours' drive or short flight from Auckland.

01 MILLARS VINEYARD

First stop on the way from Auckland, Millars is in the east coast town of Mangawhai which sits at the base of a horseshoe harbour. A quintessential and thoroughly laid-back New Zealand beach town, it's somewhat eclipsed by the narrow spit of sand, Mangawhai Heads, which sits at the harbour mouth, sheltering a seabird sanctuary.

This family-run enterprise was established in 2005 and now produces around 600 cases of wine a year from its two-hectare vineyard. You might choose from a perfumed Gewürztraminer, a fruity medium/dry Pinot Gris, flavoursome rosé or a robust Syrah. You can meet the family and taste their wines either at the no-frills cellar door or at the Mangawhai Village Market every Saturday in summer.

www.millarswines.co.nz; tel 09-431 4326; 26 Bush Ln, Mangawhai; 10am–5pm daily Labour weekend to Easter, by appt in winter

02 PAROA BAY WINERY

If a 15min drive from Russell in the Bay of Islands seems a little humdrum, why not set sail and drop anchor in Paroa Bay? The winery's stylish restaurant, Sage, lays on transport from the bay, steering you to a Mediterranean-inspired menu and fine local wines. Wine tastings also take place in the restaurant – Sauvignon Blanc, Chardonnay, Syrah, rosé and a blended red are all made from grapes grown on the property, a 4.5-hectare site.

Paroa Bay also offers a range of accommodation, including a super-luxurious retreat – personal chef and skippered speedboat, anyone?

www.paroabay.com; tel 09-403 7928; 31 Otamarua Rd, Paroa Bay, Russell; 12pm–3pm & 6pm–9pm Wed–Sun

03 OMATA ESTATE

This picture-postcard vineyard with views across the Bay of Islands nurtures around 8000 Syrah, Chardonnay and Pinot Gris vines, planted on the estate's sloping vineyard and cooled by sea breezes.

The rustic and charming Omata Kitchen takes full advantage of

01 Marsden Estate's Rod MacIvor

02 The Marsden staff

03 Appetisers at Marsden

04 Views across the Karikari vineyards

the views, serving up tempting platters and wood-fired pizzas. Flagship bottles are the Reserve Chardonnay and Reserve Syrah, but the balanced rosé and crisp Pinot Gris are great-value alternatives. A refundable tasting fee of $5 gives you the lowdown on five wines. *www.omata.co.nz; tel 09-403 8007; 212 Aucks Rd, Russell; 11am–6pm Mon–Sat, 11am–9pm Sun*

04 MARSDEN ESTATE

Named after Samuel Marsden, who planted New Zealand's first grapevines in Kerikeri, Rod and Cindy MacIvor have built up a sizeable winery and restaurant in beautifully landscaped grounds – a perfect place to pause and enjoy some of Northland's best wines. Marsden Estate has made a big contribution to Northland wine by offering contract winemaking facilities for up to 20 smaller vineyards and growers in the region. All of their wines are estate-grown except a Marlborough Sauvignon Blanc and a Viognier from Mangawhai. Buttery Black Rocks Chardonnay and smooth, peppery Syrah are their top labels while silken, fruity Chambourcin gets top marks for best-value wine. *www.marsdenestate.co.nz; tel 09-407 9398; Wiroa Rd, Kerikeri; 10am–5pm Aug–May, 10am–4pm Jun–Jul*

05 AKE AKE VINEYARD

'If nobody is at the cellar door please honk your car horn loudly and we'll be with you in 10 minutes,' advises Ake Ake's website. Welcome to relaxed Northland. If you happen to be kept waiting, you could take a self-guided walking trail exploring the vineyard, the only one north of Auckland to be fully certified organic.

Ake Ake has been producing wine since 2015, chopping and changing varieties to get the best out of their site. One of its more successful moves was to plant Pinotage, which is proving itself a winnng variety.

The vineyard's restaurant is one of Northland's best (phone ahead for opening hours outside of the summer months), set among the

05 Keeping the shelves stocked at Omata

06 The view from Sage restaurant at Paroa Bay

vines and using as much local produce as possible.
www.akeakevineyard.co.nz; tel 09-407 8230; 165 Waimate North Rd, Kerikeri; 10.30am–4.30pm

06 KAINUI ROAD VINEYARD

The small but spectacular terraced vineyard of Kainui Road is surrounded by a large area currently being regenerated – owners Helen and Alan Thompson have planted thousands of native trees and shrubs for the benefit of future visitors and are planning a nature walk.

The cellar door offers Sauvignon Blanc, Pinot Gris, Viognier, Tempranillo and Syrah, plus a rosé blended from the latter two, with Chardonnay and Gewürztraminer in the pipeline. Home in on Kainui's intense, rustic Tempranillo, a wine with serious ageing potential. At the small cafe you can also taste and buy freshly brewed Kainui craft beer.
www.kainuiroad.co.nz; tel 09-407 8040; 15 Conifer Ln, Kerikeri; 11am–6.30pm Labour weekend to Easter

07 WAITAPU ESTATE VINEYARD

With a deep blue band of the Tasman Sea in the distance, it's clear why Eric and Sandra named their two-hectare vineyard 'Waitapu', a Maori word meaning 'Sacred Water'. The couple first got planting in 2003 and after some trial and error they have settled on Syrah and Pinotage as their main varieties, accompanied by Sangiovese, Tempranillo and Chambourcin. Red wines are supplemented with whites and sparklings made from grapes grown in Northland, Gisborne and Marlborough. Don't miss the bold, peppery Reef View Syrah.

To create biodiversity and ensure the future fertility of the land, Eric and Sandra have planted tens of thousands of native trees. Visitors are invited to follow a walkway through the bush to the waterfall on the Waitapu stream. 'It requires a certain level of fitness', warns Eric.
www.waitapuestate.co.nz; tel 09-409 4939; 111 Masters Access Rd, Ahipara, Kaitaia; 10am–4pm, Sat–Sun, or by appt

08 KARIKARI ESTATE

New Zealand's most northerly winery has spectacular views across vineyards and ocean to distant North Cape. Northland isn't short of spectacular views, true, but this is among the very best. Karikari's Estate label features two whites and two reds from grapes grown in their own vineyards. Pick of the bunch is their spicy, floral flagship Syrah and seductively mellow Chardonnay. A second label, Calypso, offers three white and three red wines, some of which are made from grapes grown in other regions.
www.karikariestate.co.nz; tel 09-408 7222; Maitai Bay Rd, Karikari Peninsula; 12pm–4pm Wed–Sat Nov, 12pm–4pm daily Dec–Feb, Mar–Oct by appt

ESSENTIAL INFORMATION

WHERE TO STAY

PAGODA LODGE
Built in the 1930s by an oddball Scotsman with an Asian fetish, this lodge features pagoda-shaped roofs grafted onto wooden cottages. The property descends to the river and is dotted with Buddhas, gypsy caravans, and safari tents with proper beds, or you can pitch your own.
www.pagoda.co.nz; tel 09-407 8617; 81 Pa Rd, Kerikeri

MANGAWHAI LODGE
Smartly furnished rooms have access to a picture-perfect wraparound verandah at this boutique B&B, which also features great views.
www.seaviewlodge.co.nz; tel 09-431 5311; 4 Heather St, Mangawhai Heads

WHERE TO EAT

WOOD STREET FREEHOUSE
Craft beer has arrived in Mangawhai at this buzzing cafe, including beers from local Northland brewers such as Schippers and the Sawmill Brewery.

06

Excellent food includes burgers, gourmet pizzas and shared plates – the truffle and parmesan fries are addictive – and from Friday to Sunday fresh local oysters from Wood Street's raw bar are best devoured on the deck.
woodstreetfreehouse.co.nz; tel 09-431 4051; 12 Wood St, Mangawhai Heads; noon-late Mon-Fri, from 10am Sat-Sun

FOOD AT WHAREPUKE
With one foot in Europe, the other in Thailand and its head in the lush vegetation of Wharepuke Subtropical Gardens, this is Kerikeri's most unusual and inspired eatery. On Friday nights it serves popular Thai banquets, while on Sunday afternoons it often hosts live jazz. Adjacent is the interesting Wharepuke Print Studio & Gallery.
www.foodatwharepuke.co.nz; tel 09-407 8936; 190 Kerikeri Rd, Kerikeri; 10am-10.30pm Tue-Sun

WHAT TO DO

BAY OF ISLANDS
The Bay of Islands offers some fine subtropical diving, made even better by the sinking of the 113m navy frigate HMNZS Canterbury in Deep Water Cove near Cape Brett. Local operators also head to the wreck of the Rainbow Warrior off the Cavalli Islands, about an hour north of Paihia by boat. Both offer an array of pink anemones, yellow sponges and abundant fish life. There are plenty of opportunities for kayaking or sailing around the bay, either on a guided tour or by renting and going it alone. Cruises are also available. Note that some boat companies do not operate during the winter.

WAIPOUA FOREST
The highlight of Northland's west coast, this forest sanctuary – proclaimed in 1952 after public pressure – is the largest remnant of once-extensive kauri forests. The forest road (SH12) stretches for 18km and passes some huge trees – a kauri can reach 60m in height and have a trunk more than 5m in diameter. Control of the forest has been returned to Te Rorora, the local iwi (tribe), as part of a settlement for Crown breaches of the Treaty of Waitangi. Te Rorora runs the Waipoua Forest Visitor Centre, near the south end of the park.
www.teroroa.iwi.nz/visit-waipoua

Courtesy of Black Estate

[Canterbury]

WAIPARA

A splash of green on sunburnt plains stretching all the way to the snow-capped Southern Alps – Waipara is an oasis and possibly NZ's best-kept wine secret.

Sheltered from cooling coastal breezes by a low range of hills, the Waipara Valley enjoys hot, dry ripening conditions allowing winemakers, and not the weather, to dictate when the grapes should be picked. The region's history is short, with the first vines planted in 1978, defying warnings that they would perish from drought or frost. The vines thrived and the Waipara region has since earned a reputation for making supremely elegant wines with great potential to mature. While it accounts for less than 3% of NZ's grapes, it produces some of the country's finest cool-climate wines including Riesling, Pinot Noir and Gewürztraminer. The future of this wine region looks bright, just like the long summer days it is blessed with.

In general terms, wines made from grapes grown on the Waipara plains are lighter and suppler than those from the hills, but a wide range of soil types blurs that distinction. Limestone-derived clay on the hillsides is the secret behind some of the region's most perfumed Pinot Noir, chalky Chardonnay and bright, focused Riesling. Pinot Noir is a narrow leader in terms of vineyard area ahead of Sauvignon Blanc, then Riesling and Pinot Gris.

The region is dominated by small family wine producers although larger corporates have a growing presence. The best wines are often made in tiny quantities and disappear faster than you can say 'limit two bottles a customer'. Conveniently stretched along SH1 near the Hanmer Springs turn-off, this rural area makes for a tasty and refreshing pit stop en route to Christchurch. A good halfway point if you're travelling south from Blenheim is Kaikoura, a pretty peninsula town backed by the snow-capped Seaward Kaikoura Range. It's a dream for marine wildlife-spotting and crayfish feasting. If you're coming the other way, it's only an an hour's drive from Christchurch.

GET THERE
Waipara is an hour's drive north of Christchurch airport. Or head south from Blenheim along the coast.

Courtesy of Black Estate, Greystone Wines

01 PEGASUS BAY

A family business dating back to 1986, when the Donaldsons planted the first vines on this site, Pegasus Bay is recognised as a pioneer of winemaking in North Canterbury. It's a compelling destination, with a distinctive four-storey salmon pink tower atop the winery, restaurant and cellar door, standing amid magnificent gardens which include several lakes. Some of the district's finest wines complete the scene – there's a brace of rich and flavoursome Rieslings, from dry to very sweet; a big and complex Chardonnay; a quirky, textural Sauvignon/Semillon and a dense and especially seductive Pinot Noir.

For a modest fee you can taste the full range of 10–15 wines and be guided by friendly and knowledgeable cellar door staff. The airy restaurant, one of Canterbury's best, has contemporary art on the walls, plenty of garden seating and a regularly changing seasonal menu, carefully crafted to match the luscious wines.

www.pegasusbay.com; tel 03-314 6869; 263 Stockgrove Rd, Amberley; 10am–5pm daily

02 WAIPARA HILLS

Waipara Hills' modern building hints at 1980s American architecture, with its pitched roof echoing the peaks of its namesake hills. The midsized winery draws grapes from three local vineyards with a combined area of 210 hectares, and also makes wines from its sites in Marlborough and Central Otago. Flagship brand Equinox features wines derived only from their estate vineyards and includes a delicately fruity Sauvignon Blanc, deliciously tangy Riesling, silken-textured Pinot Gris, sleek Chardonnay and a flavoursome Pinot Noir.

A lively indoor/outdoor cafe offers shared plates and platters that change with the seasons. Visitors are welcome to wander around the adjacent Pinot Noir vineyard.

www.waiparahills.co.nz; tel 03-314 6900; 780 Glasnevin Rd, State Hwy 1, Waipara; 10am–5pm daily

01 Cycling past Black Estate's vineyards

02 Inside Black Estate

03 Busy tastings at Greystone Wines

04 Terrace Edge

05 A novel use for empties at Pegasus Bay

Courtesy of Terrace Edge, Pegasus

Kaikoura, a pretty peninsula town backed by the snow-capped Seaward Kaikoura Range, is a dream for marine wildlife-spotting and crayfish feasting

03 TERRACE EDGE

The Chapman family are happy to take the long view, and to get their hands dirty – there's been no shortage of ups and downs in converting their former sheep farm to, firstly, an olive grove and eventually a certified organic vineyard (with Tuscan olives). Like many sites in Waipara, Terrace Edge has a diversity of soil types that is managed by carefully matching different grape varieties to compatible soils. It's a labour of love, but the efforts are rewarded with a host of complex, gratifying wines – look out for the Pinot Gris, with its rich and concentrated flavours, and the moderately sweet and tangy Liquid Geography Riesling which offers excellent value in most vintages. The same goes for the flavoursome, chalky Pinot Noir.

A short guided tour, included in the tasting fee, leads you through the vineyard to a block of Syrah called 'the roasted slope', and leaves you with an understanding of the challenges of organic wine production.

www.terraceedge.co.nz; tel 03-358 4205; 328 Georges Rd, Amberley; 11am–4.30pm Thu–Sun

04 THE BONELINE

With its slightly macabre name and austere, arresting label design, The Boneline isn't your typical South Island set-up. While it might not appear traditional, in fact the estate's name harks back 65 million years to the catastrophic asteroid

Ø6 Black Estate's striking barn

Ø7 Picnicking at Terrace Edge

Courtesy of Black Estate

collision that spelled the end of the dinosaurs – the nearby K-T boundary line is a geological stratum that offers evidence of this impact.

Traces of the bones of long-gone creatures live on, of course, in the vineyard soils and ultimately have an impact on wine styles. You can find out more on a guided tour around the terraced vineyard where you'll hear more about geological features, as well as grape varieties, rootstocks and clones, and round things off with a tasting of The Boneline wines. The intense, long-lived Cabernet Franc is one of the country's best, while their mineral-laced Sharkstone Chardonnay is a steal. On Sundays, you can wander the walkway for free.
www.theboneline.co.nz; tel 03-314 8699; 376 Ram Paddock Rd, Amberley; 10am–4pm Mon–Fri, 1pm–4pm Sun

05 GREYSTONE WINES

Greystone Wines produced its first wines in 2008 but has already hit maturity in terms of wine quality. It derives its name from the unique limestone conglomerate that forms the bedrock of the organically farmed vineyards. Some of Greystone's wines are fermented in the vineyard to take advantage of vineyard-derived yeasts, giving the resulting drops an even stronger sense of place. They excel at the aromatics, Riesling, Gewürztraminer and Pinot Gris, and also produce a savoury, complex Pinot Noir, supremely elegant Chardonnay and brooding Syrah.

In 2011 Greystone bought the nearby winery, vineyards and brand of Muddy Water, a high-quality producer best known for its Riesling and Pinot Noir. You can taste both Greystone and Muddy Water wines at their cellar door, or sign up for a comprehensive tour of the vineyard and winery which includes a trip to Muddy Water, a tasting of barrel samples as well as currently released wines, and a platter lunch.
www.greystonewines.co.nz; tel 03-314 6100; 376 Omihi Rd, State Hwy One, Waipara Valley; 11am–4pm daily

06 BLACK ESTATE

The sharpest of Waipara's wineries architecturally, this striking black barn overlooking the valley is home to some excellent wine, and food that champions local producers. The wines are all made from estate-grown grapes – the three different vineyards, planted as far back as 1986, are farmed using organic and biodynamic methods.

Black Estate is best known for its three single-vineyard Pinot Noirs: Home, Damsteep and Netherwood. It's worth tasting them alongside each other to understand how each different site can influence a wine's taste and texture. Two single-vineyard Chardonnays also express their own sense of place with the flagship Netherwood offering more fruit intensity and greater complexity than the smooth-textured and weighty Home vineyard Chardonnay.
www.blackestate.co.nz; tel 03-314 6085; 614 Omihi Rd, Omihi; 10am–5pm daily

ESSENTIAL INFORMATION

WHERE TO STAY

OLD GLENMARK VICARAGE

There are two divine options in this beautifully restored century-old vicarage: cosy up with bed and breakfast in the main house, or lounge around in the converted barn that sleeps five. The splendid gardens and swimming pool are a blessed bonus. *www.glenmarkvicarage.co.nz; tel 03-314 6775; 161 Church Rd, Waipara*

ANNIE'S LOFT

Settle in to stay right in the heart of the vineyards at this luxury B&B at Waipara River Estate and soak up its awesome panoramic views. When the peace and quiet gets too much, the town of Amberley is only ten minutes away. *www.waipărariver.com; tel 03-314 6184; 169 Mackenzies Rd, Amberley*

WHERE TO EAT

PUKEKO JUNCTION

A deservedly popular roadside pit stop, this cafe in Leithfield (south of Amberley) serves delicious baked goods including gourmet sausage rolls and lamb shank pies. As well as arts and crafts, the shop next door stocks an excellent selection of local wine. *www.pukekojunction.co.nz; tel 03-314 8834; 458 Ashworths Rd/SH1, Leithfield; 9am–4.30pm daily*

AMBERLEY FARMERS MARKET

Swing by this bustling weekly farmers market to stock up for picnics or self-catering stays. All the usual suspects are on sale – local, seasonal, much of it organic, all of it mouthwatering. *66 Carters Rd, Amberley; 9.30am–12.30pm Sat*

Courtesy of Terrace Edge

WHAT TO DO

WEKA PASS RAILWAY

Hop on board a vintage locomotive and chug through the Weka Pass out of Waipara, passing vineyards, farmland and dramatic limestone landscape. Occasionally a diesel engine is used but with luck you'll be drawn by a steam locomotive. *www.wekapassrailway.co.nz; Glenmark or Waikari stations; first and third Sun of the month, but check timetable*

WALKING

There are a good number of bracing walks to be had on Amberley and Leithfield beaches with high chances of spotting native wildlife. Choose a route to match your energy level. *www.visithurunui.co.nz/hiking/amberley-and-leithfield-walks*

HANMER SPRINGS

It's worth making the trip (an hour or so by car) up to the pleasantly low-key thermal resort of Hanmer Springs. As well as soaking in the hot pools and being pampered in the spa complex, there are plenty of family-friendly and adrenaline-pumping activities on offer. *www.visithanmersprings.co.nz*

CELEBRATIONS

THE WINERY TOUR

An annual summer concert (Feb) held at Waipara Hills that recently celebrated its 10th anniversary. The place to come for a day of fantastic music and great wine among the laden vines. *waiparahillswines.co.nz/events/concerts*

01

Courtesy of Margrain Vineyard

[Wellington]

WELLINGTON

Take a Pinot Noir pilgrimage to this boutique wine region and discover where Wellington wine-lovers spend their weekends.

Wairarapa Wine Country has only recently been rebranded as Wellington Wine Country, with a nod to the cool, cultural capital on its doorstep. Winemakers from Martinborough, Gladstone and Masterton joined together to help their region gain better recognition (and avoid confusion with Waipara on the south island). Whatever you call it, this world-renowned wine industry was nearly crushed in infancy. The region's first vines were planted in 1883, but in 1908 the prohibition movement put a cap on that corker of an idea. It wasn't until the 1980s that winemaking was revived, after Martinborough's terroir was discovered to be similar to that of Burgundy. That discovery encouraged would-be winemakers to plant vines on an area of free-draining gravels that would later be known as the Martinborough Terraces. The number of vineyards has since ballooned to around 40 across the region, with Martinborough the undisputed hub of the action but vineyards around Gladstone and Masterron are also on the up.

The first wines produced in the early '80s were an instant success – low-yielding vines produced wines of real intensity and power. Wellington Wine Country's wines sit both stylistically and geographically between those of Marlborough to the south and Hawke's Bay to the north. Sauvignon Blanc, for example, has some of the punchy tropical fruit flavours found in Marlborough wines, but also gives a nod to the north with tree fruit/nectarine characters that are more characteristic of Hawke's Bay Sauvignon Blanc.

More than half of the region's vineyard area is sensibly devoted to the signature variety, Pinot Noir, which has earned an international reputation for excellence. Try to track down a Pinot Noir that's at least five years old to truly appreciate the development potential of these ageworthy wines.

GET THERE
Martinborough is an hour by car from Wellington. From Napier it's 3hrs to Wellington Wine Country's most northerly point, Masterton.

01 PALLISER ESTATE

This established wine producer has developed a strong name for consistency and excellence. With seven vineyards ranging from a petit 2.2 hectares to a hefty 25.7, Palliser has a firm place in Martinborough's big league. While relatively close together, the grapes from each vineyard offer a surprisingly diverse range of styles thanks to vine age and subtle shifts in soil composition and aspect. A complex, savoury Pinot Noir, intensely fruity Sauvignon Blanc, concentrated and complex Chardonnay and rich, yeasty *méthode traditionnelle* sparkling wine are its outstanding wines.

Palliser's light-filled cellar door is located a few minutes' walk from the centre of Martinborough. Antipasti plates prepared by Carême, Palliser's on-site cooking school, are available from October to March (Thu–Sun).

www.palliser.co.nz; tel 06-306 9019; 96 Kitchener Rd, Martinborough; 10.30am–4pm (5pm Fri–Sat during daylight saving) daily

02 MARGRAIN VINEYARD

Margrain is on the edge of the famous Martinborough Terraces, whose variable characteristics are abundantly clear from the vineyard's accommodation, the Margrain Villas: from the front door you gaze at a vista of vines, but it's all paddocks, pasture and grazing sheep from the back, which is several metres lower. Sheep don't like the arid, stony soils of the Terraces and vines don't produce their best effort on fertile pasture.

Margrain obviously have things the right way round and you can sample their greatest strength, the Pinot Noir, in their small tasting room overlooking the vineyard. Other favourites include an intense, tangy, long-lived Chenin Blanc and a bottle-fermented sparkling wine, La Michelle. The Vineyard Cafe next door serves light meals based on local produce, with daily specials. Sign up for a tour of the vineyard to hear an explanation of the grape growing and winemaking process and taste a range of currently available wines and, for a few extra dollars, a tasty platter in the cafe. In the summer months (Jan–Mar), the

01 Laying the table at Margrain Vineyard

02 Helen Masters of Ata Rangi

03 Ata Rangi in spring

04 Tending the vines at Margrain

05 Schubert Wines

cafe hosts live music by local artists every Sunday from 2pm. *www.margrainvineyard.co.nz; tel 06-306 9292; cnr Ponetahi and Huangarua Rds, Martinborough; 11am–3pm Mon–Fri, 11am–5pm Sat, 11am–4pm Sun*

03 SCHUBERT WINES

Husband and wife team Kai and Marion Schubert are both German-trained winemakers. They set their heart on tracking down the best spot in the world to grow Pinot Noir and after extensive travels settled on Martinborough. Twenty or so years later they're managing two vineyards and creating top-notch Pinot Noir. A duo of intense and stylish single-vineyard Pinot Noirs are the pride of their production which also includes a supple Syrah, delicately fruity Sauvignon Blanc, delicious rosé, a blended white called Tribianco and blended red Con Brio. Call or email ahead to check opening hours and enjoy an intimate tasting at Schubert's friendly cellar door. *www.schubert.co.nz; tel 06-306 8505; 57 Cambridge Rd, Martinborough; 11am–3pm most days, phone ahead to check*

04 ATA RANGI

One of the region's pioneering winemakers, Ata Rangi is a small family-run affair which produces one of New Zealand's most iconic Pinot Noirs. Don't stop there, though – their concentrated Chardonnays, vibrant Riesling, peppery Syrah and rich blended red, Célèbre, are also exciting wines. Founder Clive Paton was on to a good thing when he bought a patch of land here back in 1980 – Ata Rangi has witnessed Martinborough morph from a quiet country town to the bustling hub of a celebrated wine region. Their cellar door opens to visitors twice daily for an engaging hosted session that includes a tasting of six wines and covers the history of Ata Rangi, viticultural and winemaking methods and an overview of the area. *www.atarangi.co.nz; tel 06-306 9570; 14 Puruatanga Rd, Martinborough; 10am or 2pm slots to be booked in advance by emailing visit@atarangi.co.nz*

From top left: courtesy of Ata Rangi / Pete Monk (2); Margrain Vineyard

Courtesy of Schubert Wines

05 TE KAIRANGA

With four sustainably farmed vineyards totalling 105 hectares Te Kairanga would be deemed large by Martinborough standards, though fairly modest by any international measure. It's another place best known for its Pinot Noir, with three price levels to choose from, but the racy Riesling and mellow Chardonnay are not to be missed either.

The Te Kairanga cellar door is in an old farm cottage that was built in the late 1800s and was once owned by the Father of Martinborough, John Martin. It becomes a lively place on the first Sunday of the month (Nov–Apr) when it plays host to a popular farmers market.

www.tkwine.co.nz; tel 06-306 9122; 89 Martins Rd, Martinborough; 11am–4pm daily summer, 11am–4pm Fri–Mon winter, otherwise by appt

06 ESCARPMENT

Escarpment's owner/winemaker Larry McKenna was christened 'Mr Pinot' for his contribution to the development of Pinot Noir in New Zealand. Each vintage, this small winery produces six – yes, six – Pinot Noir labels, the most majestic of which is the flagship, Kupe. Mr Pinot also makes a robust Chardonnay and a bone-dry Ryan Riesling.

Escarpment takes its name from the kilometre-long 30m drop down to the Huangarua River that borders the property. The vineyards are accredited with Sustainable Winegrowing NZ and are in the process of converting to organics. While there's no regular cellar door, you can call ahead to book a comprehensive tour of the vineyard and barrel room followed by a tasting of the wines.

www.escarpment.co.nz; tel 06-306 8305; 275 Te Muna Rd, Martinborough; by appt only

07 LUNA ESTATE

Luna Estate is the union of two properties and its remodelled cellar door is a few minutes' walk from Martinborough's town square. Luna owns a vineyard next to the cellar door and the larger Blue Rock vineyard on Dry River Road, which features the famous blue rock that gives the vineyard its name.

The Single Estate labels are made from grapes grown exclusively in one of the two sites. Pinot Noir is the hero but the Sauvignon Blanc and Riesling have also impressed.

www.lunaestate.co.nz; tel 06-306 9360; 133 Puruatanga Rd, Martinborough; noon–4pm Thu–Mon

08 GLADSTONE VINEYARD

This outlying winery is a 30min drive from Martinborough but the trip via the country towns of Featherston, Greytown and Carterton is worth it. Gladstone's cellar door is in a landscaped oasis, featuring old buildings, a wooded area and vineyard. Gladstone's elegant Pinot Noir is our top drop, with a delicate rosé made from a blend of three varieties coming in a close second.

This is a family-friendly spot with a pétanque court, playground and wetlands area. Guests are welcome to bring their own picnic lunch.

www.gladstonevineyard.co.nz; tel 06-379 8563; 340 Gladstone Rd, Carterton; 11am–4.30pm daily

ESSENTIAL INFORMATION

WHERE TO STAY

CLAREMONT

A classy accommodation enclave 15 minutes' walk from town, the Claremont has two-storey, self-contained units, modern studios with spa baths, and sparkling two-bedroom apartments, all at reasonable rates (even cheaper in winters and/or midweek). Tidy gardens, barbecue areas and bike hire. Repent your cellar-door sins at the lovely old First Church nearby. *www.theclaremont.co.nz; tel 0800 809 162, 06-306 9162; 38 Regent St, Martinborough*

AYLSTONE RETREAT

Set among vines on the edge of the village, this swish retreat is a winning spot for the romantically inclined. Six en suite rooms exude French-provincial charm and share a reading room. The whole shebang is surrounded by gardens, sporting lawns, box hedges and furniture. *www.aylstone.co.nz; tel 06-306 9505; 19 Huangarua Rd, Martinborough*

WHERE TO EAT

PINOCCHIO

Pinocchio is a hip little cafe-bar wedged into a tight space behind the old Martinborough Hotel. It's hard to beat a weekend breakfast of eggs Benedict or smoked fishcakes with poached eggs at one of the forecourt tables, or burgers on Wednesday nights, roasts on Sundays and West Coast whitebait fritters in season. *www.pinocchiomartinborough.co.nz; tel 06-306 6094; 3 Kitchener St, Martinborough; 6pm-late Wed–Fri, 8.30am-late Sat–Sun*

TIROHANA ESTATE

Enjoy a casual lunch over a glass or two on the terrace at this pretty vineyard, then come back for dinner in the elegant dining room (quite the occasion). Food (salmon fishcakes, lamb shanks, bread-and-butter pudding) is amply proportioned, proficiently prepared and impeccably served. *www.tirohanaestate.com; tel 06-306 9933; 42 Puruatanga Rd, Martinborough; 11.30am-3pm & 6pm–late Mon-Sat, 6pm–late Sun*

WHAT TO DO

CYCLING

The most eco-friendly way to explore the Wairarapa's wineries is by bicycle, as the flat landscape makes for puff-free cruising. Rental bikes are comfortable cruisers with saddle bags for your booty. *www.martinboroughwinemerchants.com; www.wairarapanz.com/see-and-do/martinborough-bicycle-hire-christina-estate*

STONEHENGE AOTEAROA

About 10km from Greytown in a farmer's backyard, this full-scale adaptation of the UK's Stonehenge is orientated for its southern hemisphere location on a grassy knoll overlooking the Wairarapa Plain. Its mission: to bring the night sky to life, even in daylight. The pretour talk and audiovisual presentation are excellent, and the henge itself a surreal (and delightfully eccentric) sight. Self-guided tours are also available. *www.stonehenge-aotearoa.co.nz; tel 06-377 1600; 51 Ahiaruhe Rd, Ahiaruhe; 10am–4pm daily*

CELEBRATIONS

TOAST MARTINBOROUGH

Toast Martinborough is held annually on the third Sunday in November. Enjoyable on many levels (standing up or lying on the grass), this is a popular wine, food and music event – be quick on the draw to get a ticket. *www.toast-martinborough.co.nz*

WAIRARAPA WINES HARVEST FESTIVAL

Celebrate the beginning of the harvest with an extravaganza of wine, food and family fun. It's held at a remote riverbank setting 10 minutes from Carterton on a Saturday in mid-March. Tickets go on sale at the end of the preceding November. *www.wairarapawines.co.nz*

INDEX

INDEX

CONTRIBUTORS

Bob Campbell is one of New Zealand's leading wine writers and a Master of Wine. See www.therealreview.com; www.bobcampbell.nz and follow @VinoNZ.

Huon Hooke is a leading Australian wine expert, critic and show judge, contributing to the Sydney Morning Herald. See www.therealreview.com and follow @HuonHooke.

Michael Ellis is VinoMofo's Head of Culture with an obsession with Pinot Noir and Jamón Ibérico. Insta: @ mikey.ellis; Twitter: @ mikeyellis13; and www.vinomofo.com

Chris Zeiher is a Lonely Planet alum and has contributed to Lonely Planet's Best in Travel, Lonely Planet's Global Coffee Tour and The Best Moment of Your Life.

Kate Morgan is a Lonely Planet travel writer based on the Bellarine Peninsula in Victoria - close to some top-notch wineries. Follow her @ katemorgan_travels

First Edition
Published in September 2018 by Lonely Planet Global Limited
CRN 54153
www.lonelyplanet.com
ISBN 978 1 7870 1769 6

Printed in China
10 9 8 7 6 5 4 3 2 1

Managing Director Piers Pickard
Associate Publisher and Commissioning Editor Robin Barton
Art Direction Daniel Di Paolo
Editors Monica Woods, Yolanda Zappaterra
Cartographer Rachel Imeson
Image research Regina Wolek
Print Production Nigel Longuet
Cover Image: Courtesy of TarraWarra / John Gollings

Thanks to Nick Mee

Authors: Bob Campbell (New Zealand), Chris Zeiher (Canberra), Huon Hooke (New South Wales, Queensland, Tasmania, Western Australia, South Australia except Clare Valley and Adelaide Hills), Kate Morgan (Bellarine Peninsula), Michael Ellis (Heathcote, Macedon Ranges, Yarra Valley)

Lonely Planet offices

AUSTRALIA The Malt Store, Level 3, 551 Swanston St, Carlton, Victoria 3053 T: 03 8379 8000

IRELAND Unit E, Digital Court, The Digital Hub, Rainsford St, Dublin 8

USA 124 Linden St, Oakland, CA 94607 T: 510 250 6400

UK 240 Blackfriars Rd, London SE1 8NW T: 020 3771 5100

STAY IN TOUCH lonelyplanet.com/contact

Paper in this book is certified against the Forest Stewardship Council™ standards. FSC™ promotes environmentally responsible, socially beneficial and economically viable management of the world's forests.